Gotham City Living

Gotham City Living

The Social Dynamics in the Batman Comics and Media

ERICA McCRYSTAL

BLOOMSBURY ACADEMIC
LONDON • NEW YORK • OXFORD • NEW DELHI • SYDNEY

BLOOMSBURY ACADEMIC
Bloomsbury Publishing Plc
50 Bedford Square, London, WC1B 3DP, UK
1385 Broadway, New York, NY 10018, USA
29 Earlsfort Terrace, Dublin 2, Ireland

BLOOMSBURY, BLOOMSBURY ACADEMIC and the Diana logo are trademarks of Bloomsbury Publishing Plc

First published in Great Britain 2021

Copyright © Erica McCrystal, 2021

Erica McCrystal has asserted her right under the Copyright, Designs and Patents Act, 1988, to be identified as Author of this work.

Cover design: Namkwan Cho
Cover image © Getty Images

All rights reserved. No part of this publication may be reproduced or transmitted in any form or by any means, electronic or mechanical, including photocopying, recording, or any information storage or retrieval system, without prior permission in writing from the publishers.

Bloomsbury Publishing Plc does not have any control over, or responsibility for, any third-party websites referred to or in this book. All internet addresses given in this book were correct at the time of going to press. The author and publisher regret any inconvenience caused if addresses have changed or sites have ceased to exist, but can accept no responsibility for any such changes.

A catalogue record for this book is available from the British Library.

A catalog record for this book is available from the Library of Congress.

ISBN: HB: 978-1-3501-4890-1
PB: 978-1-3501-4889-5
ePDF: 978-1-3501-4891-8
eBook: 978-1-3501-4892-5

Typeset by Newgen KnowledgeWorks Pvt. Ltd., Chennai, India

To find out more about our authors and books visit www.bloomsbury.com and sign up for our newsletters.

Contents

Introduction 1

1 Youth and Gotham City: Raising Criminals, Training Vigilantes, and Influencing Readers 13

2 Beyond Batman: Gender in Gotham City 47

3 The Sexualized City: Violence, Power, and Liberation 77

4 Pluralism and Identity Formation: Race and Ethnicity in Gotham City 103

5 From the Slums to the Manors: Gotham City's Class Disparity 127

6 Criminal Productivity: Gotham City's Most Wanted and Most Needed 153

Epilogue 183

Notes 185
References 189
Index 209

Introduction

Since its inception, Gotham City has become the embodiment of the archetypal American city under threat. Within the Batman franchise, artists and filmmakers have imagined a depraved geography for the condition of America. Gotham City, though not directly based on a specific city,[1] represents any American city. Gotham also has the malleability to represent any temporal moment so that it may reflect real-world concerns and threats. The various depictions of Gotham City throughout the Batman franchise effectively tap into present-day cultural anxieties, and, through time, the franchise has notably represented particular cultural and historical moments.[2] In order to do this successfully, the city's social structures also reflect American society, making the social fabric of the city recognizable to readers and viewers. While each creative team may take a unique approach, the franchise has, over time, often delivered messages promoting social progress. Social, political, and economic tensions are exacerbated through the criminal activity within the city, and Batman, in offering his services to Gotham, also provides hope for continued progress in urban America.

In order to create an iconic, lasting hero, Batman creators Bob Kane and Bill Finger first had to establish some ground rules for their character. Batman first appeared in *Detective Comics* #27 in 1939, and Gotham City was created as Batman's home in *Batman* #4 in 1940. Early on, the city existed as a backdrop for crime, and the comics mainly focused on Batman's detective skills and crime fighting. Amid Second World War anxieties, Batman provided an outlet for an audience that was consumed by wartime propaganda (Brooker 2001, 84). As Batman grew in popularity, the parallels to particular historical moments and cultural values increased. The 1950s brought pressures to create content deemed appropriate for the target youth audience. The Space Age also greatly influenced the comics, resulting in an influx of science-fiction storylines in the Batman comics (Weldon 2016, 57–8). Then in the 1960s, Batman became defined by the campy television series *Batman*, which was playful and tongue-in-cheek. This set a tone that the comics of the 1970s worked to move away from (Weldon 2016, 112–13).

Glen Weldon (2016, 67) compares early depictions of Gotham City to "a studio back lot." In the 1960s, though, he argues that it "grew into a larger and more idiosyncratic metropolis that for the first time evinced a grubby, lived-in character." A pivotal transition to the franchise came in the 1980s. Frank Miller's iconic graphic novels *The Dark Knight Returns* (illustrated by Klaus Janson [1986] 2002) and *Batman: Year One* (illustrated by David Mazzucchelli [1987] 2005) reimagined the Batman franchise through a Gothic approach using tropes such as darkness, uncertainty, and the intrusion of the past on the present. Terrence R. Wandtke (2007, 91) notes, "Miller portrays the city as truly Gothic in appearance and the series is colored in a way that accentuates the bleak desperation." The city itself has become a harbinger of evil. Critics also find *The Dark Knight Returns* deeply concerned with US politics, particularly Reaganism amid the Cold War. For Richard A. Iadonisi (2013), the graphic novel is "an enactment of the Reagan mythos" and mocks "soft body" politicians (75), likening Batman to a "Reaganite Hard Body" (78). Wandtke (2007, 94) further considers the problems of the city as lying with the people: "*The Dark Knight Returns* works as a social commentary about a society that won't acknowledge its own shortcomings and inconsistencies." Miller's social and political statements make for a much more serious text than its predecessors. It uses the darkness of the Gothic to expose problems in urban America.

Miller and Janson's ([1986] 2002) graphic novel is also deeply concerned with the layers of vigilantism and different perspectives of criminal versus heroic behavior. In *The Dark Knight Returns*, Batman is "the *good* kind of criminal, the kind needed to restore order to the chaos that is America" (Iadonisi 2013, 79). However, due to the overarching political implications, Batman's actions become increasingly complicated, especially in the way he contrasts with national authority. For Mike S. Dubose (2007, 922), "Batman is a political liability because his morality is fiercely independent. He only fights those *he* (not the government) believes are wrong and is consequently treated as a vigilante—vigilante being the key term for those who will not fall in line to authority's domination." Batman is not only a powerful figure in this DC universe but also an authority in the readers' eyes, which makes his efforts and intentions impactful in the real world. Regarding *The Dark Knight Returns*, Wandtke (2007, 95) notes that Batman "is publicly embarrassing the president by bringing the decay of Gotham and in turn, the president's misguided domestic policy, to light." Batman exposes the social and class problems in Gotham City, which reflect the failings of this universe's American government. In doing so, Miller and Janson's work also invites readers to reflect on their own social and class structures and the effectiveness of federal action in real-world America.

When Gotham City was brought to the big screen, audiences were given access to navigate the city with a new kind of visual and auditory mobility that offers fresh perspectives of the urban environment. While the comic books have reflected the social structures within urban America and continue to do so, the films have been most successful in creating a visual space that viewers will recognize and relate to as representative of the American cityscape. The film representations speak to viewers, reminding us that Gotham City exists in our own world through our conscious analogizing. Tim Burton's films *Batman* (1989) and *Batman Returns* (1992) include a Gotham City that, following Miller and Janson's lead, is visibly Gothic in its darkness and architecture while increasingly inciting fear and encouraging the uncanny. In terms of crime in society, the films turn away from more global concerns to focus on the threat of gangsters in *Batman* and the corporate body in *Batman Returns*. Marc DiPaolo (2011, 67) notes that in *Batman Returns*, "white-collar, corporate criminals are the most dangerous after all, and the most in need of being brought to justice by any means necessary." In these films, the citizens of Gotham need to look inward to find the corruption within their city's walls.

The subsequent Joel Schumacher films *Batman Forever* (1995) and *Batman and Robin* (1997) return to some of the campiness of the 1960s TV series and are often negatively critiqued by both fans and critics. They show an eclectic, garish side of Gotham, which can be added to a catalog of its iterations throughout the franchise. This Gotham is a visible representation of excess and showmanship. Christopher Nolan's reboot in 2005 marked a new era of Batman, concerned with post-9/11 fears and set in a Gotham City that has the visual likeness of several twenty-first-century American cities (DiPaolo 2011, 51). DiPaolo notes that in *Batman Begins*, Gotham's "overall feel is certainly inspired, in part, by the archetypal 'corrupt' New York of the 1970s … But *Batman Begins* blends the visual feel of the dirty, overtly 'immoral' New York with the more subtle corruption that infests the cleaner, tourist friendly New York of today" (51). The threat of corruption within a recognizable, safe space is a technique of the Romantic Gothic in the domestic space that Nolan has brought into the urban environment. Nolan's use of the Gothic may also be found through the power of terror over the imagination, what Douglas Kellner (2013, 164) calls "spectacles of terror," which, he says, "are so powerful in Nolan's trilogy that it is possible for audiences to identify with some of the terrorist characters and their acts of destruction." The infiltration of the terroristic Other also arouses Gothic fear. Dan Hassler-Forest (2011, 144) argues, "this break with tradition, relocating the main threat from inside Gotham to a sectarian rebel militia in the Far East, is the first element that connects *Batman Begins* with post-9/11 discourse." Critics of Nolan's trilogy find a similar anxiety present in *The Dark Knight* and *The Dark Knight Rises*.[3] Like Miller's graphic novels, Nolan's films have been argued as politically imbued: "Nolan's *The Dark Knight* and *The Dark Knight Rises* present a critical allegory about the corruption, violence, and nihilism of the Bush/Cheney era" (Kellner 2013, 163). Social, political, and terroristic threats may all be found in the films and may resonate with audience members with similar concerns for real-world America. On the other hand, viewers may also find the films illustrative of showing a darker, more corrupt potential for America.

Nolan's *Batman Begins* and Bruno Heller's TV series *Gotham* (2014–19), both of which show the condition of the city before Bruce Wayne becomes Batman, illustrate a dilapidated environment rampant with criminal activity. Even the police department is laced with deeply rooted corruption. The arrival of Batman actually allows for the cyclical pattern of depravity in the city, where Batman removes a criminal threat just before another arrives. While William Uricchio (2010) argues that the franchise is rooted in Batman's origin story, I argue that the origin story provides psychological explanation and motivation for his donning the mask but does not explain the roots of crime-ridden Gotham City. Embedded pathological depravity is inherent to the city and must be viewed as always already part of the metropolitan social fabric.

The impact and success of Gotham as representative of urban America greatly depends upon its visual depiction. In many film and television representations, Gotham is the amalgamation of multiple American cities. New York City is a frequent filming location but altered in order to illustrate a unique metropolis. Schumacher describes his Gotham as "Manhattan on steroids" (qtd. in Natale 1995). Heller's *Gotham* was filmed on New York City's streets, but its skyline is a composite of New York City and computer-generated imagery (CGI) buildings with added gargoyles. According to *Gotham's* visual effects supervisor, Tom Mahoney, the show's Gotham City is "a blend of neo-Gothic, art deco and beaux arts elements" with sky replacements to create the appearance that "there's always a storm brewing over Gotham" (qtd. in CoSA VFX 2014). The various point-of-view shots and angles provide the audience with a constructed Gotham, a visual creation that is itself an art piece. These visual effects reflect the Gothic atmosphere of which the city thrives.

Nolan's (2008) *The Dark Knight* was filmed mostly in Chicago with recognizable buildings used in several scenes. In *The Dark Knight Rises*, Nolan (2012) further "builds a familiar setting for his film" (Ioannidou 2013, 235). Filming for *The Dark Knight Rises* took place mainly in New York City and Pittsburgh and included scenes at recognizable landmarks, such as the Queensboro Bridge and 23 Wall Street in New York City and Heinz Field, PPG Place, and Carnegie Mellon University in Pittsburgh. Using a combination of landmarks makes this Gotham City the amalgamation of urban America. The terrorism brought to Gotham may incite fear in the audience because the attack is on familiar space rather than the constructed, artistic sets that Tim Burton used in his films.

While Nolan's Gotham is constructed to be recognizably American, Tim Burton (1992) filmed *Batman Returns* on set and used miniature models of the city. Production designer Bo Welch argues, "Gotham City represents the old American city, kind of rotted, kind of corrupt, but full of character and life." He calls this Gotham "a caricature of a city" (qtd. in Nasr 2005). In contrast, Cory A. Reed (1995, 39) sees Burton's Gotham as "a futuristic Gotham, development run amok, in which the triumphs of technology literally overshadow humanity." In this way, Burton's Gotham also taps into contemporary anxieties. Gotham represents the old and the new, as its Gothic appeal simultaneously recalls the past while pushing toward the future. Visibly, it is not recognizable of or mirroring a specific city because it represents any city plagued by criminal threats. Tom Duffield, the supervising art director, says that the city that they created has an "international style … it's kind of a generic Fascist neoclassic architecture" (qtd. in Nasr 2005). Because the city was entirely constructed, the designers could blend this "international style" with Gothic architecture to make an exaggerated cityscape. Reed (1995, 48–9) also considers Burton's Gotham as reflective of Mikhail Bakhtin's grotesque realism: "Burton's world … is not the real world or a stylized comic-book world; the aesthetic of grotesque realism exaggerates reality to sensationalistic—and entertaining—extremes." For Bakhtin (1984, 48), in the grotesque, "all that was for us familiar and friendly suddenly becomes hostile." He also remarks, "The grotesque image reflects a phenomenon in transformation, an as yet unfinished metamorphosis, of death and birth, growth and becoming" (24). The city is a Gothic organism that illustrates this liminality as it allows for the coexistence of abundance and depravity and is visually distorted, uneven, and limitless. Burton's Gotham is visually exaggerated because it is not intended to model a real space (but can still tap into real-world problems). Highly stylized, dark, and grotesque, Burton's Gotham City is a work of art that arouses terror in the imagination through its active employment of darkness and lack of uniformity.

At times, works within the DC multiverse seem to create a dark/light dichotomy. Ultimately, though, they prove that light and dark cannot actually be polarized. In Walter Simonson's (2007) "Legend" in the comic book miniseries *Batman Black and White*, a mother tells her child the history of Gotham City: "Once upon a time ... the city was a Gothic realm of eternal night. Full of pain ... and grief ... and a people ... broken by evil" (68–9). She then describes how Batman emerged to save the city from the "four horsemen of the apocalypse" (69–70). The irony of the tale, which takes place in the "far future and in a stainless steel city of light" (67), is that the future is no better than the past. The militants that govern the city, wielding their black fist insignia, do not indicate that the city of light is better off than the city of darkness. The reality is that Gotham is perpetually under threat because its apocalyptic condition has been normalized, regardless of its luminosity.

Gotham City's darkness can tap into readers' and viewers' own psychological complexities. The "dark-deco" style of *Batman: The Animated Series* (1992–5) creates an urban space where both criminals and vigilantes lurk in the shadows, making audiences think about the uncertain and the unknown. For Charles Holland (2008), the darkness of Gotham City in *The Dark Knight* reflects the inner intricacies of the individual watching the film: "The film suggests that it is impossible to design out darkness. It is a product of our own desire, and a nightmare lurking in the same places that also give us comfort. It is not an alternative world so much as the dark side of our affluent lives." Holland suggests the city represents the self, and the audience can identify with the darkness rather than displace it as fantastic. The terrors associated with darkness can arise from the everyday comforts of our own lives. Darkness, even symbolically, pervades all aspects of life.

With new creative teams writing and illustrating Batman comics and producing new film and TV iterations, Gotham City continues to exist as a space for perpetual reconstruction of an iconic American city. Readers and audience members take in each version, collecting the various Gothams in their mental catalog. No version is less Gotham than another, and while one may be personally preferable, they all coexist as Gotham City. Thus, the reimagined city is simultaneously one and many, a recognizable space that has been described, built, and crafted through a variety of methods and media. New creative teams and technology will continue to provide opportunities for Gotham to be freshly envisioned while still remaining recognizably American. As such, readers and audiences can take this recognizable city and look inside at the relationships between Gotham's people. Gotham embodies the social conditions of America, and its heroes and villains help make visible social issues regarding class, race, ethnicity, gender, and sexuality. The people of Gotham are the people of America, and the franchise uses both comic books and films to illustrate struggles of adolescence and promote identity development while also encouraging social progress to transcend perceived social inequalities.

The following chapters examine the social fabric of Gotham City as representative of urban America. Gotham is an organic space that simultaneously encourages destruction and offers hope. Contemporary American society is reflected in the characters through their relationship with the city. Henri Lefebvre ([1979] 2009) argues that space is socially produced. The social production of space occurs in representations of Gotham City throughout the franchise from an external and an internal perspective. Externally, the public has often influenced the content of comic books, and internally, Gotham becomes recognizable as a space built from its social relations. For Lefebvre ([1979] 2009, 186), "Space is social: it involves assigning more or less appropriated places to the social relations of reproduction, namely, the biophysiological relations between the sexes, the ages, the specified organization of the family, and to the relations of production, namely, the division of labor and its organization." Children growing up in Gotham are subject to the city's adverse conditions, and the effect can be developmentally deleterious, while others may rise up and become heroes. The city also makes class divisions visible as the poor live in visibly depraved conditions. The space of Gotham City is where identities are developed and fostered. It is also a space for women to experiment with their femininity and apply it to superheroics or villainy. Batman is the one constant, though. He traverses all corners of the city, giving readers and viewers access to such impactful spaces and the social dynamics within the city.

In the 1950s, the comic book industry was under the microscope and criticized regarding the appropriateness of content for youth readers. The Batman franchise has repeatedly made efforts to favor the pathways toward moral goodness and continues to speak to youth readers by including relatable adolescent characters. Bruce Wayne essentially skips his childhood to don the cowl and assume a post of moral defender. In various storylines, the city nurtures children to become moral citizens or criminals. Though Batman repeatedly reaches out to Gotham's youth, the city's innate criminal nature and the franchise's need for conflict require that some children take the pathway toward criminality. Batman does successfully guide and mentor the various Robins, demonstrating the proclivity for children of trauma to rise up from tragedy and be morally serviceable. As Tim Drake faces trials that are common to American teenagers—such as bullying, gun violence, and suicide—his character emerges as a strong representation of and role model for American youth. Stephanie Brown's experiences with teenage pregnancy and sexual abuse allow young female readers to witness her coping mechanisms and sympathize or empathize with her character. Through these examples and others, the Batman franchise effectively displays and provides commentary on the burdens of American adolescents as they grow and develop.

Turning to gender, the Batman franchise embraces its female characters, as women have become increasingly powerful in Gotham City, both as superheroines and as supervillainesses. From Catwoman to Batwoman to Poison Ivy, Gotham's female characters assert themselves as power figures rather than prescribe to gender roles. Both superheroines and supervillainesses have redefined and repurposed notions of femininity and the feminine ideal. While there may be social implications to gender performance, the Batman franchise has pushed against normative gender prescriptions and embraced femininity as equally superheroic as masculinity. The ways that women have been historically depicted in the Batman comics illustrate the social progress of women in America. At the same time, supervillainesses embrace their feminine prowess and use it effectively to manipulate men, illustrating power inherent to their gender. As the Batman franchise continues to reflect a socially progressive climate in America, the *Batgirl* series has also included trans characters, which stimulates additional conversations regarding gender performance and social assumptions.

Much of the power of the female characters in Gotham stems from their sex appeal. Though often controversial, representations of sexuality throughout the Batman franchise have significantly evolved over the years. Early on, the Comics Code maintained strict regulations against the sexualization of women, but the comics and films in the Batman franchise now embrace sexuality and use it as a form of empowerment. Many villainesses use their sexual prowess as a weapon to gain the upper hand over male adversaries. This can be dangerous, though, as the *Batwoman* series (Vol. 2) illustrates the perils of rape and sexual manipulation. The Batman franchise also has a long history in its approach to sexuality. Fredric Wertham's writings and the Comics Code aimed to maintain heteronormativity within the comics. However, twenty-first-century works in the franchise embrace LGBTQ characters. In particular, *Batwoman* comics consider the personal and social impact of silencing and encourage openness with one's sexuality. The transition of the social politics of sexuality in comics, TV, and film in Gotham City shows how the Batman franchise now does not need to promote heteronormativity and can embrace sexuality.

The franchise has also shown to be socially aware regarding race and ethnicity. Since Gotham City's population has remained predominantly white, it may appear that it fails to reflect the cultural pluralism of American cities. However, I argue that the Batman franchise's creative teams have not neglected race as an exclusionary practice. Instead, they have catered to their intended audience and adhered to the Comics Code, which intended to encourage role model citizens by eliminating exposure to prejudiced or stereotypical depictions of nonwhite characters. Comics in the twenty-first century have aimed to reflect racial conflicts of twenty-first-century urban America. Robyn Wiegman's (1995) theories of race as constructed based on what people see and Michael Omi and Howard Winant's (2015) theories of racial formation provide a lens for examining the franchise's approach to racial conversations and conflicts in urban America. The Batman franchise has produced works that reflect social anxieties related to ethnic and racial difference, communal problems that can occur with gentrification, and racial conflicts with the police. Such topics encourage reflection on racial and ethnic identity formation in America and the social implications of assumptions and prejudices.

Gotham City's wealthy and poor classes simultaneously illustrate urban growth and degradation. The comics and films show great disparity between socioeconomic classes in the city and the conflicts—and typically crime—that tend to arise as a result. Marxism offers an approach to discussing class and classlessness in Gotham and, in turn, the socioeconomics of urban America. The comics and films often focus heavily on the dire situations of the poor, which seem to be perpetuated through capitalistic hegemony. The class-related problems inherent to Gotham, an environment with extremes in its social hierarchies, are exacerbated throughout the comics and films. However, Batman requires a capitalist system in order to exist as a vigilante. Criminals in Gotham may be from any class, as Batman has tracked crime to financially desperate men and also fought power-hungry white-collar criminals. This illustrates the city's proclivity to cultivate criminals despite their background. At the same time, a relationship between space and socioeconomic groups in Gotham City exists and offers commentary on capitalism in urban America in both the twentieth and twenty-first centuries.

Gotham City is a breeding ground for criminality, which then spreads like a disease, contaminating more individuals. Gotham City's miscreants—whether they be petty criminals or supervillains—maintain a relationship with a city that encourages criminal activity. As an organism, Gotham requires a constant surge of criminals to maintain its depraved condition. The franchise also needs to ensure that Batman always has an adversary. The criminal characters in Gotham reflect contemporary urban anxieties in America regarding violence, terrorism, and criminal influence. Nineteenth-century psychiatrist Henry Maudsley (1880) examined the root of criminality through a classification of criminal types. His theories can be applied to Gotham's criminals and supervillains to better comprehend reasons for their inclination toward criminal activity. Vigilantism has emerged as a response to crime in Gotham City, and Batman and his cohorts operate according to their own set of rules. The city that is under perpetual threat suggests that such deviancy is in fact needed to quell crime.

Just as Gotham City aesthetically and visually reflects urban America, the people of Gotham are the people of America, and the concerns raised throughout the Batman franchise are those that prey upon the American populace. The following chapters take a close look at the comics and films that have built a fictional American city that represents real-world urban America and its social dynamics. As Gotham continues to evolve, it remains current and relevant for Batman readers and audiences.

1

Youth and Gotham City: Raising Criminals, Training Vigilantes, and Influencing Readers

The comic book industry has traditionally catered its content to its youth audience. Historically, concerns about the negative impact of sex and violence on young readers caused the entire comic book publishing industry to self-regulate and establish "appropriate" standards of content. While the principles of appropriate content have changed greatly over time, comic books still often speak to young readers in a variety of ways to entertain, inspire, or educate. The Batman franchise uses all three purposes as it illustrates the complexities of growing up in an urban environment rife with crime. Many stories contain troubled youths—some who turn to crime and others who embrace heroism. Batman often tries to morally steer Gotham's youth away from criminal influences, as he realizes that children and adolescents are greatly impacted by their surroundings. Through Lawrence Kohlberg's theory of moral development, this chapter looks at the ways in which Gotham's youth cultivate moral judgment.

Batman's efforts are also motivated by personal experience. Bruce Wayne was a child of Gotham who skipped adolescence to become a vigilante due to childhood trauma. This chapter examines adolescence through James Marcia's theory of identity formation as well as trauma theory to see the impact of trauma on child development in Gotham. Through Robin's character, the Batman franchise has been able to create a relatable young hero, one who develops from boy to man and grapples with teenage troubles while simultaneously serving the city as a vigilante. While there have been multiple Robins throughout history, the existence of Robin serves as an inspiration to American youth. Both his experiences and Batman's guidance of Gotham's young population impart wisdom and life lessons to young comic book readers, while children of Gotham who become criminals illustrate corruptive influences within the city.

The Comic Book Industry and America's Youth

The comic book publishing industry has a history of criticism regarding the appropriateness of content for young readers. The fear, especially in the 1950s, was that crime, violence, and sex in comic books could have a dangerous influence on children. A largely vocal and influential critic of comic books, psychiatrist Dr. Fredric Wertham, began his crusade in 1948 in an article in *Collier's Magazine* that published the results and conclusions of his research. He continued to publish and speak at events declaring the dangers of comic books on the youth of America. Titled "Horror in the Nursery," the 1948 article quotes Wertham saying, "The comic books, in intent and effect, are demoralizing the morals of youth. They are sexually aggressive in an abnormal way. They make violence alluring and cruelty heroic. They are not educational but stultifying" (qtd. in Crist 1948, 22). He considered the glamorization of sex and crime detrimental to childhood development. The apparent lack of educational substance made comic books even less appealing in the eyes of critics, who found no redeemable qualities in such reading materials.

Public responses to the comic book problem included comic book burnings across the country.[1] On October 26, 1948, in Spencer, West Virginia, 600 grade school students burned two thousand comic books. Thirteen-year-old David Mace, who led the "burial service," said, "Believing that comic books are mentally, physically and morally injurious to boys and girls, we propose to burn those in our possession. We also pledge ourselves to try not to read any more" (qtd. in *The Washington Post* 1948). Then on December 10, 1948, students at St. Patrick's Parochial School in Binghamton, New York, burned a mound of two thousand comic books and pictorial magazines. Students of SS. Peter and Paul Parochial School in Auburn, New York, followed suit on December 22, 1948, burning comic books that they gathered from their homes. In Cape Girardeau, Missouri, on February 24, 1949, students of St. Mary's High School conducted a mock trial where comic book characters " 'pleaded guilty' to various charges of leading young people astray and building up false conceptions in the minds of youth." A Girl Scout troop initiated a crusade against the comics, which ended in a comic book burning. The students at both St. Mary's High School and grade school pledged not to read or purchase "objectionable publications" and to boycott retailers who sell comics (*Southeast Missourian* 1949).

In December 1948, in a letter to be read at all masses in churches in the Albany Diocese, Bishop Edmund F. Gibbons called for a boycott of comic books and pictorial magazines: "Another evil of our times is found in the pictorial magazine and comic book which portray indecent pictures and sensational details of crime. This evil is particularly devastating to the young, and I call upon our people to boycott establishments which sell such literature" (qtd. in *New York Times* 1948). The involvement of religious institutions and individuals in the protest and destruction of comic books deemed them immoral and contrary to sacred teachings. Across America, there was a call for a widespread control of content and exposure. Those in positions of higher moral authority preached and influenced others to effectively self-censor by refusing to read.

However, some individuals disagreed with the claims that comic books were dangerous to young readers. In an article published in the *Journal of Educational Sociology* in December 1949, Professor Frederic M. Thrasher criticizes Dr. Wertham's claims, arguing that his evidence is inadequate and unjustly projects vexations with the state of society onto the comic book industry:

This extreme position which is not substantiated by any valid research, is not only contrary to considerable current psychiatric thinking, but also disregards tested research procedures which have discredited numerous previous monistic theories of delinquency causation. Wertham's dark picture of the influence of comics is more forensic than it is scientific and illustrates a dangerous habit of projecting our social frustrations upon some specific trait of our culture, which becomes a sort of "whipping boy" for our failure to control the whole gamut of social breakdown. (1949, 195)

Aside from criticizing the lack of research behind the claims, Thrasher finds that comics critics are neglecting opposing research and instead creating a narrative to respond to "social frustrations." Instead of scrutiny into the real root of the problems with youth delinquency, Wertham and other comics critics imagine a negative social and developmental influence. Thrasher also finds Wertham's conclusions merely unsubstantiated opinion (200). The inconsistency of research would make Wertham's claims purely theoretical; however, his criticisms gained tremendous public acknowledgment.

Wertham combined all of his findings and arguments in his book *Seduction of the Innocent* ([1954] 2004, 164), where he argues, "Our researches have proved that there is a significant correlation between crime-comics reading and the more serious forms of juvenile delinquency." He also states that comic books contribute to maladjustment in children (10). Wertham deeply criticizes not only comic books themselves but also society. He argues that a society that produces seductive, violent comic books is guilty of contributing to detrimental effects that comic book reading may have on a young reader (12). Additionally, he believes, "Even more than crime, juvenile delinquency reflects the social values current in a society" (149). An uptick in juvenile delinquency—which is a result of the comic books according to Wertham—would indicate a misalignment of social values of the society that created the comic books.

In response to the controversy, the US Senate Committee on the Judiciary created an investigative subcommittee and held hearings in April and June 1954 to investigate the impact of the comic book industry on juvenile delinquency in America. After hearing from expert witnesses, its interim report *Comic Books and Juvenile Delinquency* was released in March 1955 and presented the following conclusion: "The subcommittee believes that this Nation cannot afford the calculated risk involved in the continued mass dissemination of crime and horror comic books to children" (United States Congress 1955). The recommendation was not for governmental censorship but for parents, publishers, and citizens to actively seek to eliminate the exposure of youth to crime and horror in comics. The subcommittee called upon the comic book industry to ensure that "the comic books placed so temptingly before our Nation's children at every corner newsstand are clean, decent, and fit to be read by children" (United States Congress 1955). The main concern of Wertham and the subcommittee was how American society was educating its youth through reading materials.

Anxiety that comic book reading could influence social behavior prompted the formation of the Comics Magazine Association of America (CMAA) and the adoption of the Comics Code in 1954. The code set regulations of appropriateness for content in comics. After going through some revisions over the next sixty years, the code was completely abandoned by comic book publishers by 2011. Today, concerns have shifted to debates on the impact of violent media on adolescent behavior. As early as the 1960s, researchers began running studies to determine the effects of violent television and movies on adolescent antisocial and aggressive behavior.[2] The Motion Picture Association of America's modern ratings system was established in 1968. The Telecommunications Act of 1996 encouraged the entertainment industry to create voluntary ratings of television programs to give parents information about content, and in December 1996, the TV Parental Guidelines were created.

In 2005, Senator Hillary Rodham Clinton proposed the Family Entertainment Protection Act (United States Congress 2005–6). The bill sought to prevent businesses from selling or renting video games rated Mature, Adults-Only, or Ratings Pending to anyone under the age of 17. The bill claimed that research demonstrated that violence in media causes individuals "to exhibit higher levels of violent thoughts, anti-social and aggressive behavior, fear, anxiety, and hostility, and desensitization to the pain and suffering of others" (To Limit the Exposure 2005). However, Congress did not enact the bill.

Then in 2011, in *Brown v. Entertainment Merchants Association*, the Supreme Court ruled to overturn California legislation that prohibited the sale and rental of violent video games to minors. The court ruled that video games—regardless of their content—are protected by the same first amendment rights as books, plays, and film.

Violence in media continues to be a hot debate, and as so many comic books have been adapted into TV shows, films, and video games, the industry is constantly scrutinized for its content and influence on youth. Despite the presence of crime, violence, and sex in the Batman franchise, the comics and adaptations impart many lessons for young readers to learn. The franchise includes several adolescent characters whose experiences allow for the exploration of child and teenage development—whether toward crime or heroics. These characters also have to grapple with the everyday struggles of teenagers, which makes the comics more relatable to young readers. The fictional characters, especially Robin, serve as representations of America's adolescent population.

Criminal Influences

The children of Gotham City are often depicted as products of their environment. Gotham is rife with criminality and poverty that can have a big impact on childhood development. Gotham's youth are vulnerable to criminal influence that can strip them of their innocence and turn them into a new generation of criminals to plague the city. While Batman needs to combat any threat that comes his way, he also needs to find ways to provide for and support Gotham's youth if he wants to repair an ongoing cycle of criminality.

Batman's efforts to morally steer Gotham's children and adolescents started very early in the franchise. In *Batman* #3 (Finger and Kane 1940e), Batman fights a group of thugs—one of whom turns out to be a boy. After following him to a deserted warehouse in the slums, Batman discovers that a criminal has been serving as a teacher at a crime school at the warehouse, instructing boys on how to pick pockets and crack safes and encouraging them to admire criminals. Bruce tells Dick Grayson, "We've got to make these boys **hate** crime and evil, and not look up to a racketeer like Big Boy Daniels who is probably their ideal!" To reverse the situation for these boys, Bruce first rents a barn to make a gym for underprivileged children living in the slums. Then, Dick showcases his fighting skills to the boys. He encourages them to join the new gym and teaches them to be honest in sports. Batman and Robin provide an outlet for the boys that focuses on fair play and tries to steer them away from criminal activity. When Big Boy Daniels later goes to the crime school to recruit boys for his mob, Batman warns the boys and scares them into staying out of trouble. Batman fights Big Boy, and Dick rallies the boys on Batman's side, saying that Big Boy did not fight fair. The narrator states, "The campaign for fair play and honesty bears fruit as the boys turn on their former idols." At this point, the boys illustrate their moral development. The youth are easily impressionable as they have not yet developed a moral compass. This example illustrates Lawrence Kohlberg's theory of moral development, which argues, "Moral judgment, while primarily a rational operation, is influenced by affective factors such as the ability to empathize and the capacity for guilt. But moral situations are defined cognitively by the judging individual in social interactions. It is this interaction with one's environment which determines development of moral reasoning" (Kohlberg and Hersh 1977, 57). Whether from lessons imparted by Big Boy Daniels or Batman and Robin, the social environment impacts and steers the boys' moral development.

According to Kohlberg's theory, individuals move through different levels as their moral reasoning progresses. A child who falls under the preconventional level "is responsive to cultural rules and labels of good and bad, right or wrong, but interprets these labels either in terms of the physical or the hedonistic consequences of action (punishment, reward, exchange of favors) or in terms of the physical power of those who enunciate the rules and labels" (Kohlberg and Hersh 1977, 54). The boys who look up to Big Boy Daniels are influenced by his power and status. However, Batman and Dick encourage the young would-be hoodlums to become upright citizens who understand fairness and honesty. In doing so, they help the boys morally develop beyond the preconventional level into the conventional level. Specifically, the boys show moral progress toward stage 4, the "law and order orientation," where "there is orientation toward authority, fixed rules, and the maintenance of the social order. Right behavior consists of doing one's duty, showing respect for authority, and maintaining the given social order for its own sake" (55). Batman and Robin morally educate the boys to gain such respect for authority, law, and social order. Batman imparts his lesson upon the boys: "I hope this proves to you what sort of underhanded yellow rats criminals are." The boys eagerly agree, marking success for the vigilantes in steering Gotham's youth down a moral path. The issue ends with Bruce telling Dick, "It's up to other cities to do the same[,] build more playgrounds, gymnasiums—encourage youngsters to join school and church organizations[.] Do this and we will wipe out crime!" (Finger and Kane 1940e). The vigilantes make it their mission to promote positive moral development through improving the environment. For Kohlberg, "the teacher must help the student to consider genuine moral conflicts, think about the reasoning he uses in solving such conflicts, see inconsistencies and inadequacies in his way of thinking and find ways of resolving them" (Kohlberg and Hersh 1977, 57). Batman and Robin aim for Gotham's youth to achieve such a moral education.

This issue serves as a public service announcement to Americans to change and rework urban environments to make safer places for children to grow up. The youth need places where they can develop morals and values that are productive. Cities need to promote goodness rather than serve as breeding grounds for criminals. America faced high child poverty rates during the 1930s, which were at nearly 70 percent (Corsaro 2005, 259). The comic urges Americans to improve these conditions. Batman's message clearly reflects the extant intentions for improving society in the real world, as during the 1940s, child poverty rates in America declined (259).

The existence of a crime school in Gotham occurs again almost fifty years later in *Batman* #408 (1987). Located in Crime Alley, Ma Gunn's School for Boys opens, taking in runaways to help and educate them. A well-run school aimed at targeting the problems of this section of the city could help deter criminality in the youth who witness it every time they step outside. Batman tells Ma Gunn, "I for one **admire** what you're trying to do. The only way to turn Crime Alley around is by helping the **next** generation" (Collins and Andru 1987). However, this image of a moral and admirable institution turns out to be a rouse—Ma Gunn's school is actually a crime school. In *Batman* #409, she teaches the boys about different types of guns and encourages them to drink alcohol. She also brings them to an art museum to steal jewels for the Joker. The only lesson that Ma Gunn teaches her students that is not criminal is proper grammar (Collins and Warner 1987). In Gotham, adult criminals and sympathizers aim to direct the moral development of the children.

In *Batman* #408, Batman catches Jason Todd stealing the tires from the Batmobile. Jason is a cigarette-smoking orphan whose mother overdosed on drugs and father is believed to have been killed by his boss, Two-Face. Batman says that he is going to tell the juvenile authorities about Jason, who replies, "I can fend for **myself** just fine! I know how to make it on the streets—and I **like** it there!" (Collins and Andru 1987). Jason has survived on the streets so far, demonstrating willpower and independence. He was forced to grow up when his mother died and now practices any means for survival. When Batman asks him about school, Jason says, "I graduated a **long** time ago—from the streets of Crime Alley." Jason seems to have received plenty of education in criminal behavior simply from his daily life. But he has no role models, no morally upright individuals guiding him or teaching him about respect, self-care, health, and appropriate behavior. The only path for a boy of Crime Alley is toward crime.

Batman sends Jason to Ma Gunn's, thinking that she will help the troubled child. Despite his apparent criminal nature, Jason does have a sense that this school is inappropriate and dangerous. He calls it "a kindergarten for crime" and tells Batman, "I don't wanna learn to be no *crook*. I just boost what it takes to *survive*" (Collins and Warner 1987). Jason is not motivated by greed, lust, or adventure. He understands right and wrong but feels that he has no other means of survival. Jason is difficult to classify according to Kohlberg's stages. On the one hand, he behaves according to stage 2 of the preconventional level, where "right action consists of that which instrumentally satisfies one's own needs and occasionally the needs of others" (Kohlberg and Hersh 1977, 54–5). However, Jason also has a grasp of right and wrong in terms of society's rules. He does a civic duty (Kohlberg's stage 4 under the conventional level) in providing Batman with the truth about Ma Gunn's school. Jason does not morally develop following a particular sequence of stages.

His morality is impacted by his surroundings. While he demonstrates moral behavior consistent with stage 4, he also creates his own rules and justifies them based on necessity for survival. Jason illustrates the ways in which moral development is more complicated than a set of stages, and perhaps a moral compass exists within an individual despite environmental influences. Jason also illustrates the capacity to understand right and wrong without the guidance of a moral role model. His justification for breaking the law is similar to Batman, who also creates his own rules in order to protect others.

Environment can certainly influence a child's development, but it may create stereotypes or assumptions. When Batman refuses to believe Jason's warnings about Ma Gunn's school, Jason yells, "Just 'cause I'm a *kid* from Crime Alley don't make me a *liar!*" (Collins and Warner 1987). Jason is aware that his upbringing may make him morally questionable but is firm that he is telling the truth. Ultimately, Jason helps Batman stop Ma Gunn and the other boys, and Batman decides to take him in to become the new Robin. What had been a pathway to crime takes a redeeming turn toward vigilantism. Batman recognizes that both he and Jason hold similar moral values. They both create their own interpretation of the law but with good intentions.

The moral malleability of Gotham's youth provides Batman with the opportunity to guide and educate. As the city's renowned protector, he is in a position of influence. Despite Batman creating his own laws through his vigilantism, his moral compass remains intact, aligning with selflessness and the duty of protecting the people of Gotham. He is concerned with the lessons that he can impart to the city's youth rather than the methods that he must use. In *Batman* Vol. 2 #44 (2015), while Batman investigates the murder of 15-year-old Peter Duggio in the Narrows, a poor project in Gotham, he observes some kids standing around outside: "They look at him like they want to talk. But not about the case. About their lives, about everyday concerns." The children have a need for social interaction with a potential mentor figure. Rather than approach the kids in need, Batman scares them away. Later, he unravels Peter's story—from dealing with the Penguin to taking a drug that temporarily transformed his body. Peter grew wings and flew off but then fell to his death. Batman realizes that while there were criminals involved, "above all, the one to catch was the boy. Before he fell" (Snyder, Azzarello, and Jock, 2015). Batman notes a critical period in this child's development where intervention could have saved him from a premature death.

According to Maria Montessori ([1948] 2007), children morally develop during a stage that begins at age 7. She refers to the time of moral development as a "sensitive period" (6). Teachers are encouraged to take a "delicacy of approach" to morality at this age (6). Also, Montessori argues that at this age, "the concept of justice is born, simultaneously with the understanding of the relationship between one's acts and the needs of others" (6). Montessori finds that the child needs "to escape the closed environment" (7) during this time. In *Batman* Vol. 2 #44, Peter never could escape his environment. He was enclosed within the Narrows, thus limiting his ability to socially and morally develop. While he did not turn criminal, his associations with criminals put his life at risk. He was unable to escape his surroundings even though he literally grew wings.

Under such conditions of the closed environment, a child can easily fall into a life of crime or become associated with criminals. The child's capacity for social and moral development is stunted. In *Batman* Vol. 2 #44, Batman realizes this, which brings him to return to the boys he had previously scared away. Batman tells them to talk to him, ending the issue with the hope that Batman can reach the youth of Gotham. For sociologist William A. Corsaro (2005, 275), "heightened fears about children's safety are, to a large degree, a reflection of our own adult anxieties about our lack of control in a rapidly changing world." Batman wants to maintain a controlled environment, one where rules are followed and laws are obeyed. He sees the chaos of Gotham and the ways that it can negatively impact the youth of the city. He tries to restore and rebuild after devastation hits, but there are too many alleyways in Gotham City. He cannot fix every space, but he will try—either as Batman or as Bruce Wayne. Batman can talk to the kids and learn about their lives, their needs, and the dangers that they face. He can be a positive influence and role model and bring them out of their closed environments. Then Bruce Wayne can use his influence and finances to try to build and develop safer spaces.

Despite the closing of crime schools in the comics, adolescents in Gotham may have other pathways to criminality. Gotham City (and Batman) needs thugs, thieves, and supervillains to bring action to the franchise. Gotham will always be a breeding ground for criminality no matter how productive or proactive Batman is. However, the comics can use adolescent crime as a subject for imparting lessons upon America's youth readers.

Selina Kyle is another child of Gotham who, like Jason, turns to crime for her own survival. *Catwoman* Vol. 2 #0 (Moench and Balent 1994) and *Catwoman* Vol. 2 #81 (Carlton and Johnson 2000) show Selina growing up in the poor slums of Gotham City. Her father is an abusive alcoholic, and Selina discovers her mother dead in a bathtub of blood after cutting her wrists. A few years later, when she is about 13, Selina finds her father's dead body after having drank himself to death. Selina runs off and tries living on the streets, but she is caught stealing after a week and is sent to Seagate Juvenile Home for Girls, an institution for orphan girls who are "runaways and other underage offenders who would be criminals if not for a technicality of the law," according to the director. The director says, "You've had your chance at being dear sweet innocent children—and you've forfeited that chance and that luxury, every last one of you!" (Moench and Balent 1994). Selina has to cope with the trauma of discovering both her parents' dead bodies, resulting in a loss of her innocence. She chooses to survive on her own rather than through the help of social services but is ill-equipped for living on the streets. In *Catwoman* #0, Seagate proves to be a corrupt environment, so Selina leaves. The issue then traces her development as a thief from her early, reckless days to age 18 when she had "refined her techniques" as a cat burglar (Moench and Balent 1994). But in Gotham City, the line between vigilantism and criminality can often be blurry. Selina's troubled adolescence may have corrupted her in some ways, but she often helps Batman, demonstrating some moral sensibility; thus, she serves as a liminal character—not quite a heroine or a villainess. She intrigues Batman because he too exists as a liminal character where he does not abide by the law but maintains moral superiority.

In Bruno Heller's TV series *Gotham* (2014–19), Selina (Camren Bicondova) is a teenage orphan living on the streets. She witnesses the murders of Bruce's parents Thomas and Martha Wayne. Seeing a murder at such a young age could be traumatizing for an adolescent, but Selina remains a tough, headstrong young woman. She does not show emotion readily, aside from frustration. Like her original comic book character, Selina cannot be categorized as a heroine or villainess because she aligns herself with both factions. She conducts criminal behavior, but she also helps Bruce and James Gordon. However, she does seem somewhat dulled to murder as she pushes Reginald Payne out a window to his death (Woodruff 2015). Selina commits murder to protect Bruce, so her intentions are noble, but her actions make her a teenage killer. According to Kohlberg's levels, Selina's morality would fall under the preconventional level because she does not follow the law but justifies her actions based on her intentions. She is self-serving; even though she helps Bruce, she does so because he is her friend. Travis Langley (2012, 101) describes the characters of Selina Kyle and Jason Todd as exhibiting "adaptive delinquency"; their transgressions can be described as "an attempt to adjust to the manifold disadvantages of poverty and inner-city living." Such a description positions the characters as responding to their dire situations.

Despite aiding Bruce on numerous occasions throughout the TV series, Selina also joins the ranks of the villains, including Fish Mooney's posse, which she calls "the coolest gig ever" (Heller 2015). Selina fluctuates working for and with whoever is most convenient for her. She does not attend school but learns from living on the streets and from the criminals in her surroundings. In fact, Selina becomes a master of survival on the streets of Gotham. In Season 2, she even teaches Bruce how to live on the streets because she can skillfully navigate the city and has networks spread throughout. She is resourceful, agile, and fast thinking. Selina is perhaps the embodiment of all that exists in Gotham City: she is a heroine, villainess, broken youth, and survivor.

Even youth with healthy upbringings can turn to crime. Despite his father being Gotham City's police commissioner, James Gordon Jr. becomes a criminal with violent impulses. His father may be an upholder of the law, but James Jr. makes his own rules and does not hold the same moral code as any member of the Gordon family. *Detective Comics* #875 (2011) contains a flashback story where Commissioner Gordon's ex-wife calls him to tell him that a boy who was bullying James Jr. ended up in the hospital from something he ate, implying that James Jr. may have contaminated his food. Barbara brought James Jr. to different doctors, and one wanted him to take a psychopathology test. As Gordon remembers the past, we see how as a baby, James Jr. never cried. As a young child, he mutilated birds, and for Halloween one year, he dressed as the Joker (Snyder and Francavilla 2011a). Since he was an infant, there were indicators that he would take a pathway to crime.

Langley (2012) defines James Gordon Jr. as both a sociopath and a psychopath, noting that the terms are often used interchangeably (101). He describes symptoms of psychopathy, including "grandiose self-concept, lack of empathy, and rejection of responsibility for one's own behavior" (104). Langley also says psychopaths "should know the difference between right and wrong, but at heart they don't understand it and they don't care" (104). James Gordon Jr.'s upbringing should have provided him moral guidance, but his tendency toward criminality and his lack of empathy suggest that he was never able to morally develop due to this psychological condition. James Jr. began his criminal escapades as a teenager. In *Detective Comics* #881, Barbara Gordon, his adoptive sister, recalls a time that James Jr.'s bus driver called him "four eyes." A year later, the driver was attacked in an alley, her face slashed with a razor blade matchbox weapon that James Jr. concocted. The woman was disfigured as a result of the attack. Barbara tells James Jr. that his attack was not for revenge: "You were out to **hurt her** for the sake of hurting her. Because you **enjoyed** it. You always have. That's you, James. You **want** people to pick on you. You want them to give you an excuse to do what you're dying to do already … torture them" (Snyder, Francavilla, and Jock 2011). Barbara finds that James Jr.'s nature—from childhood into adulthood—is sadistic.

While psychiatrist Richard Krafft-Ebing, in his 1894 edition of *Psychopathia Sexualis*, certainly finds sexual elements in many cases of sadism, he qualifies different types of sadistic impulses, arriving at a basic, summative definition: "the wish to inflict pain and use violence" (148). James Jr. recalls that when he was a teenager Gordon had him locked up in Arkham to try to scare him into behaving better. He was a couple of cells from the Joker, whom he claims to have gotten along with. Certainly, they both share a sadistic pleasure from committing crimes and causing harm to others. James Jr. tells Barbara that he told the Joker all about her and had the idea of her attack, but then he says he is kidding (Snyder, Francavilla, and Jock 2011). He has a manipulative, perverse sense of humor in claiming credit for the attack that paralyzed his sister and caused her severe trauma.

Holding onto childhood grudges, an adult James Jr. tortures and dismembers Ben Wolff, who took his glasses when James Jr. was a kid (Snyder and Jock 2011). James Jr. is fueled by his criminal nature and even tries to perpetuate criminality in Gotham. In *Detective Comics* #879, Barbara and Commissioner Gordon realize that James Jr. has reversed the effects of a medication and plans on putting it in infant formula. Gordon says, "He's hoping to turn people into … psychopaths like him" (Snyder and Francavilla 2011b). James Jr. plays the role of criminal deity, wanting to create a breed of psychopathic humans by corrupting them as infants. This plan is similar to those that have been concocted and attempted by the Joker.[3] Despite being the son of Gotham's police commissioner—whose life's purpose is to uphold the law and maintain order in the city—James Jr. was born with a toxicity reflective of supervillains in Gotham.

James Jr. even claims that he is a product of Gotham City. He recalls to Batman his mother telling Gordon that Gotham "is a city of nightmares" (Snyder, Francavilla, and Jock 2011). Batman (who is Dick Grayson in this issue) replies, "I think she meant that raising kids in Gotham is tough." Dick knows the challenges of childhood and adolescence in the city. James Jr. finds the city created him as a contrast to Batman with the intent on psychopathy being the dominant human trait of future generations. He says:

> This place is special, Dick. It is a city of **nightmares.** And I'm yours. I'm the **face you see in the glass.** A man with no conscience. No empathy. Gotham made me to challenge you. You and my father and Barbara and all the heroes who don't see the truth. Because the truth is that men like me, men like the ones in that study, **we're** the future. We're the next step for humanity. We're not damaged. We're superior. I am **Gotham's son,** and the city made me so I could help usher in a new generation of children, true children. (Snyder, Francavilla, and Jock 2011)

James Jr.'s perspective makes him an Antichrist tasked with bringing forth "true children"—babies that he has poisoned in order to populate the city of the future with psychopathic criminals. His beliefs deny Gotham's natural children legitimate existence. It also may be argued that Bruce and Dick are Gotham's sons made to quell corruption and crime. If the city can birth both moral and immoral children, is Gotham good or evil? James Jr. appears inherently—or perhaps, psychologically—evil, whereas Batman's moral compass steers him toward defending and protecting innocent people.

Many factors could contribute to James Jr.'s stray from upright citizenry. However, Langley (2012, 99) observes, "James Gordon Jr. is a product of more than genes, upbringing, and head injury. He's a child of Gotham City, the city that killed the Waynes and gives rise to a never-ending line of hoodlums and freaks." The city itself is an agent of crime, creating criminals to maintain its decrepit condition. Langley accuses Gotham for murdering the Waynes rather than the individual criminal who actually shot them. James Gordon Jr. is, in a sense, a victim of the city, a city that has failed him and its citizens in general. It does not matter that he is the offspring of the police commissioner; Gotham's toxic nature makes the city a breeding ground for criminals. For Kohlberg (Kohlberg and Hersh 1977, 57), "moral development results from the dialogue between the person's cognitive structure and the complexity presented by environment." While James Gordon Jr. may be a psychopath, his environment also contributes to his moral decay. Despite the interventions of the Bat Family, Gotham is a place that fosters criminality. But it is also a place that gives birth to superheroes.

Pathways to Heroism

Developmental psychologist James Marcia (1980, 159) defines identity as "a self-structure—an internal self-constructed, dynamic organization of drives, abilities, beliefs, and individual history." Marcia finds identity to be dynamic, a process that spans infancy through old age (159–60). However, Bruce Wayne's life does not fall under such a delineation due to his deliberate transition from child to vigilante. While the Batman identity is a self-construct as a result of childhood trauma, when Bruce dons the cowl, his identity as Bruce Wayne no longer develops. From here on out, Bruce Wayne is the mask, and Batman is the adopted identity of this individual.

Bruce Wayne's development into Batman illustrates a coping strategy and matured mentality following childhood trauma. Research professor of social work Brené Brown (2017, 241) argues, "Of all the things trauma takes away from us, the worst is our willingness, or even our ability, to be vulnerable." Bruce is typically depicted as 8 years old when his parents are murdered. The first appearance of the murder occurs in *Detective Comics* #33 (Finger et al. 1939). The narration states, "The boy's eyes are wide with terror and shock as the horrible scene is spread before him." Days later, Bruce prays at his bed and declares, "And I swear by the spirits of my parents to avenge their deaths by spending the rest of my life warring on all criminals." In prematurely growing up, Bruce loses his vulnerability. Bruce's trauma gives his life purpose and a goal. His vow is a deliberate declaration of identity. While Marcia (1980, 161) argues that with identity formation, "decisions are not made once and for all, but have to be made again and again," Bruce's decision to become Batman does not follow such identity development. Instead, he makes a single commitment and essentially gives up his identity as Bruce. Bruce Wayne will no longer develop; his vow catapults him prematurely into adulthood. In *The New Titans* #65 (1990), Dick Grayson tells Tim Drake, "I don't think Bruce was *ever* young. At least not after his parents were killed. I think he became an *adult* in that instant. He certainly didn't allow himself to enjoy growing up" (Wolfman and Grummett 1990). Bruce skips adolescence and focuses his energy on his newfound purpose rather than on himself. He denies experiencing the pleasures of childhood because they would not help him achieve his agenda of fighting crime.

Tom King (2018) takes a different approach to Bruce's identity development. In *Batman* Vol. 3 #50, Selina writes a letter to Bruce where she claims that he is actually still a child underneath the mask:

You hide your eyes because they reveal you fully. There's nothing in the blue, beneath the blue, on the blue. Because there you are. Not the flawed hero. But the boy in pain. The boy longing not to be alone. The plea of: please, someone help me. Just be there. Be here. With me. And no one comes, and you head out into the night. Not despite that longing but because of it. You fight for this city. You save the city. This world. This everything. That's your power, Bruce. More than anything else. You look upon the world with the eyes of a child. (King 2018)

Unlike Dick's explanation of Bruce's development, Selina sees a trapped child who adopted this role to hide his pain. Selina writes, "You are still a child, Bruce. A hurt child." She sees his pain that no one else has been able to see. With this perspective, Batman is able to exist only because Bruce has not grown up. He never coped with his pain; instead, he bottled it and put on a mask. His fearlessness and selflessness stem from the persistence of youth.

Brown's (2017, 276) theory directly addresses the ways in which children react to feeling vulnerable: "As children we found ways to protect ourselves from vulnerability, from being hurt, diminished, and disappointed. We put on armor; we used our thoughts, emotions, and behaviors as weapons; and we learned how to make ourselves scarce, even to disappear." This description is perfectly fitting of Bruce when he takes the oath. His armor is his cape and cowl. Any purpose for Bruce Wayne disappears, and that identity becomes the mask for his true self. However, Brown considers a healthy approach to vulnerability for adults as she continues, "Now as adults we realize that to live with courage, purpose, and connection—to be the people we long to be—we must again be vulnerable. The courage to be vulnerable means taking off the armor we use to protect ourselves, putting down the weapons that we use to keep people at a distance, showing up, and letting ourselves be seen" (276). Bruce Wayne/Batman will not be vulnerable. He will remain behind the mask because he has decided that the man underneath does not matter; the greater purpose is more important. Bruce sacrifices his vulnerability and his opportunity for healthy relationships with others when he sacrifices himself. While this has been the traditional approach to Batman, King (2018) gives Bruce the opportunity to achieve this vulnerability by marrying Selina. He allows the man to emerge. However, when Selina realizes this, she decides not to marry Bruce so that Batman can live on.

Tom King and Mikel Janín (2017a) portray Bruce's response to his trauma in a way that even more deliberately illustrates his identity sacrifice as a child. In *Batman* Vol. 3 #12, Bruce confesses in a letter to Selina that his parents' deaths left him feeling so hopeless that he attempted suicide. He describes putting a razor blade to his wrist but then letting it fall to the ground. He writes, "I'd done it, I'd surrendered. My life was no longer my life." At this point, he declared his oath and committed his life to being a vigilante. He writes, "It's the choice of a boy. The choice to die. I am Batman. I am suicide." Bruce admits here that his suicide was the death of his childhood and essentially Bruce Wayne. He completely gave his life up in order to become Batman; thus, his identity does follow Marcia's definition in that it is a self-construct. Arguably, it may also be considered a self-sacrifice. King and Janín's approach to Bruce is that identity is a choice. He kills the Bruce Wayne identity and takes on the role of Batman. According to Marcia's (1980, 161) four identity statuses, Bruce would best fall under "identity achievement," which describes "individuals who have experienced a decision-making period and are pursuing self-chosen occupation and ideological goals." However, Bruce's decision-making occurs abruptly without consideration of other potential roles for himself rather than over the course an exploration period. Being Batman becomes his ideology, and he pursues this path with vigor.

Heller's TV series *Gotham* provides an adolescent Bruce Wayne whose drive to avenge his parents' deaths brings him to work with Gordon, live on the streets of Gotham, and train to fight. In Season 2 Episode 14, in a letter to Alfred Pennyworth, Bruce explains that he needs to live on the streets of Gotham in order to better understand the people of Gotham that he has been sheltered from:

> You can't kill murder. You can't get revenge on evil. You can only begin to fight such things by not doing them. And you can only fight them where they live, not just at Wayne Enterprises. In the streets, in the slums, in the bad parts of town ... I'm not going to start battling muggers or anything. But one day, I am going to do something to help the people of Gotham. I don't know what yet, but I will. Meantime, I need to learn stuff. Number one: I need to learn how to live in the same world other people have to live in. Selina's giving me a place to sleep and will show me the ropes. (Harper 2016)

Bruce feels this experience will prepare him for the future where he will be better equipped to help Gotham's people. This is an opportunity for discovery—both of himself and of the inner workings of Gotham City. Bruce gains a better understanding of the social fabric of Gotham and the ways in which criminals operate by immersing himself in their geographical space. He also tests himself, getting into a fight that provides the self-realization of his own inner strength (Hull 2016). The fight is therapeutic for Bruce, allowing him to compartmentalize and process his emotional struggles and then feel confident in himself.

Aside from *Gotham*, in most accounts, Bruce essentially skipping adolescence makes him harder for fans to relate to. Even though Robin has had multiple identities, the character has become the heroic figure who can best represent and inspire America's youth. Batman creators introduced Robin as a boy named after Robin Hood specifically to be relatable and recognizable to readers (Langley 2012, 179–80). Robin's (Dick Grayson's) first appearance is in *Detective Comics* #38 (Finger and Kane 1940f). The first page declares, "Introducing in this issue ... an exciting new figure whose incredible gymnastic and athletic feats will astound you ... a laughing, fighting, young daredevil who scoffs at danger like the legendary Robin Hood whose name and spirit he has adopted ... Robin The Boy Wonder." This issue also provides Dick Grayson's backstory, where he is a member of the Flying Graysons, a family of acrobats (father, mother, and son). They are performing outside Gotham City when Dick overhears confrontations between the circus owner and gangsters who threaten him for money. The next night, they put acid on the ropes, and Dick's parents plummet to their deaths. Batman tells Dick that he cannot go to the police because the gangsters will kill him. He relates to the boy: "My parents too were killed by a criminal. That's why I've devoted my life to exterminate them." Dick asserts that he wants to do the same and that he is not afraid. Batman makes Dick swear an oath: "that we two will fight together against crime and corruption and never to swerve from the path of righteousness!" This declaration allows Bruce to protect and guide Dick and establish a partnership built on shared values, goals, and motivations.

Robin is described as "a sturdy, lithe figure with a dare-devil grin on his young face" (Finger and Kane 1940e). Meg Downey (2015) traces the aging progression of Dick's character, much of which occurs due to the controversies of the mid-1950s:

The beginning was a bit of a slow burn. Writers began to allow Dick Grayson to age. This was a protracted reaction to Wertham's accusations of sexual deviancy, which often touched upon the pederastic nature of an adult man and a young boy living in such close proximity with one another. It didn't happen all at once, but by the 1970[s] Dick was a "teen;" by the mid-70s he was officially college age.

Dick leaves for college in *Batman* #217 (Robbins and Novick 1969d). He proclaims, "I'm a **man** now!" as he leaves Wayne Manor to head off to Hudson University. Dick's development through puberty that was depicted in the comics through the 1970s was uncommon in comic books, especially because these universes are typically stagnant (Downey 2015). This makes Dick a realistic representation of a coming-of-age adolescent who is relatable to American youth and also a role model as an educated superhero who found purpose in his life following trauma.

Dick Grayson, like Bruce, is a child of trauma, similarly witnessing his parents' deaths at the hands of a criminal. In the podcast *The Arkham Sessions*, psychologist Andrea Letamendi (Letamendi and Ward 2014) analyzes Dick Grayson's trauma in the episode "Robin's Reckoning Part I" of *Batman: The Animated Series*. She defines trauma as "an event that includes actual or threatened death or injury. This could include experiencing it yourself or witnessing someone else experience something like that." She continues, "There's no doubt that [Dick Grayson] experienced what we would consider a traumatic event." After witnessing his parents' deaths, Dick wants to track down Tony Zucco, the man responsible for their demise. Letamendi finds Dick's feelings and behavior as normal given the circumstances: "There's really nothing that we see here that's necessarily unhealthy in terms of Robin's determination, his level of anger, his level of resentment. I think that's all natural. I think that's all, as I said before, all developmentally normal as well as emotionally—of course he wants to be involved in taking down the man that killed his parents." Dick's inner drive for revenge is different from Bruce's feelings after the murder of his own parents. Bruce almost immediately gave up his identity for a larger cause, whereas Dick's emotions are targeted at the man who killed his parents. Dick's emotional response to his trauma is perhaps more realistic for a child than Bruce's abrupt decision to give up his childhood. We also do not typically see much emotion from Bruce, but Dick shows his pain and anger. Therefore, young readers and audiences may be able to emotionally relate better to Dick.

No matter who is under the suit, Robin is a victim of trauma who was taken in by a vigilante to be trained as a sidekick. While these circumstances seem to be extraordinary, they may still be inspirational to young readers who may see themselves in the boy. Letamendi (Letamendi and Ward 2014) says, "We know that about 68–75% of children under 18 will experience some kind of trauma." Even though Bruce also experienced similar trauma to Dick, since the franchise tends to skip his adolescence, Robin exists as the character who is more relatable to young readers. In "Robin's Reckoning Part I" of *Batman: The Animated Series*, Dick asks Bruce, "Does the hurt ever go away?" Bruce replies, "I wish I could say yes. But it will get better in time" (Rogel 1993). Letamendi (Letamendi and Ward 2014) offers to listeners: "It's really not so much about the idea that something bad happened to you, but that it's what you do with that traumatic event; it's how you make meaning out of that and how you move past it." This is the way readers and audiences can also approach their own traumas. Michael Brody (2007, 116) notes, "like myths and fairy tales, [comics] provide an externalization of inner conflicts. The child can now see his inner difficulties more clearly and reflect on a variety of solutions." Whether experience with trauma or any other conflict, children reading the comics may be able to relate and subsequently cope with their own difficult situations.

In *Batman Chronicles: The Gauntlet* (1997), Batman sends Dick out on the streets of Gotham as his final exam. The test is whether he can survive the streets of Gotham without being caught by Batman. Instead of hiding, Dick ends up collecting evidence against a crime boss and taking down a syndicate of Gotham's organized criminals. Bruce tells Alfred,

> The whole concept of Robin is important to Dick, old friend—and it's important *for* Dick. When I lost my parents I had no way to release my anger, my—*grief*. Though he hides it well, those same emotions are churning away inside Dick. Robin will be his release

valve, a way to exorcise that darkness before it can corrupt his soul. (Canwell and Weeks 1997)

Bruce knows how to channel his own emotions into productive vigilantism, so he effectively serves as a guide and role model for Dick. Dick can use his pain toward good rather than toward causing additional suffering. But in Gotham, tragedy can steer a child in either direction. In *Batman* #436 (1989), Tony Zucco is up for parole. A flashback of his youth shows Tony witnessing his father being murdered by mobsters. Tony's mother was also killed, and Tony was separated from his siblings and brought to St. Jude's Orphanage. Tony then ran away and killed the men who killed his parents. A nun from the orphanage found him and tried to help, but it is implied that he killed her too. He joined up with one of the major crime families, eager to learn from them. The present-day parole hearing compares Dick to Tony since both were children whose parents were murdered. Alfred says to the committee, "Zucco was brought up with hatred, and that's what he returned to the world. Richard Grayson was brought up with love—and not even Zucco's act of murder could change that" (Wolfman and Broderick 1989). Zucco shut out opportunities to be morally guided because he was so consumed by the death of his parents that it drove him to become a killer himself. This issue shows how despite sharing a similar tragedy, these youths chose different paths. Dick embraced the help and guidance of a morally upright citizen, while Zucco actually became the type of criminal that had initially triggered his personal loss of innocence.

Dick eventually grew out of being Robin and became the hero Nightwing.[4] Jason Todd was next in line to serve as Batman's sidekick. Jason makes his first appearance in *Batman* #408 (1987). This version of Robin was reimagined Post-Crisis as "a cigarette-smoking street urchin in the process of boosting the Batmobile's tires the first time Batman meets him" (Langley 2012, 184). Apparently, readers were not too keen on the new boy wonder (185). Jason did not last long. In Jim Starlin and Jim Aparo's four-part miniseries *Batman: A Death in the Family* (*Batman* #426–29; 1988–9), the Joker beats up Robin and then leaves him locked up in a room with a bomb. Readers were then given the opportunity to call in and vote whether or not Jason should be killed. The last page of *Batman* #427 states, "Robin will die because the Joker wants revenge, but you can prevent it with a telephone call" (see Starlin and Aparo 1988a). The statement was phrased in a way to encourage readers to save Robin's life. Readers were invited to call one of two numbers to cast their vote over a two-day period. In a very close final tally—5,343 to 5,271—readers voted to kill off Jason Todd's Robin (Dullea 1988). The circumstances of the vote were not well received by Batman creative team members. "Bob Kane hated the stunt" (Langley 2012, 185). Frank Miller expressed utter disgust about it: "*A Death in the Family* should be singled out as the most cynical thing that particular publisher has ever done. An actual toll-free number where fans can call in to put the axe to a little boy's head" (qtd. in Sharrett 2015, 35). Essentially, the readers, not the Joker, killed the boy. The public demand shows that many fans had no qualms about killing a young superhero, which could suggest questionable moral values of these readers. However, we may also consider this as a way for readers to be involved in the creative process. Unfortunately, it came at the expense of a main character's—and a child's—life.

Jason's death weighs heavily on Batman, as he reassesses his decisions in training the boy to become Robin. In his search for Robin's body, Batman thinks, "Why didn't I see that you were too young for this kind of work? How could I have been so stupid?" (Starlin and Aparo 1988b). Batman recounts his experiences with the boy, regretting mistakes he made in raising Jason as his protégé. The depiction of Jason's death is gruesome. Robin's body is bloody and battered. His Robin suit is torn to shreds. A devastated Batman carries the boy's body, cradled like a baby. Batman was father figure and role model to Jason, and now he must face his violent death.

The loss of Jason Todd causes Batman to prefer to continue defending the city solo, but his refusal to have a partner is short-lived. In *Batman* #441 (1989), 13-year-old Tim Drake recalls seeing Dick and the Flying Graysons at the circus the night that Dick's parents died (Wolfman and Aparo 1989). Then, in *Batman* #442 (1989), Tim saves Batman wearing the Robin costume. After Jason's death, Batman says that he will not put another child in danger. He has finally realized that his actions have been endangering a child, but it took a death for Batman to gain such a perspective. Despite Batman's new view, Robin is still a necessary figure. Tim argues with him that Batman and Robin's costumes serve as symbols of law and justice. He says, "Batman *has* to have a Robin," and "Batman *needs* a Robin" (Wolfman, Pérez, and Aparo 1989). They have a reciprocal relationship as the older mentor guides the youngster while Robin provides Batman a sidekick to help in his plight against criminality and be a potential replacement if Bruce retires or dies. As he is a symbol of justice, it seems Gotham City needs a Robin as well to continue to show the way that youth can rise above destructive environmental influences and become productive—and lifesaving—role models.

The Robin identity comes to life when the individual finds a purpose and controls emotions. In *Batman* #455, Tim attends his mother's funeral. He says he knows why the vigilantes put on their suits: "They're **angry**. Full of **rage.** They want to **hit back**. They want to fill the **hole** that's **burning** inside them!" (Grant and Breyfogle 1990a). Bruce encourages deeper introspection, saying that Tim needs to live with his anger rather than fight against it because "one day it'll be your friend." Bruce has developed a productive way to cope with, control, and use his emotions. He imparts these lessons to his young pupil. Dick Grayson remarks on the cycle of coping with pain as a child: "But I guess we all need **some**thing to help us make **sense** of it all. We need to find **meaning** in the **pain** … **patterns** in the **chaos**. **Tim** needs it now, as I once needed it. As Bruce did before me." In the Batman franchise, vigilantism proves to be therapeutic for children of trauma. But this kind of therapy has a delicate integration process. Tim wants to become the next Robin, but Bruce says he is not ready because he needs to understand the commitment and be able to control himself:

> When you put on the suit you become larger than life. You become a **symbol**. And then you don't have a choice. You **have** to live up to what you've made yourself into. The mask hides your fear. No one knows what you're thinking. And it's double-edged. It frightens your enemies and feeds your strength. But **no** suit—**no** mask—can **ever** hide **you** from **yourself!** (Grant and Breyfogle 1990a)

Being Robin requires deliberate identity manipulation and control of emotions. The adolescent assuming the role must acquire a complete understanding of the symbol and of the self. And Batman—as a former child who suffered trauma—can help guide other trauma victims down a path of righteousness.

The process of becoming Robin continues in *Batman* #457. Scarecrow attacks Tim with fear gas, and Tim becomes tormented by a hallucination. During the hallucination, Tim sees the former Robins, who encourage him: "Don't fight it, Tim! **Live** with it! **Confront** it!"; "It's nothing to be ashamed of. But just because you're **afraid**—doesn't mean you can't **act!**"; and "You don't **need** the **suit!** You don't **need** the **mask!** It's in **you!** You make **yourself** a **hero!**" (Grant and Breyfogle 1990b). This allows Tim to fight the Scarecrow despite his fear. Tim reappropriates his fear to foster self-discovery. He overcomes fear—his own inner strength overpowering emotional duress—which makes him emerge as a hero. After this, Batman calls Tim by the name Robin. Tim has defeated his own emotional inhibitors and simultaneously proven himself as capable of being a vigilante.

In *Robin* Vol. 2 #124–5, Tim's father, Jack, eventually learns that his son is Robin and demands that Tim give up the gig (Willingham and Rodriguez de la Fuente 2004a and 2004b). He tells Tim to "get out of that ridiculous play-suit" (Willingham and Rodriguez de la Fuente 2004b). Describing Robin's suit as a "play-suit" makes it sound childish, as if being Robin is some kid's game. Meanwhile, Tim argues, "I've found my purpose in life." He tries to make his father understand by comparing himself to his grandfather who snuck into the military at age 15 to fight in the Second World War. Adolescent readers may be able to relate with this battle between parent and teenage child—the teen fighting to be who he wants to be and the parent trying to protect his child. Tim respects his father enough to agree to quit being Robin, but events that occur during the "War Games" arc bring Tim to return to being Robin, and his father eventually, though reluctantly, accepts his decision. Jack is concerned about his son, even saying to him, "You're sixteen years old. You shouldn't be running around in a mask and cape" (Meltzer and Morales 2004). But in the same conversation, Jack tells his son that he is proud of him. Jack is a conflicted parent who understands that Tim is doing a great service to the city as Robin but worries about his son constantly putting his own life in danger. Very soon after, Captain Boomerang kills Jack, leaving Tim an orphan just like the other Robins with Bruce as a protector and father figure.

Batman holds Tim tight as he cries over his father's dead body and says, "I've got you" (Meltzer and Morales 2005). Batman assumes the role of support. He will always hold onto Robin no matter who is in that role.

Tim eventually becomes Red Robin, and Bruce's son (born from Talia al Ghul), Damian, takes over as the next long-term Robin.[5] Damian Wayne was trained by the League of Assassins, and at age 10, he becomes Robin. In *Batman and Robin* Vol. 2 #2 (2011), Bruce says, "What the hell did Talia do to this kid to turn him into such a … killing machine …" (Tomasi and Gleason 2011). Bruce hopes that he can nurture Damian to quell his violence and stop him from killing. For Langley (2012, 189), "Damian is too dangerous to leave unguided," so Bruce needs to try to help his son to prevent him from turning into a villain. When Bruce grounds Damian as punishment, the boy leaves anyway, telling Alfred, "The city needs me" (Tomasi and Gleason 2012a). Despite his young age, Damian adopts the responsibility of being a defender and protector of Gotham. In trying to shift Damian's moral compass, Batman teaches his son, "You can't build a better world by killing criminals—it bankrupts your soul **and** society's by reinforcing the same cycle of violence" (Tomasi and Gleason 2012b). Batman imparts his wisdom to his son to disrupt patterns of murder and to morally train Damian.

Bruce Wayne serves as a father figure to Dick and all the subsequent Robins. But he is also their vigilante boss, coach, and role model. "Batman gives each Robin the mentor he himself didn't have and a father figure who's not on the payroll" (Langley 2012, 191). Leaving these boys without a mentor—especially in Gotham City—is too risky. Alfred says to Bruce, "You've given all the boys a moral and ethical road to follow. You've been their compass" (Tomasi and Gleason 2011). While the Robins have an older, experienced vigilante to learn the trade from, Bruce also gains from his relationship with a young pupil. "Identification reminds Bruce why he does this: to keep others from suffering what he once suffered. He goes out to serve the kid he once was. Identification provides a connection to his inner child—before his parents died, when they died, and afterward" (Langley 2012, 191–2). Bruce had to grow up quickly after his parents' deaths. The boys who become Robin also face difficult events in their own lives. Even though they turn to vigilantism, as Bruce did, they can still be boys and experience the adolescence that Bruce skipped. Tim Drake, especially, has been depicted in ways that highlight the triumphs and difficulties of growing up. Tim struggles balancing his schoolwork with his nighttime activities as Robin, but the inclusion of his teenage troubles makes him relatable to adolescent readers and the embodiment of American youth.

Teenage Troubles

The series *Robin* (Vol. 2) addresses many common problems that adolescents face daily. *Robin* #59 (1998) includes school bullies who antagonize Tim Drake's friend Philmont during gym class. Philmont is soon after found beaten to death. Tim and his friend Ives are with Philmont when the bullies approach him but do not take any action. After the tragedy, Ives says, "I just thought they'd rough him up like **usual**. We should have **done** something" (Dixon and Johnson 1998b). Ives feels guilt for his lack of action, but he notes the bullying had been a frequently occurring event. This issue shows the devastating potential outcomes of school bullying. It also illustrates a commonplace acceptance of bullying as a part of the students' day at school.

The 2000 report *Indicators of School Crime and Safety* released by the United States Department of Education found that "in 1999, about 5 percent of students ages 12 through 18 reported that they had been bullied at school in the last 6 months." The annual National Crime Victimization Survey conducted by the United States Department of Justice has shown the trends in violent victimization at school for youth aged 12–17. Between 1992 and 2010, the accounts peaked in 1994 (Finkelhor 2013). *Robin* #59 was released in 1998, during a time when violent victimization at school had started to decline. The comic contributes to awareness of bullying and allows youth readers to consider the potential outcomes of passivity and acceptance of bullying. The issue argues that no one should accept bullying as normal because it can have detrimental results. In a 2001 study of bullying on elementary school playgrounds, D. Lynn Hawkins, Debra J. Pepler, and Wendy M. Craig (2001, 512) found that "peers were present in 88% of bullying episodes and intervened in 19%." Tim and Ives are much older—high schoolers—but still lack the courage to intervene when Philmont is bullied. Eyes on Bullying reports that most bystanders "**passively accept** bullying by watching and doing nothing. Often without realizing it, these bystanders also contribute to the problem. Passive bystanders provide the audience a bully craves and the silent acceptance that allows bullies to continue their hurtful behavior" (Education Development Center 2008). The bully gains superiority over the victim, and the witnesses may also be intimidated by the actions. Tim has the skills and abilities to fight the bullies in school but must protect his identity as Robin. In *Robin* #60, Robin tracks down the bullies and beats them up—avenging his friend's murder. Unfortunately, Tim's actions come too late for Philmont, but the issue intends to teach young readers to avoid being bystanders and take action to stop bullying. With the combined efforts of school resource officers and bullying and violence prevention programs, bullying in American schools has been on the decline since the mid-1990s (Finkelhor 2013). *Robin* provides another means for reaching youth who may be victims, bystanders, or even bullies themselves.

Robin also helps a young man who wants to commit suicide in *Robin* #156 (2007). Robin spots someone on the edge of a tall building, planning on jumping. He goes to the rooftop and sits on the ledge and initiates a conversation. The young man is an unnamed college freshman, who represents any adolescent who struggles with heavy problems in life. Robin makes himself relatable, telling the young man, "I was out swinging around, thinking about all the ways I've screwed up and stuff" (Beechen and Williams II 2007). After Robin asks why he wants to jump, the college student starts talking. He says, "I hated high school. Always felt like I was outside looking in, never part of any group or anything." He says that he went to college as a way to "reinvent" himself but was not successful. He tried to be social but could not find anyone to connect with, and eventually he gave up his efforts. Earning poor grades and sleeping all the time, the student began displaying signs of depression. After returning home, his high school girlfriend broke up with him. The combination of everything brought him to the rooftop, where he tells Robin that other people have bigger problems, which might make him be viewed as weak. But Robin tells him, "Your problems are worse than anyone else's … because they're yours." This statement speaks to all readers. Individuals who may assume that others will trivialize their problems can garner comfort from Robin's words. While someone may be able to relate, no one can fully fathom the weight that an individual's troubles carry. So any problem, no matter how small it may seem, is worth attention and tending to in order to reduce its emotional and mental impact. Robin explains that even a superhero does not have it easy. Since Robin struggles with similar problems as other young people, he is relatable. He is not just some untouchable idol; he suffers and carries burdens like anyone else. Robin tells the young man that he copes with his struggles by reminding himself that things do get better, and when he is really having a hard time, it is helpful for him to talk to someone. Someone with a different perspective can give advice or just offer a listening ear. The young man embraces this suggestion as worth trying and leaves the rooftop with Robin. The issue ends with the phone numbers for the National Suicide Prevention Lifeline. According to the Centers for Disease Control and Prevention (CDC), in 2007, the suicide rate for individuals aged 15–24 was 9.7 per 100,000 (Xu et al. 2010). In 2007, suicide was the third leading cause of death among individuals ages 1–24 (Miniño et al. 2007). *Robin* #156 addresses a relevant issue for young people in America and offers advice and methods for easing pain and coping with daily burdens.

Another relevant issue present in *Robin* is teenage gun violence. In *Robin* #25 (1996), Karl, a classmate of Tim's at Gotham Heights High School, shows him his gun and says, "You see what's **happening** to our school? All kinds of punks from Gotham are coming here. They're going to turn this place into a **warzone**. You think **they're** not strapped?" (Dixon and Wieringo 1996a). Karl feels threatened by the potentially violent students, saying, "We don't stand up to these guys, then Gotham Heights High is finished." While Karl believes there is a need to have a gun in order to protect not just himself but the school too, Tim fears guns at school. High school violence is very much a concern for the adults as well. Karl's father tells Tim's father that these days, "you send your kid to school and he could get **killed** by some lowlife." Tim's father does not think teenagers are old enough to possess a weapon, whereas Karl's father feels that his son has the maturity to handle it. He wants his son to be protected. But the gun fails as a protective measure. Some punks start a fight with Karl at school that turns into guns being pulled and fired, and Karl is killed. Robin says that Karl "thought that gun made him invincible. It just made him a target" (Dixon and Wieringo 1996b). The issue makes the case that guns offer a false sense of security.

The National School Safety Center reported high numbers of homicides and deaths resulting from school shootings in the early 1990s (K12 Academics n.d.). In an article published in 1993, *The Baltimore Sun* reported the results of a poll of over 2,500 sixth- to twelfth-grade students nationwide conducted by the Harvard School of Public Health. Strikingly, 59 percent of students said that they could get a handgun if they needed one. "Nine percent said that they had shot a gun at someone," and "eleven percent [said] they have been shot at during the past year" (Banisky 1993). The poll showed that this was not just a problem in urban environments; rather, it extended into the suburbs and rural areas of America as well. Karl's storyline in *Robin* was responding to an existing concern in the 1990s regarding guns and youth. While the Batman franchise has always contained violence, it also shows ways to balance that violence with lessons. These *Robin* issues show that being in possession of a gun cannot ensure protection. In fact, Karl was shot because he had the gun. The comics argue that objects of violence inherently carry violence with them despite the individual's intentions. The issue encourages conversations about the dangers of guns in school and indirectly addresses policy by appealing to the readers' emotions.

The *Robin* comics also deal with teenage pregnancy. In *Robin* #58 (1998), 15-year-old Stephanie Brown (Spoiler) tells Tim that she is pregnant and that the father ran out on her. Stephanie's mother takes her to Gotham county social services. After her mother tells the counselor that Stephanie is keeping the baby, the counselor hands them some literature and says, "There's no need to make a mistake you'll regret" (Dixon and Johnson 1998a), implying that Stephanie should consider having an abortion. Stephanie is firm in her decision to continue her pregnancy: "I let some **jerk** knock me up. I'm not going to make my baby pay because I was stupid." Stephanie takes responsibility for the outcome of her choice to be sexually active. She and her mother then go to a man's office and discuss giving the baby up for adoption. His corporate rhetoric makes adoption sound as if it is a business transaction: "I'll have the usual contracts drawn up," and "I can assure you that you'll be well compensated for your services." Stephanie interjects, "My baby is not a business," taking a firm and mature stance on the future of her unborn child. In *Robin* #59, Stephanie further discusses the situation with her mother, who encourages her daughter to learn from her experience and tells Stephanie that she is proud of her decision (Dixon and Johnson 1998b). Stephanie is still a teenager, balancing her schoolwork and physical condition. In *Robin* #65, Stephanie gives birth to her baby. She has decided to give the child up for adoption, and she does not even want to know the sex of the baby (Dixon and Rosado 1999). Stephanie has to make difficult decisions, which illustrates her maturity in recognizing her limits—as both a teenager and a superheroine—in raising a child. She also detaches herself emotionally from her pregnancy and child's birth so that she can more easily move forward from her decision.

In 1994, teen out-of-wedlock births peaked in America (Corsaro 2005, 268). The comics do not address heightened sexuality in teenagers. Instead, they show the life-changing impact of engaging in sexual behavior. Even superheroines have to deal with the challenges that American youth face daily. While becoming a superheroine is itself a moment of maturation, Chuck Dixon's story allows Stephanie to grow up through these issues. She ultimately acts more mature than some of the adults who treat her and her baby as objects. Despite the relevancy of the issue of teenage pregnancy, presenting it in comics requires delicacy in order to reach and maintain the fanbase. Langley (2012, 1987) observes, "Through Stephanie, the *Robin* series addressed teenage pregnancy and adoption sensitively and somewhat realistically while also stirring controversy for covering them at all." The inclusion of this story allowed *Robin* to continue to reflect contemporary America and provide young readers—especially females—the opportunity to sympathize or empathize with the trials that these teenage characters experience. The issue also raises awareness to teenage male readers who may be sexually active to show them the potential outcomes of such activity and what their partners may have to face.

Robin has also addressed child molestation and sexual abuse and harassment. In *Robin* #111 (2003), Stephanie tells Tim that when she was 11 years old, her father's friend Jim Murray was her babysitter. She recalls Murray's creepy comments, like asking her about boyfriends and suggesting that she model her favorite outfit for him. One time, he put his hands on her arms and moved toward her. She bit his face and ran away. For a couple of years afterwards, Stephanie would not let herself be alone with any male (Lewis and Woods 2003). The events forced her to prematurely grow up. She also tells Tim that it took her a couple of years to realize that she did nothing wrong. The issue allows readers to see not only the difficulties a victim of sexual abuse faces but also how she might rise above them. These events may have driven Stephanie out of childhood, but she has remained a strong person. She clearly still carries the trauma of the event but, in explaining her realization of her innocence in the interactions, shows readers who may be able to relate that the child is the victim and not a culpable party. Stephanie serves as role model for young female readers, not simply because she is a superheroine as Spoiler but also because she shares her personal struggles—burdens that make her relatable—and offers inspiration to rise above any obstacle.

* * *

The Batman franchise has made great efforts to present scenarios identifiable with America's youth. *Robin* has been a valuable series depicting teenage troubles and teaching lessons on how to overcome them. While the Batman comics have historically been criticized for the inappropriateness of content, they have always made efforts to educate adolescent readers and create characters who serve as role models. The franchise has traced the paths of child development in both heroes and criminals and shown the impact that an urban landscape can have on maturation. While some adolescents fall victim to Gotham's innate criminal nature, the various Robins and Stephanie continue to serve as representative of positive moral development capable within America's youth.

2

Beyond Batman: Gender in Gotham City

While Batman and Robin were the original defenders of Gotham City, the Bat Family has expanded to include female members as well. Batwoman, Batgirl, Huntress, Oracle, and Black Canary, among others, patrol the streets of Gotham and fight for the safety of its people. While Batman's strength and skills may be considered as masculinizing the image of a superhero, these women have demonstrated the ways in which femininity is also superheroic. Women in Gotham have also been represented as supervillainesses, often using their sexuality as power against men and also redefining and even exploiting femininity for their advantage. The twenty-first century has also brought a couple of transgender characters into Gotham and, in doing so, joinined the growing social conversations about public self-identification and normative gender roles.

In *Female Masculinity*, Judith Halberstam (1998, 1) theorizes about the fluidity of notions of gender, arguing, "Although we seem to have a difficult time defining masculinity, as a society we have little trouble in recognizing it, and indeed we spend massive amounts of time and money ratifying and supporting the versions of masculinity that we enjoy and trust." Comics publishers have traditionally aligned superheroism with masculinity and created visual signifiers of such masculinity because this has been an effective strategy for selling their product. Comics scholar Trisha L. Crawshaw (2019, 91) criticizes the approach as appropriating power for masculinity: "Modeling the 'appropriate' expressions of gender, comic books provide visual templates for emphasized femininity and hegemonic masculinity." However, this perspective neglects to note the power that women are also afforded through their femininity. The comic book industry has created recognizable visual representations of gender, and comics culture has therefore adopted an understanding of masculinity and femininity as a result. Crawshaw (2019, 91) further critiques that the representations are often "two-dimensional models of idealized social standards." However, when fans find pleasure in consuming comic books and films, there is not necessarily a risk of social peril. Fans can enjoy the comics for their idealizations without necessarily projecting such heightened standards on individuals in the real world. Certainly, Superman is a successful and impressive hero because he is physically strong and has the ability to fly. Thor's muscular physique has also been highlighted (and even mocked when he has neglected his body—see the 2019 film *Avengers: Endgame*), but he is a god with powers connected to universal elements that keep fans on the edge of their seats. These superheroes may display idealized masculinity, but they also have powers and abilities that impress and engage readers. The intention is not to establish social expectations of gender but to entertain through exciting action that is only possible because of the heroes' strength and power.

The Batman franchise has consistently portrayed Batman in ways that align masculinity with the strength, speed, and cunning of the hero. Batman is a typical male idol, intended to be a positive role model for male readers and audiences. He is strong, fearless, and confident. The films contain heightened images of such masculinity. Joel Schumacher's films, in particular, highlight the male anatomy in the costumes. Batman in Tim Burton's (1992) *Batman Returns* is sexualized when Catwoman strokes his suit. But in Schumacher's (1997) *Batman and Robin*, Batgirl's suit is also a distinct silhouette of her curves, demonstrating that anatomy becomes body armor. Therefore, the male and female form provide the heroes protection. The relationship between gender and superheroism has evolved over time in Gotham City. Batman has consistently represented the masculine ideal, while female characters have served as barometers of the changing social perspectives of women in America. In doing so, they also present a transformable feminine ideal that is projected through both heroines and villainesses.

Judith Butler's ([1990] 2007) theories on gender align it specifically with performance, which makes it an act directly related to social expectations. To understand gender, then, is to view the power and pressure of society on effecting a particular display of behavior. Butler argues:

> That the gendered body is performative suggests that it has no ontological status apart from the various acts which constitute its reality. This also suggests that if that reality is fabricated as an interior essence, that very interiority is an effect and function of a decidedly public and social discourse, the public regulation of fantasy through the surface politics of the body, the gender border control that differentiates inner from outer, and so institutes the "integrity" of the subject. (185)

Butler finds gender reality as essentialized through social influence and determination. The "outer" body and the "inner" essence are regulated through a "gender border control," which is a public creation. Butler's arguments suggest a power of society to define and influence gender reality. In this case, then, popular culture, by its very essence of needing to appeal to a large fanbase, must keep in mind the social expectations of gender. As a visual medium, too, comics and their adaptations also must deliberately think about gender performance in their artistic renderings of characters.

Just as superheroes have to negotiate two identities, playing the roles of both hero and regular citizen, gender roles in Gotham City may also be considered performative, especially when heroes and villains use their gender to gain an advantage over a foe. People in Gotham, especially women, actively perform, embrace, and highlight their gender—or, as Candace West and Don H. Zimmerman (1987, 126) say, "do" gender: "Doing gender involves a complex of socially guided perceptual, interactional, and micropolitical activities that cast particular pursuits as expressions of masculine and feminine 'natures.'" West and Zimmerman call it "a situated doing" because it is a social action; others understand the behavior as associated with such gender (126). The superheroines in Gotham, especially, simultaneously embrace their gender and put pressure on stereotypical understandings of femininity. They show how qualities and objects deemed feminine can be powerful and heroic—just in ways different, understandably, from masculine heroism. The Batman franchise also reflects changing perspectives of identity in urban America over time, and the shifting presentation of gender contributes to discourse on gender social politics in America.

History of Superheroines in Gotham City

The Dynamic Duo are noted for their strength, cunning, speed, and dexterity through which they protect the people of Gotham. They are not heroes with superpowers but with particular skill sets that make them effective as public defenders. Such skills are regarded as masculine, especially as the comic books aim to inspire and entertain their young male target audience. Carol A. Stabile (2009, 87) finds, "The central premise of superhero lore is that someone out there needs to be protected." Batman capitalizes on such thinking as the masculine superhero charged with servicing the vulnerable public. And as the superhero embodies hypermasculinity, "the someone in need of protection is invariably female or feminized" (Stabile 2009, 87). Females have historically been viewed—and subsequently depicted—as more vulnerable than men (91). The superhero genre has traditionally relied on such gender representations to create exciting conflict to engage its young male readers. Batman and Robin are successful heroes because they can save those who need protecting and inspire young men to care for vulnerable women. Critics may find that this reduces females to objects in need of protection rather than autonomous figures who can not only protect themselves but also defend and protect others. Thus, the franchise has also grown to include powerful female superheroines.

Simone de Beauvoir's ([1949] 2011, 283) notable theory on the origination of gender argues for social influences: "One is not born, but rather becomes, woman. No biological, psychic, or economic destiny defines the figure that the human female takes on in society;

it is civilization as a whole that elaborates this intermediary product between the male and the eunuch that is called feminine." To apply this argument to comics, when the superheroine is born, it would not be her body that makes her a female superhero but society's determination of femininity that classifies her. In contrast to de Beauvoir's comment about biology, the powerful women in Gotham use their bodies to their advantage. Superheroines assume a role initially created for men and therefore associated with masculinity. For female superheroes to separate themselves, they need to impose femininity on their performance as heroes. Over time, the women of Gotham City have changed this trend and revised how superheroism can be defined. The evolution of empowered women in Gotham City also illustrates the shifting definition of femininity and a feminine ideal in America. While early depictions of women embrace attributes and objects associated with women of the 1950s and 1960s, such as makeup and graceful fighting skills, the modern woman of Gotham has more diversified combat skills. Women play roles that simultaneously embrace socially situated femininity and also push audiences to reassess their ideas of females as capable of being superheroic.

Batwoman was Gotham City's first female superheroine, but she was not created entirely with the intention of empowering women. In 1956, with DC under scrutiny after Fredric Wertham ([1954] 2004) declared that gay subtexts were becoming visible between Batman and Robin and with the Comics Code of 1954 establishing parameters for sexual content in comics, Batman was offered a love interest through Katherine Kane—Batwoman. Even though she was created to maintain heteronormativity, Batwoman's first appearance actually put pressure on hypermasculinized superheroics. Batwoman made her debut in *Detective Comics* #233, with the exclamation on the cover: "Featuring The Bat-Woman!" (Hamilton and Moldoff 1956b). Batwoman enters the scene on the cover page to save Batman and Robin—a bold declaration that the male defenders have become the vulnerable figures in need of rescue. As the issue begins, a pair of crooks see Batwoman's silhouette on the wall. When they realize it is not Batman, one comments, "Why, it's a Bat-Woman! Ha, ha! What can she do?" Despite her cape and cowl, the criminals doubt her abilities as a vigilante simply because she is a woman. Later, a thug sees the trio and says, "The girl doesn't count!" The narration follows, "But this girl **does** count, in a fray!" Batwoman has to prove herself in order to "count" as a superhero. She is not an immediate threat to the thugs because women have not previously been associated with superheorism; rather, they have been situated as vulnerable and in need of rescue from the men.

West and Zimmerman's (1987) gender theory allows us to see the way performing gender both reinforces social norms and reinscribes them. They find that gender "is the activity of managing situated conduct in light of normative conceptions of attitudes and activities appropriate for one's sex category" (127). In order to change the prescriptions of women as victims and men as the sole superheroes, Batwoman redefines what may be constituted as superheroic through the integration of femininity. Batwoman repeatedly succeeds foiling thieves with much help of her powder, bracelets, compact mirror, perfume flask, and hairnet—her "flashing feminine trick[s]!" (Hamilton and Moldoff 1956b)—inside her shoulder bag utility case. Her socially defined feminine gadgets help her defeat the criminals, essentially equalizing her abilities to those of her male counterparts. The repurposing of feminine tools gives Batwoman unique versatility that makes her just as effective as the male superheroes. While this may appear reductive and essentially reinforcing notions that females are not as strong as men, Batwoman demonstrates that females are just as capable of defeating evil—and perhaps even more capable since they possess means beyond the male superheroes' potential. Batwoman is a protector and savior to those in peril. Her feminized objects empower her, showing women that their accessories are more than supplements to their physical appearance. Over time, the female superheroes developed stronger physical abilities, especially in their martial arts skills, but for the 1950s, Batwoman's status as a heroine and successful crime-fighting capabilities were still progressive. She projects a feminine ideal of power, skill, and resourcefulness that intended to expand superheroics beyond strength and brawn.

In Batwoman's first appearance, she is described as "a flashing feminine figure" (Hamilton and Moldoff 1956b), drawing awareness to her gender through positive, catchy rhetoric. Despite her success defeating criminals, Batwoman does have to fight for gender equality, even with Batman—who argues that the law in Gotham City says no one can wear a Batman costume. Batwoman replies, "The law says 'no **man** can wear it.' I'm a woman!" She uses a loophole in the law—gendered rhetoric—to her advantage, noting the assumptions that the legal system has made that only a man would try to be a superhero. For Crawshaw (2019, 91), "comic book writers reinscribe the notion that women are helpless without men." However, female superheroines have shown that they can create their own version of superheorism. I also argue that comics do not capitalize on the helplessness of women but on the excitement of a hero who can rescue anyone in need. Since a female superheroine was a novelty during the 1950s, the response to her behavior draws concern, especially for her safety. Batman says, "I do worry about the risks she's taking!" When an armed man attacks a club, Batman and Batwoman both arrive on the scene. Batman says, "This is no place for a girl—let me handle it!" He adds, "Batwoman, to you this is just a thrill—you don't realize that fighting crime is a dangerous business!" (Hamilton and Moldoff 1956b). Batwoman foils the idea that a dangerous situation is "no place for a girl," as she does not embody the vulnerability typically associated with women. Batman is not misogynistic but protective of women. His lack of progressive thinking is because he is used to his role as a protector, which is not demeaning but chivalric. This comic contains a reversal of typical gendered scenarios, where Batman becomes the vulnerable figure in need of protection, and Batwoman serves as the successful heroine who saves his life. The moment does not emasculate Batman but unravels stereotypical presentations of gender to showcase the abilities of a woman. This does not go unquestioned, though. Robin exclaims, "A girl saving **you?** It's ridiculous!" (Hamilton and Moldoff 1956b). Batwoman has to prove herself in order to be accepted as a superheroine—even to the Dynamic Duo, who are supposed to be models of fair treatment. Robin's response may be viewed as the natural response to a society that has not yet seen many women as superheroes. Robin is not necessarily being misogynistic here; he is in disbelief that Batman—the epitome of hypermasculinzed superheroics—could need saving. Batman has always been the standard for masculinity and superheroism in Gotham City. Batwoman shows that femininity can be superheroic as well. A woman can accomplish the same things as a man, even if it is with a compact instead of a fist.

With Batwoman serving to disprove accusations of Batman being gay, DC decided that Robin also needed a love interest. This sparked the introduction of Bat-Girl (Devore 2017, 195). Bat-Girl was created by Bill Finger and Sheldon Moldoff in 1961 (*Batman* #139) as Betty Kane, Kathy's niece and a sidekick to Batwoman, but only lasted until 1964. In 1967, James Gordon's daughter Barbara, a librarian at Gotham City Public Library, made her first appearance as Batgirl (Fox and Infantino 1967). Following her introduction in the comics, Batgirl also made her screen debut in September 1967 in the *Batman* TV series (played by Yvonne Craig) in an attempt for the series to appeal to female viewers (Lucas 2017, 173). The show's producers first created a seven-and-a-half-minute presentation film showcasing their new superheroine to ABC executives. In the presentation film, the narrator states, "Gotham City, like any other large metropolis, abounds in girls of all shapes and sizes—debutantes, nurses, stenographers, and librarians" ("Batgirl— Unaired Pilot" 1967). The narration casts females into particular professions, which reflects the working culture of women in 1960s America. But in making Barbara Gordon simultaneously a librarian and Batgirl, the show demonstrates the ways in which a woman can both fulfill the typical roles of women in society and also put pressure on gender norms. The narrator also says that Batgirl is "modeled after her idol, Batman," which may seem to suggest that the female superhero exists in the image of a man. However, her similarity to the Caped Crusader is part of Batgirl's allure and actually empowers her. She becomes a superheroine worthy of inclusion in the "triumphant trio" because she shares a likeness to Batman—though one that has been feminized. Her costume is purple and shimmering, she drives a Batgirl Cycle, and her electronic Batgirl compact has a laser beam. Like Batwoman in the comics, the TV Batgirl has a unique, feminine tool that makes her an effective fighter. She repurposes situated aspects of femininity to redefine who can be a superhero.

Batgirl creates opportunity for other aspects of femininity to be associated with superheroism as well. In the episode "Catwoman's Dressed to Kill" of the TV series *Batman*, Batgirl wins an award for the best-dressed crime fightress in Gotham City. Commissioner Gordon says, "This award just goes to prove that there is room for style even in crime fighting" (Ross 1967). Fashion can be tied to superheroism without diminishing the power and influence of a superheroine. In fact, it is an honor to be the best-dressed superheroine, as part of Batgirl's feminine prowess is her style.

While twenty-first-century viewers might criticize some aspects—Batgirl's fighting skills have been compared to the kicks of Broadway showgirls (Early and Kennedy 2003, 136)—an in-the-flesh female superheroine was a progressive model for women during the 1960s.[1] Yvonne Craig (1967) defines the feminine ideal that Batgirl embodies and emanates:

> And while Batgirl is an active type, she is also very feminine. None of that smacking people low with karate and gung-fu. In my opinion, three karate chops, and you've lost your femininity. If a girl goes on a date and a fellow gets fresh, she can't very well give him a karate chop for a good-night. But if she ducks, she's simply adept and feminine. (2)

Craig's Batgirl proudly brings femininity into superheroism. Batgirl is a defensive fighter rather than an attacker, capitalizing through a less aggressive approach than the male superheroes. In doing so, Batgirl revises notions of superheroics to include both masculine and feminine skills. In the episode "Enter Batgirl, Exit Penguin" (Rudolph 1967), Batman and Robin are impressed with Batgirl's skills. Robin exclaims, "Holy agility, I'll say." Batgirl has feminine agility rather than masculine strength but proves that such strength is not required to be successful. In this episode, Batgirl's dainty kicks effectively put the criminals out of commission.

Craig (1967) also comments that Batgirl is a sidekick, not the frontrunner: "Batgirl will be aiding and assisting Batman and Robin, not constantly rescuing them. I like that, too." At this point in social history, her success as a superheroine is an achievement for women. Not only can women save men, but they can also fight side by side and reinforce them. Aware of the potential influence on young women, Craig also connects Batgirl's behavior to the real world through her comment about proper behavior while dating. Instead of questioning the ways in which women in society were expected to behave, she hybridizes heroism for a culture that is not ready to accept brute force from a woman. She retains the societal expectations of femininity while also showing the strengths unique to women that can propel them into heroine status. Craig is proud of Batgirl's feminine qualities and wants to show the capabilities of women—that they can retain their feminity while being a heroine. Over time, the image of the female superheroine has changed, with the current Batgirl and Batwoman depicted as dexterous, strong fighters, which seems to be a response to the shifting ways women "do" gender. But for the 1960s, Batgirl was a perfect role model for females. She was a powerful and positive figure who still retained her feminine identity and, in doing so, redefined femininity as simultaneously agile, defensive, resourceful, stylish, and superheroic. Batgirl, like Batwoman, serves as a cultural icon who demonstrates that it is possible to be both feminine and superheroic.

Despite Batgirl's effective crime fighting, Batman is still hesitant about her role as a vigilante. In the episode "Catwoman's Dressed to Kill," when Barbara suggests using Batgirl as bait to catch Catwoman, Batman exclaims, "Never! ... I wouldn't dream of endangering that fair lady's head. No, you better leave the crime fighting to the men" (Ross 1967). Batman is concerned with Batgirl's safety, just as his character was toward Batwoman in her comics debut. When Batgirl rescues Batman and Robin from Catwoman's capture, Batman says, "We can fight our own battles!" Batman fails to give Batgirl credit as a crimefighter not because he is misogynistic but because he wants to protect such a "fair lady." Batman retains a code of chivalry, and his gender ideology is so inscribed that he has difficulty viewing women as proactive agents.

As Batgirl repeatedly proved herself as a superheroine, she became a public icon. Although the *Batman* TV series was canceled in 1968, Yvonne Craig appeared as Batgirl in a 1974 public service announcement promoting equal pay for women. As Batman and Robin are tied up next to a ticking bomb, Batgirl swings in to the rescue. However, she will not let the Dynamic Duo free without first commenting on the injustice that she is paid less than Robin: "Same job, same employer means equal pay for men and women" (Craig 1974). Batman thinks she is making a joke, to which Batgirl corrects him and makes note of the Federal Equal Pay Law.[2] Batgirl serves as an advocate for gender equality. This public service announcement actively draws awareness to a problem in America, as even a superheroine faces gender inequality in the workplace, and even such a noble hero as Batman does not provide equal pay. Since Batman is tied up, he appears weak in the announcement, and the focus is on Batgirl's strengths and abilities. She is the savior here and deserves to earn pay that measures up to her work.

Barbara Gordon/Batgirl has become an icon for the advancement of women in America. In *Detective Comics* #423–4 (1972), Barbara Gordon runs for United States Congress with the goal of reforming prisons. She wins the election after earning the confidence of the citizens of Gotham not as Batgirl but as Barbara (Robbins and Heck 1972b). Her campaign is not based on being a woman but on being young in contrast to the "same old pros" (Robbins and Heck 1972a). In fact, her gender is never mentioned; it is simply acceptable that a woman in Gotham can run a successful congressional campaign. The citizens of Gotham see her strength of character and have confidence in her ability to represent them. Barbara is a powerful female both as herself and as Batgirl; she simply acts in the best interests of the people of Gotham City. The superheroines of Gotham have historically embodied a progressive agenda for women and redefined the relationship between superheroism and femininity. Through the Batman franchise, the feminine ideal becomes visible—where a superheroine, through her feminine skills and tools, is as capable at crimefighting as a male superhero.

Gotham's Modern-Day Superheroines

When the first female superheroines appeared in Gotham City, they resembled the image of Batman. Even their names are the female versions of the male hero. But for that cultural time period in America, this was still a progressive moment for females. As Batwoman and Batgirl have evolved over time, creators have found other ways for their characters to demonstrate female power that is not necessarily in the image of a man. The New 52's Batwoman draws inspiration to become a vigilante from Batman, but this comes only after she has established her life's goal to protect others. In Greg Rucka's

Batwoman: Elegy (which contains *Detective Comics* #854–60, 2009–10), Kate Kane joins the military, but when she is released due to her sexuality, she becomes lost. She says that without being in service, "I've got nothing," and "I don't know what to do, what to be." When she is jumped in an alley, she fights the thief off, saying, "You don't know I'm a soldier" (Rucka and Williams III 2010a). Kate identifies as a fighter and defender. The thief assumes that as a woman, she is an easy target. He is ignorant to the strength and skills his female target could possess. Batman arrives to help, which is unneeded, as Kate does not require a man to protect or defend her.

As Batman makes a grand exit, there is no dialogue, only illustrations of Kate suddenly inspired as she stands looking upwards, Batman's shadow behind her, offering the image of wings spreading from her own body. In the final illustration, Kate looks up at the bat signal, as at this moment, it calls to her rather than to Batman (Rucka and Williams III 2010a). In *Detective Comics* #860, Kate feels that the bat signal is "a call to arms." She says, "I finally found a way to serve" (Rucka and Williams III 2010b). While being a superhero in Gotham has been a man's job, at this point Kate finds that her purpose to serve and protect others can now only be fulfilled if she becomes a superheroine. Ultimately, being a superhero is not about being a man or a woman, but it is a fulfillment of purpose; it is a calling.

Kate, in finding herself through becoming Batwoman, takes on a role that differs from her public self. Like the male superheroes, Kate must negotiate a double life, both of which compose her entire self. Identity becomes performative for superheroes when they don their disguises and patrol Gotham. Andréa Gilroy (2015) argues, "Kate Kane performs her identity through her actions within the story in multiple, gendered ways that challenge stereotypes and assumptions about gender, especially as they relate to superheroes and the superhero genre." Gilroy points to Batwoman's feminized physical appearance in contrast to her "much more punk/goth/butch persona" as Kate. One of Batwoman's feminine qualities is her long, flowing red hair, which Batman criticizes in *Detective Comics* #854 because he thinks it could be hazardous (Rucka and Williams III 2009a). However, Batwoman's hair is actually a wig; thus, the image of femininity that she creates is a ruse. The modern Batwoman "does gender" by taking a socially situated feminine appearance and using it as a prop for deception. For West and Zimmerman (1987, 135), "doing gender consists of managing ... occasions so that, whatever the particulars, the outcome is seen and seeable in context as gender-appropriate or, as the case may be, gender *in*appropriate." The wig is part of Kate's disguise as she plays the role of feminized superheroine, while her pedestrian self publicly displays an edgier persona. The modern Kate/Batwoman teaches us on the one hand not to trust preconceived notions of gender. But she also shows the ways in which an individual can play gender and manipulate gender to fit the needs of a situation.

Modern-day Barbara Gordon/Batgirl has also evolved over time and shows the ways in which superheroics can be both feminine and non-gendered. Creators have expanded Barbara Gordon's educational background.[3] Carolyn Cocca (2014) notes Barbara's skills: "Much of her power in the DC Universe stems from her extraordinary eidetic memory, her level of education, her economic resources, her network of well-resourced peers, her pre-paraplegia super-athleticism, and her ability to pass for a non-disabled male." While Barbara is praised here for her aptitudes, the idea of "passing" for a male could suggest that superheroic masculinity is at a superior level to femininity and that Batgirl's successful passing reduces her autonomy. Though this could be seen to reinforce gender hierarchies, more recent versions of Barbara redefine femininity to position it as, in fact, indistinguishable from or even superior to masculinity. Barbara's strengths are mental, social, and physical, and they collectively work together to make her an effective superheroine. Even when she is disabled after being shot by the Joker in Alan Moore and Brian Bolland's ([1988] 2008) *The Killing Joke*, her superheroism is reborn through the role of Oracle, a tech whiz, and she proves to be an integral contributor to the successes of the superheroes who are on their feet.

In Gail Simone and Ardian Syaf's (2012) *Batgirl* Vol. 4 #3, Barbara has recovered from her paralysis and reclaimed herself as Batgirl. She questions Batman and Nightwing's concerns about her, assuming they doubt her abilities. Batgirl's interior narration reads, "All my life, I've had well-meaning guys hovering over me, protecting me when I didn't need it or want it." Nightwing is concerned about Barbara's physical recovery from her paralysis. He says to Batgirl, "Batman and I were worried, yes. Not because we doubt you. It's because we love you." Like Batman's chivalry of the past, Batman and Nightwing express their love and concern for Batgirl. Their attention toward her has nothing to do with her gender but with her health.

Comics creators have also empowered women in Gotham City in groups. Originating in 1996, the female superhero group the Birds of Prey have included Oracle, Black Canary, Huntress, and Lady Blackhawk. The cover of *Black Canary/Oracle: Birds of Prey* #1 says, "Some situations require ... a **woman's** touch!" (Dixon and Frank 1996). The group operates out of Gotham, as the city has a need for a powerful female force. The message on the cover suggests that Batman cannot handle all situations in Gotham. The city needs the female superheroines because they offer feminized superheroics that may be the only way to defeat particular supervillains. Here, the feminine ideal has become collective femininity that is empowered by numbers. In Barbara's case, it also has become something indistinct and indefinable, as it need not necessarily be situated in contrast to superheroic masculinity but simply be acceptable as equally superheroic.

Violence against Women

While female superheroines in Gotham City fight alongside their male compatriots, women are still the victims of violence in unequal proportion to the violence committed toward males. In 1999, comic book writer Gail Simone (n.d.) created a web page called Women in Refrigerators to track the female superheroes who had been "killed, maimed or depowered." Simone argues, "Male characters seem to die nobly, as heroes," whereas women are frequently "butchered." When women are attacked and brutalized, they regain some of the vulnerability that had seemed to decline when women became superheroines. Such depictions also fetishize the female body, as a butchered or maimed woman is reduced to an object; this draws attention to her body parts rather than her heroic identity.

One direct example of this occurs in Alan Moore and Brian Bolland's ([1988] 2008) graphic novel *The Killing Joke* after the Joker shoots Barbara Gordon. The Joker is dressed like a resort tourist in this scene with a camera slung around his neck. As such, he is a sadistic spectator, taking photos of Barbara's naked body suffering in pain, which he later exhibits in his fun house to torture her father.

Barbara is reduced to an objectified body on display. The suffering female body is fetishized and used as a weapon to try to make Gordon go mad. Simone argues, "The story itself treats Barbara as a prop ... there's just no effort in it to treat her as a human being" (qtd. in Rogers 2012). Cocca (2014) uses Simone's terminology in critiquing the plot: "The violence done to Barbara was a classic 'fridging' in that no one in the story ever asks her how she's feeling after it happens. The whole point of the story is how her father and Batman feel about it." Barbara is the victim of horrific violence and trauma, but the focus is on her father, who becomes the unfortunate spectator of the violence. The book ends without showing readers whether Barbara is even still alive, further decentralizing her character's trauma. Simone argues that during the time that *The Killing Joke* was published, female characters' "primary value was as shock elements for revenge fantasies. There was a feeling of expendability to the female characters, a real sense that no female was reading these books anyway, so who cares what we do to these characters?" (qtd. in Rogers 2012). Simone criticizes the dehumanization and objectification of female characters in comics. Such occurrences arguably masculinize the comics and reinforce the idea that women are vulnerable objects in need of rescue rather than strong, empowered individuals. The argument is that female bodies are fetishized spectacles for male readers to consume. Such depictions receive criticism for being socially unhealthy disparagement: "Normalizing—and justifying—violence against women for the sake of a story arc contributes to a misogynistic culture" (Crawshaw 2019, 99). Crawshaw finds entertainment value a poor excuse for violent treatment of female characters. This viewpoint, though, fails to perceive the potential for empathy, sympathy, and social awareness.

Showing violence toward women may actually provide a glimpse into reality that is beneficial for social awareness. When the avoidance of violent objectification of women is deemed more appropriate for the female audience, such censoring or limitations could actually validate and heighten the very notions of masculinity critics argue against.[4] Therefore, showing women as victims of violence may not necessarily dehumanize them but, instead, prompt attention to real-world events and empower women to fight against such violence. William Proctor (2016), a lecturer in media, culture, and communication, argues,

"There can be catharsis found in such representations; survivors can feel able, and empowered even, to speak out about their own personal traumas or identify with such depictions as a healthy coping strategy." Following this argument, then, *The Killing Joke* would be a work that allows trauma victims to connect with Barbara, and those who have not experienced trauma can perhaps sympathize with her character. Such a perspective humanizes the female as a source for human connectivity.

Barbara's paralysis has not stopped her from being a useful member of the Bat Family, and in 1989, she made her first appearance as Oracle in *Suicide Squad* #23 (Ostrander, Yale, and McDonnell 1989). Cocca (2014) looks to Barbara's disability as a way for her to "both subvert the privileged and masculinized construction of the superhero body and at the same time also shore up the normalization of those non-disabled superhero bodies through her contrast to them." Oracle is a nonnormative superhero—a disabled superheroine. While Cocca argues that she simultaneously puts pressure on masculine normativity while also reaffirming it, Barbara Gordon's existence as Oracle has allowed her to actually expand female superheroism in Gotham City. Teamed with Black Canary, Oracle helps found the Birds of Prey, which positions her as a leader and role model for women. Her disability does not hinder her work; in fact, as Oracle instead of Batgirl, Barbara successfully unites female forces and normalizes nonmasculine superheroics. This does not necessarily mean that superheroism has been feminized. The way that femininity is defined in terms of superheroism has changed so much over time that currently, it is hard to define at all. Instead, modern superheroism may be considered as perpetually revising notions of gender. Both superheroes and superheroines have excelled in quashing crime in Gotham City so that gender cannot be a determining factor in the abilities, success, or identity of a superhero(ine).

During the New 52 reboot, Barbara Gordon becomes Batgirl once again. Her past still involves the shooting at the hands of the Joker, but she has recovered from temporary paralysis. In the *Batgirl* comics, written by Gail Simone, she must cope with post-traumatic stress disorder as a result of the incident. In an interview with *Newsarama*, Simone describes:

We have seen very little about this in superhero comics, really. People return from the dead, people are tortured, the world is threatened, and the next day, it's as if it was all forgotten. Many trauma survivors don't have that option. My favorite superhero stories are always about survival. Kicking people in the head is great, but heroism holds to a much higher standard. (qtd. in Rogers 2012)

Simone observes the ways in which comics typically return to the environment's status quo. New villains attack, new threats emerge, and after the superheroes defeat them, everything reverts to a semblance of normality. However, real-world trauma victims have to cope for extended periods of time. *Batgirl* allows Barbara to deal with the aftermath of her event. It is not forgotten in the reboot; it is something she copes with every day. For Simone, this makes Barbara an even more impressive heroine. She is not just a fighter but a survivor—an ideal, true superheroine not according to a male standard but empowered to revise such a standard.

Supervillainesses

Gotham City's supervillainesses are also powerful female figures who illustrate and redefine notions of femininity in America. For Shannon Austin (2015, 294), "Batman's female villains ultimately exemplify what it means to be women forced to cope with the gender biases prevalent in a male-dominated society." However, I do not find these women coping with bias as Austin argues. Instead, they reappropriate femininity in order to exploit men. These supervillainesses deliberately use particular aspects of their femininity as sources of power. Austin also argues, "The women in the Batman universe seem to be penalized for their crimes more because they are powerful women. As women in positions of power and dominance, they are seen as a threat and must therefore be controlled or otherwise diminished by men" (286). Punishing women more harshly may reify gender inequality or it may show a fear that men may have that women are actually more powerful than them. Whether they use their skills for good or evil, Gotham's women cannot be ignored or taken for granted.

Selina Kyle is a remarkable figure, one of the most powerful forces in all of Gotham City because she serves as both superheroine and supervillainess. Since Selina flourishes as both, she is a force that cannot be stopped. Bob Kane (1989, 107) states that Catwoman was created "to give the strip sex appeal." The creators also wanted to bring in a character relatable to female readers. Catwoman made her first appearance in *Batman* #1 (Finger and Kane 1940a) as "The Cat," a jewel thief. In *Batman* #3 (Finger and Kane 1940d), citizens of Gotham exclaim, "The Cat is making the police look ridiculous!" and "Imagine being made a fool of by a mere girl!" A female criminal in Gotham finds success by making a mockery of the police department. The people of Gotham assume that the men should be able to catch her, which reinforces notions of masculine superiority during this time. They do not complain that she should be caught just because she is a criminal but because it is a woman who is committing these crimes. The social hierarchy not only positions members of law enforcement as above criminals but also men above women. However, such a perspective of women makes Catwoman's actions all the more impressive. She defies the odds and causes society to reassess the capabilities of women.

In *Batman* #210 (Robbins and Novick 1969a), Catwoman serves as a spokeswoman and freedom fighter for women. The cover of the issue declares a "Battle of the sexes!" Catwoman recruits eight inmates from the Women's House of Detention to join her. She tries to rally them by saying, "We all have a common cause—a common enemy … Men! It was men who led us astray—men who put us behind bars like caged tigers!" She tells them that together they will get revenge on the men who put them in prison. After Catwoman whips the women into physical shape in order to meet her crime-fighting standards, each woman of the crew dons a Catwoman costume in order to foil the men and steal valuable jewels. In this issue, female criminals band together and use their shared antagonism toward men as a driving force and motivation. They seek to prove that men cannot suppress or control them. Even though their plight is unsuccessful, they still draw awareness to an existing gender division and the mayhem that a collective female force can cause. However, Tim Hanley (2017) argues that this issue was in fact "a direct jab at women's lib." Exaggerations and even mockery of women's rights could be counterproductive to the aims for social progress for women. Regardless of its intentions or how it is read, *Batman* #210 does encourage dialogue on the topics of women and power in America.

Over the years, Selina's character has changed but always embodies strength in a way that puts pressure on preconceived notions of femininity. Frank Miller and David Mazzucchelli's *Batman: Year One* ([1987] 2005) introduces Selina as a dominatrix. In such a role, she would be performing a position of dominance over a man. However, it is a performance not a real gender role. It is done at a man's bidding for his own sexual arousal. So Selina's performance is only to stimulate a man, not to empower her own self. Despite performing such a role, Selina is still independently driven. She is a protector, looking out for and defending other women. She is a skilled fighter and thief and realizes her potential for greater achievements by becoming a masked figure. Selina, like the New 52's Kate, sees what Batman is capable of as the Caped Crusader. She is inspired to be more effective throughout the city (whether within legal realms or not), and donning a costume is a proven means for achieving that in Gotham. When Selina becomes Catwoman and starts committing cat burglaries, the news reports that it was Batman, which frustrates Selina since she wants the credit. She wishes to show off the skills of a female criminal in Gotham. Later, the news refers to "a woman with claws—presumably Batman's assistant." This irritates Selina as well, as she says, "**Assistant**. Now I'm his **assistant**. I'll have to do something **really** nasty, next time ..." (Miller and Janson [1986] 2002). Selina desires complete autonomy from Batman. She does not want to be associated with him, especially in an inferior position. In these examples, the newscasters project a role upon her. In the first report, the assumption is that only Batman could be a potential "Robin Hood," as the reporter suggests. In the second report, Catwoman is denied autonomy. Her actions are assumed to be at the bidding of the dominant male vigilante in Gotham.

The Batman films have made Catwoman into a sexy, skilled fighter. In Burton's (1992) *Batman Returns*, Catwoman (Michelle Pfeiffer) initiates a fight with Batman (Michael Keaton). When he eventually hits her back, she says, "How could you? I'm a woman," to which Batman stammers, "I'm sorry, I ... I ..." and approaches her to help her up. She attacks him again, saying, "As I was saying, I'm a woman and can't be taken for granted." She briefly plays the role of vulnerable, battered woman in order to exploit Batman. Batman is susceptible to her game, demonstrating his sensitivity toward women—which proves to be a weakness. Catwoman is aware of her power as a woman to use her gender to her advantage. Catwoman is destructive, violent, and eager to murder Max Shreck. Instead of treating her like other supervillains, though, Batman hesitates and shows gallantry toward her. Yet, treating her differently has consequences, as Catwoman proves that female and male criminals can be equally threatening and menacing. She also says to Batman, "Life's a bitch; now so am I." With this comment, she announces a shift in what it means for her to be a woman. She is not a vulnerable damsel—as Selina was before Shreck tried to murder her. Now, she is a "bitch," a hardened, violent woman.

In Nolan's (2012) *The Dark Knight Rises*, Selina (Anne Hathaway) is locked up with male inmates in the department of corrections, as "the Dent Act allows non-segregation based on extraordinary need." Selina does not need to be segregated from the male inmates because she can hold her own among them. As she is escorted to her cell, a male inmate says, "A little closer baby," to which Selina replies, "Why, honey? You want to hold my hand?" while grabbing his hands and twisting them as she completes a cartwheel. The inmate cries out in pain, and the warden assures a guard, "She's gonna be fine." The male inmates do not intimidate Selina; instead, she poses a threat to them—not because she is masculine but because she is an unstoppable and unpredictable force. She defies traditional standards of femininity and, in being "fine" amid the men, makes masculinity and femininity indistinguishable. In the comics, Catwoman often fluctuates from being a supervillainess and a superheroine, and in Nolan's film, Selina also turns toward moral goodness and helps Batman save the city. Since she has been both supervillainess and superheroine, she cannot be contained to one category. Her redefined feminine strength empowers her and allows her to fit in among superheroes or supervillains, men or women.

Catwoman has turned into more than just a strong, sexy woman. She demonstrates that superheroic masculinity (specifically, Batman) is not superior to femininity. She also proves that femininity is not reductive, as Catwoman's femininity is constantly in flux. As a powerful woman in Gotham, Catwoman redefines femininity into something that can be wild, daring, and inconsistent. Catwoman is ever-changing and evolving, demonstrating that femininity is not a fixed state. The feminine ideal changes with the times and is not necessarily derived from or reflective of the image of man.

Several other female supervillains exist in Gotham City and show the ways that they can effectively "do" gender. The supervillainesses use their femininity as a strength to their advantage, essentially performing femininity. Shannon Austin (2015, 287) notes, "These women, in order to obtain and keep their power, must also use a mask of femininity to survive in a male-dominated society, forcing them to sometimes use typical female displays of sexuality and seduction to fight back." Though Austin claims the use of femininity is forced, I find the supervillainesses embrace their abilities to use femininity to exploit men. Pfeiffer's Catwoman employs this "mask of femininity" to her advantage when battling Batman. Poison Ivy is the embodiment of sexualized villainy, as she seduces her victims in order to overpower them. Ivy's overt, hypersexualized behavior is a ruse for gaining advantage over men. She too "does gender," performing sexualized femininity to empower herself (see Chapter 3). In their content analysis of Modern Age American comic books, Matthew Facciani, Peter Warren, and Jennifer Vendemia (2015, 2) argue, "Women in comic books are depicted in a hypersexualized way, with physical beauty often taking precedence over their achievements and non-physical qualities." However, Ivy uses her beauty and sexuality to empower herself. Like superheroines, who use feminine tools to battle criminals and foil their expectations of a female's capabilities, the supervillainesses often use feminine tools, specifically, their seductive prowess, as weapons to gain advantage.

As femininity empowers supervillainesses, they show impressive and impactful capabilities that contrast with male characters. When the Joker inspires Dr. Harleen Quinzel to turn into the supervillainess Harley Quinn, he acquires masculine dominance over her. In Paul Dini and Bruce Timm's (1994a) *Batman Adventures: Mad Love*, Harleen turns to crime after falling in love with the Joker. Her harlequin costume, too, may be viewed as in the image of the Joker. However, her character has transformed immensely since its inception. Her first appearance was in *Batman: The Animated Series*, where she is presented as the Joker's sidekick (Dini 1992b). But in the episode "Harley and Ivy" (Dini 1993), Ivy tries to show Harley that she can be her own woman, independent of the Joker. Harley rationalizes the Joker's abusive treatment: "Don't get me wrong, my puddin's a little rough sometimes, but he loves me, really." Ivy tells Harley, "You just need some lessons in good ol' female self-esteem." Ivy tries to serve as a role model for Harley, with heightened female power through the debasement of men. Ivy infiltrates the Peregrinators Club and criticizes them for being a group of all men: "The joke ... is this obsolete, sexist mockery you call a men's club. Now I ask you, what kind of adventurers refuse to admit women?" Ivy has a progressive agenda and fights for women's rights. Even though she is a supervillainess, her approach makes the men appear disgraceful since they perpetuate gendered divisions in society. She feels that sexism is a greater crime to society than her frequent acts of theft. Ivy may be breaking the law, but the men are disrupting social progress. Ivy is also determined to prove her capabilities as a female supervillain. After she and Harley capture Batman and chain him up, she says, "Here we have the typical male aggressor, fittingly imprisoned within the bonds of female domestic slavery." Ivy uses Batman's body as representative of all men. She materializes and twists the sentiment that women are domestically bound by chaining him up with an espresso machine, mixer, iron, and vacuum, literally binding the male to the household gadgets designated to a housewife. The tools hold the male body in place and grant the female superiority. Ivy then says to Batman, "Admit it darling, you didn't think two women were capable of bringing you down." Her goal was not a personal vendetta against Batman but to prove that a woman could defeat a powerful man. Batman does not discriminate, replying, "Man or woman, a sick mind is capable of anything." In this case, villainy is an equalizer. He does not find gender as a signifying differentiator of any who are criminal. This differs from the Joker's perspective, as he says at the end of the episode, "Next time I start a gang, no women." The Joker finds that Harley and Ivy are disruptive to his agenda because they are women. His view of women is more debasing than Batman's, as he assumes better success when only surrounded by men.

Even though Harley and the Joker have a romantic relationship, he physically and emotionally abuses her. The Joker is so tied to Gotham that Harley actually needs to leave Gotham City to become an autonomous woman. When she moves to New York City in Amanda Conner and Jimmy Palmiotti's (2013) *Harley Quinn* of the New 52 series, she becomes a professional working woman, living life free of the Joker's abuse. Harley gains the female self-confidence that Ivy tries to imbue upon her only after leaving the man who has repeatedly oppressed her. Harley's storyline illustrates the debasement of women under an objectifying eye. Though she lacks self-esteem, she develops the strength to remove herself from a toxic situation.

The female camaraderie between Harley and Ivy demonstrates the effective power of collective femininity. With the addition of Catwoman, Paul Dini and Guillem March's series *The Gotham City Sirens* (2009–11) brought together these three supervillainesses to work as a unit and protect one another. Their group's name also illustrates the mythos of female power. These women are enticing, seductive, and dangerous. They hold power as a group that makes them effective against both vigilantes and other supervillains. Both the Birds of Prey and the Gotham City Sirens are indicative of the power of a female syndicate. In being entirely composed of women, though, the groups simultaneously draw awareness to gender as they attempt to eradicate gender distinctions. So while they are empowered, the groups still reify the gender divide. However, since these characters often work with or against Batman, Robin, Nightwing, and other male members of the Bat Family, they prove that women can comparatively achieve the same success as men.

The Trans Inclusion

Women have clearly made a powerful impact in a formerly male-dominated comic book universe. DC has continued its attempts to expand its socially inclusive practices by creating trans characters and prompting conversations about trans people in America. The inclusion of trans in comics studies raises questions as to how popular culture visualizes gender in a way to tap into its fanbase.

Halberstam (1998, 27) argues that a binary is enforced despite its failure to adequately encapsulate all people: "Precisely because virtually nobody fits the definitions of male and female, the categories gain power and currency from their impossibility. In other words, the very flexibility and elasticity of the terms 'man' and 'woman' ensures their longevity." Despite acknowledging that the terms are flexible, Halberstam still raises issue with them existing as binaries. While trans could distinguish fluidity of gender, an understanding of it requires an understanding of a distinct binary.

So far in the Batman franchise, only the series *Batgirl* has included trans characters and has received both positive and negative feedback regarding its approach. In Gail Simone and Daniel Sampere's (2013) *Batgirl* Vol. 4 #19, Barbara's roommate Alysia Yeoh tells Barbara that she is transgender. Barbara gives her a hug and simply says, "The people I love call me Babs." Barbara's response is positive and embracing. Alysia is and continues to be an important part of Babs's life. Alysia telling Barbara that she is transgender strengthens their friendship as Alysia has entrusted Barbara with sensitive information, and Barbara reassures Alysia of her love. It is a powerful moment that illustrates a strong bond between individuals where gender and identity are not complicated or divisive.

In an interview with *Wired*, Simone said that while the comic book industry was built from its characters who are "white, cis-gendered, straight, on and on," the industry needs to evolve. For Simone, Alysia is "a character, not a public service announcement … being trans is just part of her story. If someone loved her before, and doesn't love her after, well—that's a shame, but we can't let that kind of thinking keep comics in the 1950s forever" (qtd. in Hudson 2013). Simone reports her efforts to challenge and broaden the gender norms of comics. A trans character in Gotham reflects a diverse urban population in twenty-first-century America and shows that plot does not always have to rely on cisgendered characters. Though Simone asserts that she is not making a public service announcement through Alysia's character, she is deliberately expanding the population of Gotham City and making efforts to normalize non-masculine (and non-feminine) identities.

With Simone's efforts, *Batgirl* began to build a more expansive universe that houses gender diversity reflective of the social conversations of present-day America. However, after Simone left the series, readers accused the creative team of *Batgirl* vol. 4 #37 of transphobic content. The villain of the issue, Dagger Type, has been impersonating Batgirl (Stewart, Fletcher, and Tarr 2015b). When Batgirl tracks down the imposter, her shocked reaction to a man under the wig and cowl has been argued as transphobic. The public outcry against the issue prompted the creative team—Cameron Stewart, Brenden Fletcher, and Babs Tarr—to issue an apology on Twitter. The responses to the tweet were both appreciative and accusatory. Some individuals said that the team should stand by its creative choices rather than apologize for them. These readers view the work as a creative piece, not a statement of social prejudice or stereotyping. The creators remained sensitive to the criticism of transphobia, though, and rewrote and redrew some parts of the issue for the trade paperback edition. In this case, the public response directly informed and even revised the comic. The rewritten *Batgirl* #37 in *Batgirl Volume 1: Batgirl of Burnside* (Stewart, Fletcher, and Tarr 2015a) changes Batgirl's expression from confused to determined when she winds up with Dagger's cowl and wig in her hands. And instead of saying, "**Dagger Type?** But you're a—" (Stewart, Fletcher, and Tarr 2015b), she says, "**Dagger Type?** So **you're** the—" (Stewart, Fletcher, and Tarr 2015a). With the emphasis on "you're," the comment becomes a revelation of the truth behind a mystery rather than an assumption about Dagger's gender. In the original version, Batgirl saying "but" seems to imply that a male could not pose as a female. The outcry from fans seems to read the original as containing a lexicon of gender bias and perhaps even gender formation.

The response of angered fans to the issue shows how comic books can serve as cultural artifacts of perceptions of stereotyping and sensitivity to gender bias. Jessica Lachenal (2014) finds that such occurrences can hurt the comic book industry and have a negative social impact:

> Transmisogynistic stereotypes like these are what really set back the industry, because it reinforces negative preconceptions of an entire community to a greater population of readers, especially younger readers which this book seems to be geared for. These stereotypes are tools which are often used to justify the

marginalization of these already incredibly overlooked and abused groups.

In revising the issue, the creative team aimed to avoid the perpetuation of stereotypes that it initially—though unintentionally—contained. Batgirl makes assumptions about gender in the original, but the demands of the readers, in compelling a revision, have allowed gender to be strictly performative.

With an imposter villain, the issue illustrates the art of performativity. Dagger, in dressing as Batgirl, performs a role, which, ironically, is a performance of a performance, as Barbara performs Batgirl, and then Dagger adapts Barbara's performance. For Judith Butler ([1990] 2007, 34), "gender proves to be performative— that is, constituting the identity it is purported to be." In this case, the layering of performance actually confuses identity. Dagger's performance as Batgirl is essentially the creative adaptation of a female performing a role previously reserved for a (Bat)man. Batgirl's confusion in the original comic over Dagger's reveal is because she views Batgirl as a role for a female. This issue makes aesthetics a social statement, especially in the way it presents bodies as works of art. Dagger is an artist, and at his art show, he displays several moderately sexualized images of Batgirl. Upon seeing them, Barbara comments, "I feel so violated" (Stewart, Fletcher, and Tarr 2015b). Dagger turns Batgirl the person into a work of art and a performative piece, and Barbara's response is feeling a loss of power. Dagger not only puts her image on display, making her an object, a spectacle for others to gawk at, but also sexualizes her in a way that is inconsistent with her identity. For Barbara, her performance as Batgirl is not a sexualized female, but in modeling a man, she actually embodies the masculinity of the bat-figure and adds her own femininity to her performance. In Halberstam's (1998, 2) theory about female masculinity, she argues, "What we understand as heroic masculinity has been produced by and across both male and female bodies." Barbara's performance as Batgirl, then, may be argued as a feminized version of heroic masculinity. But when Dagger assumes the role, the male body takes back the heroic masculinity but in the feminine cowl. The conflation of gender binaries in this example creates identity confusion. However, since many readers felt that such confusion was a transphobic reaction rather than an illustration of the complexities of gender identification and conversation in present-day America, the creative team felt the need to make changes. In complying with reader reactions, though, the newer publication loses some of its opportunity to speak to readers about gender layering, expectations, and social cues.

Dagger also showcases a piece that he created called *Vulnerable*, a sculpture of Batgirl in a wheelchair with her head down, which physicalizes an emotional response to her trauma (Stewart, Fletcher, and Tarr 2015b). When Dagger dons his Batgirl costume, he transforms her identity from work of art into artistic performance. His various costumes include one that dazzles in glittering gold and another of glittering silver. Dagger appears on stage in costume, revealing himself as both the artist and the subject. The audience complains and boos, calling him a "faker" and "an ad." What is intended to be performative art for Dagger turns into a failed attempt to gain patrons who are more impressed with the real Batgirl. In criticism of this, J. Skyler says, "I think Batgirl #37 illustrates the fact that gender outside of cis normativity is assumed to be a performance. As in trans people aren't 'real' in the strictest sense of the word—we're just putting on a show for the rest of the world to gawk at" (qtd. in Scott and Kirkpatrick 2015, 165). Rather than viewing gender performance as art, Skyler finds that performance objectifies trans individuals and ruins their opportunities to be viewed as real humans with equal footing as cisgendered individuals. Poison Ivy deliberately performs gender to gain advantage over men, so perhaps we can view Dagger's performance as a way to gain fans and overtake Batgirl. Dagger feels empowered by playing a role on the streets because in the real world, his performance blends with reality. But on stage, he loses power when the audience rejects his performance, expressing preference for the real Batgirl. Batgirl's original reaction to the imposter's identity may be considered transphobic, but at the very least, the comic does make efforts to illustrate the ways that gender can be empowering.

The issue ends with Barbara as Batgirl posting a posed photo of herself on social media, where she says, "This is the way I choose to be seen" (Stewart, Fletcher, and Tarr 2015b). Batgirl is also performing a role because she wants to be visible to the citizens of Gotham in a particular way. The criticism, though, is that a male performing the role of a female is made to be villainous. The sexualized images of Batgirl objectify her female body, which, ironically, since Dagger is the model, is a male body. The male body has transformed into a sexualized female body, and when that is exposed, Batgirl's shocked reaction has been read as perpetuating opinions of trans individuals that could be judgmental, unaccepting, or nonnormative. For Mey Rude, this reaction is an illustration of transmisogyny:

> I think Batgirl #37 is a perfect microcosm of trans representation in comics right now. It had a trans woman in it, but she was only there for a few panels and didn't really do anything that impacted the story. It also featured Batgirl reacting terribly when she pulled the wig off of someone she thought was a woman, and a trans misogynistic trope. So I think it shows that although some people are trying, we've still got a really long way to go. I think that discussions about transphobia fit in very nicely with discussions about misogyny and sexism and homophobia in comics. First of all, most of the 'transphobia' is actually transmisogyny. (qtd. in Scott and Kirkpatrick 2015, 164)

In this issue, femininity reigns because Batgirl is preferable to Dagger as Batgirl. This situation would seemingly empower women; however, it creates the potential for transmisogyny since the trans individual is viewed as less real. The fan outcry to *Batgirl* #37 demonstrates a collective mindset about the trans population in America and the hope for the acceptance from cisgendered people. Batgirl is an icon and role model, so her reaction in the comic seems to be a step backward in social acceptance. However, the community of fans who raised issue with the comic for being narrow-minded illustrates an American social ideal for peaceful, accepting coexistence of all individuals regardless of identifying factors such as gender. At the same time, however, the changed reprint limits conversation about social expectations and perceptions.

With different artists and writers creating and recreating the stories of comic book characters, every character embodies a unique assortment of perspectives, mentalities, and emotional responses. Batgirl has been both inviting and hesitant toward trans individuals. She can be accepting and shocked because she embodies multiple perspectives toward identity. She is an American, and Americans do not all share a collective social mentality. Batgirl is also shaped by her fans' response to her, and both versions of *Batgirl* #37 reflect the social perspectives of American people. So, her character illustrates the pluralistic mindsets of Americans and invites conversations on social inclusion and how identity is shaped, performed, and understood.

* * *

While superhero comics historically embraced masculinity to target a male audience, Gotham City has been gender diverse and has demonstrated the ways in which both superheroines and supervillainesses can redefine popular conceived notions of gender. Portrayals of femininity, especially, have evolved over time to reflect the different ways in which women can be as successful as men. While the current Batwoman, for example, may no longer need a compact as a weapon, any version of her character empowers American women. The men of Gotham City have continued to be strong, fast, and clever figures. Superheroic masculinity has not changed much over time, though modern-day Batman is perhaps more accepting of females into the Bat Family, aware that these women do not need his protection and can well serve their cause and the people of the city. Femininity in all its incarnations has a formidable place in Gotham City. And although trans people have only appeared in *Batgirl* so far, DC is clearly opening up the universe to even further expanded gender diversity. The Batman franchise's evolution of the social genetics of Gotham City reflects a hopeful landscape of diversified character renderings both within the city and for urban America.

3

The Sexualized City: Violence, Power, and Liberation

Like the popular portrayal of women in comic books, the Batman franchise has often sexually glamorized its female characters. Such sexualization may give some characters power, but it also problematizes sociocultural perceptions of women. Comics creators have the difficult task of keeping up with an environment that shifts in its collective perceptions of sexuality. Because the comic book industry is so socially potent, the comics also stimulate conversations about eroticism, sexual violence, and sexual orientation. The Batman franchise has historically been accused of including content with latent gay subtexts. DC's initial response was to illustrate the heteronormativity of superheroism. But now, in the twenty-first century, DC has opened closets and embraced queer representation instead of refuting it. Gotham City continues to exist as a space that reflects the ongoing social tensions regarding sexuality in America, allowing for readers and viewers to think critically about their own social perspectives.

This chapter analyzes sexualization, sexual expression, and sexuality throughout history in Gotham City. It looks at having sex appeal as a powerful and dangerous force over others. This chapter also turns to rape theory to analyze sexual exploitation in the Batman comics. Sexual expression is also tied to sexual identity. Specifically,

Batman's sexuality went under scrutiny in the past, whereas in the twenty-first century, Batwoman's openness about her queer identity serves to critique public policy and illustrate confidence in being true to oneself. However, regardless of sexual orientation, the Batman franchise repeatedly illustrates that healthy romantic relationships cannot be maintained for heroes or villains in Gotham City. The call to either defense or crime serves a greater priority for many of these characters. Yet, sex and sexuality still hold significant power in Gotham, making this discussion important to a larger understanding of Gotham's social dynamics.

Sexualization and the Male Gaze

The physical appearance of women in comics has gone through great scrutiny and regulation as the industry has often aimed to deter objectified sexualization of the female form. This started with Wertham's *Seduction of the Innocent* ([1954] 2004, 179), where he criticized sexualizing women as dangerously seductive to young readers: "In very young children comic books set up confusion and create a sadistic interpretation of sex." Wertham points to frequent practices of comics creators to extenuate the female body: "One of the stock aphrodisiacs in comic books is to draw girls' breasts in such a way that they are sexually exciting. Wherever possible, they protrude and obtrude" (178). Wertham finds the enhanced female body as obtrusive. It draws attention to itself as a sexual stimulant, which, he concludes, is dangerous for young readers who may develop sadomasochistic fantasies (177). Wertham also finds a connection between violence and sex associated with the primitive nature of human beings. He argues that comic books tap into this part of the mind (179). In linking sex and violence, Wertham makes a case for sexualization as dangerous to the minds of the youth of America.

In fear of the potential harmful impact of content on adolescent readers, the Comics Code of 1954 (Comics Magazine Association of America, Inc. 1954) established regulations on the depiction of the female form. For one, the code states, "Females shall be drawn realistically without exaggeration of any physical qualities." This suggests that a female figure drawn proportionally to scale lacks sexual intrigue. Once a woman's curves are extenuated, she becomes a sexual object. Ironically, the same is not said about men. Male characters can wear skintight suits that enhance their physique but not be deemed as sexual objects. The woman's curves, for the 1950s certainly, were those that needed illustration regulations according to the code. The fear was that the female body could provide fetishistic pleasure for males, which was deemed inappropriate exposure for young readers, so the code's intentions were to reduce the sexual objectification of women. Aside from Wertham's link between violence and sex, the code's efforts can also be read as trying to protect women from being objectified by men and, therefore, holding the female body as more sacred than the male body.

The code's demands were not to tone down the female body at the expense of feminine freedoms but to suppress what we may refer to now as the male gaze. Laura Mulvey first defined the "male gaze" in her theorizing about cinema in 1975. Mulvey (1989, 19) argues, "In their traditional exhibitionist role women are simultaneously looked at and displayed, with their appearance coded for strong visual and erotic impact so that they can be said to connote *to-be-looked-at-ness*." For the comic book medium, the extenuation of a woman's curves, panels that focus on sexual body parts, and women in seductive or sexual positions may also illustrate the ways in which women are drawn to be looked at as sexual objects. Meg Downey (2015) argues that the problem in the comic book industry is that, for decades, women have only been depicted as sexy: "Imaginary ladies designed by men to be consumed by them, and served up to them on silver platters." The consuming of women occurs through the male gaze. Women are turned into objects that appeal to the scopophilic instinct, which Mulvey (1989, 25) defines as "pleasure in looking at another person as an erotic object." Another concern may be that comics could encourage voyeurism. According to Mulvey, voyeurism "has associations with sadism" (21). This is precisely what Wertham accused the industry of creating—fetishized sex objects that appeal to sadistic impulses.

Early Batman comics occasionally present sexualized women, but the focus is predominantly on crimes, mysteries, supervillains, and Batman and Robin's crime-fighting efforts. In *Batman* #49 (Finger, Kane, and Schwartz 1948), one panel depicts Vicki Vale in her home wearing a low-cut slinky dress with a fur sleeve that has slipped off one shoulder. She is seated, legs crossed, wearing high heels, with both legs exposed from the knees down. Later, Vicki wears a backless strapless dress with a deep V in the back. In these panels, she appears as an alluring figure. Her exposed skin sexualizes her in these two illustrations, but her character is not sexually objectified. The panels glamorize her rather than position her as a sexual commodity.

    Catwoman has historically been depicted as a sexy, alluring character. In the pre-code comics, her attractiveness often causes Batman to lower his guard and even let her escape. Hanley (2017) notes, "Catwoman met all the femme fatale criteria. She was a beautiful woman committed to a life of crime who used her feminine wiles to corrupt Batman and make him do what she wanted." Her power over Batman marked a vulnerability in the superhero. In both *Batman* #3 (Finger and Kane 1940d) and *Batman* #10 (Schiff, Robinson, and Ray 1942), The Cat kisses Batman to catch him off guard and escape before he can turn her in to the police. Batman's attraction to The Cat gives her an advantage over him. Since Batman is often inclined to let Catwoman go, he is making a statement that the law does not apply to everyone, especially if they are sexually attractive. Sacrificing his moral code and giving concessions based on sexual intrigue perpetuates criminality. Catwoman also exposes a weakness in Batman. He is supposed to be a symbol of justice, but his attraction to a female criminal reveals the man underneath. While young Bruce gave up his identity when he declared his oath to war on criminals in *Detective Comics* #33 (Finger, Fox, Kane, and Moldoff 1939), his submission to Catwoman shows that the heterosexual desires of the man beneath the cowl cannot be eradicated entirely. Sexual desire is too powerful a force to be completely suppressed. Catwoman was removed from the comics after the code was enacted because she was deemed too sexy for readers: "The code, by forbidding suggestive postures, demanding realistic drawings of women with no exaggeration of any physical qualities, banning glamorous or sympathetic criminals, and requiring punishment for all crime every time, left little room for the sexy thief who steals Batman's heart" (Langley 2012, 210). Under the code, sexual desire could not dominate moral authority, so Catwoman was deemed no longer appropriate for the comics.

Over time, as the code became obsolete, female characters in Gotham grew increasingly more sexualized. In one sense, regaining their sexuality provides women with a chance to be empowered by their bodies. On the other hand, the comics continue to attract the male gaze, which would again suggest objectification and the consuming of female bodies. Similarly, in real-world America, there are ongoing controversial opinions regarding representation and perception of women. Women have often celebrated their bodies and used them as a voice for power. During the 2017 Women's March protest to advocate for women's rights in Washington, DC, women wore vagina costumes and "pussy hats." They wrote signs referencing female body parts, thus using their bodies to make a social and political statement. While a protest for women's rights would be against objectification, the costumes and hats may be viewed as essentially doing exactly what they are protesting against. The focus on female genitalia during the march was also criticized for excluding the transgender community.[1] Such neglect is the very same exclusionary practice that the protest was intended to fight against, which complicates social attempts for unification. Sexualized bodies in comics create similar social conflict. Sexuality can empower women at the same time that it could objectify them. Ultimately, the reader's social perspectives determine the interpretation, which allows for diversified reading experiences and can prompt debate.

The social aspects of sexuality are often paradoxical and difficult to negotiate. What is offensive to one person may be empowering to another. Comic books and their film adaptations are perfect examples of how sexual representation can take on different meanings. Multiple readings of Mindy Newell, J. J. Birch, and Michael Bair's 1989 four-part series *Catwoman* may pit glorification against oppression. The miniseries imagines a Catwoman story that aligns with Frank Miller and David Mazzucchelli's ([1987] 2005) *Batman: Year One* where Selina is a prostitute turned masked thief. For Deborah Elizabeth Whaley (2011, 12), "Miller's sexualized Catwoman was congruent with a growing trend in 1980s comics to present latex and leather clad angry women ass-kickers, such as Barb Wire, Lady Rawhide, Witch Blade, Fatale, Black Widow, and She-Hulk." However, Hanley (2017) argues that in Miller's depiction, Catwoman's "sexuality no longer belonged to her; it was controlled and dictated by a series of men."

This changes in Newell, Birch, and Bair's approach. In the miniseries, Selina's abusive pimp gives her a catsuit. But Selina ultimately fights back and uses her costume for empowerment (Newell, Birch, and Bair 1989a). In wearing the costume required by a superior male, she may be judged as adopting a prescribed sexualized role of inferiority. On the other hand, she also may be viewed as taking a symbol of oppression and exploiting it. In doing so, she claims power over her oppressor and redefines the symbolic meaning behind the catsuit.

Even though the Comics Code was not concerned with the sexualization of male bodies, the representation of sexuality in the Batman franchise also caters to the female gaze. Downey (2015) discusses the ways in which women in the Batman comics have repeatedly made comments about Dick Grayson's body or have taken advantage of his body. These women are portrayed as acting inappropriately toward him. One example of a female exploiting Dick is from *Batman Family* #1 when Batgirl kisses Robin to stop him from telling her that she shouldn't be a superhero (Maggin and Grell 1975). This sparked controversy from readers who felt the age gap between teenage Robin and 20-something Batgirl was inappropriate.[2] Batgirl may be argued as sexually manipulating Robin in gaining the upper hand through the kiss. Downey (2015) finds other similar occurrences when Dick is objectified in the comics and argues that "Dick was allowed to freely express sexual desire, and freely allowed to be the recipient of sexual desire, but only when he was the one who is in control of the moment. The moment he became the object of the gaze, or the object of someone else's desire that he did not directly control, he expressed discomfort." This perspective argues that the comics condone sexual initiative for male characters but not female characters. Women who gaze upon Dick or act sexually toward him are regarded as inappropriate. Such a representation is illustrative of a social perspective that feels as though women should be passive. However, if the male is the instigator of sexual behavior or if a woman is the object of the male gaze, at what point does this too become regarded as inappropriate? The #MeToo movement of 2017 demonstrates a collective outcry against men who speak or act upon women sexually in undesired and potentially abusive situations. Therefore, twenty-first-century popular culture has to tread delicately in its portrayal of men making advances on women. An ongoing tension exists in negotiating appropriate sexual behaviors between men and women in America.

Sexuality and Violence

The Batman franchise illustrates a relationship between power and sexuality that is often made visible through the villainesses. Poison Ivy, for example, is empowered by her sex appeal and by sexual violence. Ivy was introduced in 1966 in *Batman* #181, where she is described as "a luscious nemesis—the unique villainess—the irresistible Poison Ivy!" She is also called a "vivacious villainess" and "delightful but dangerous." Ivy boasts that she is not only more beautiful but also a better criminal than any of the other female villains. When she states her name to the crowd, she proudly says, "Poison—as in arsenic! Ivy—as in irresistible!" (Kanigher and Moldoff 1966). Her seductive prowess serves as her superpower. She is also referred to as "the slithering siren," and she effectively embodies the mask of beauty and the threat hidden underneath.

Ivy is dangerous because she takes advantage of men's inclination to be attracted to her. When Bruce meets Ivy in *Batman* #181, he says, "You are luscious, dreamboat!" (Kanigher and Moldoff 1966). The villainess's beauty serves as a distraction to draw the superhero's attention away from her criminality. In using her sex appeal to exploit men, Ivy reveals their vulnerability. Batman says, "I was thinking of how cute Poison Ivy is—I hate to put such a beautiful doll behind bars!" Batman struggles to overcome her seductive powers and potentially sacrifices his code of conduct simply because she is "cute." Like Catwoman does on several occasions, Ivy exposes a weakness in Batman—one that reduces him from idealistic superhero to mere man driven by primitive sexual instincts. Physical appearance holds manipulative power over men—even superheroes. Ivy is still a villainess regardless of her beauty, but her captivating attractiveness clouds the perceptions that men have of her. In this issue, she also draws Batman in to kiss her and attempts to disorient him with chloroform lipstick (Kanigher and Moldoff 1966). Like a Siren, Ivy's sex appeal becomes a weapon against the Caped Crusader and provides her dominance over a powerful man.

In Joel Schumacher's (1997) film *Batman and Robin*, at a charity auction, Poison Ivy (Uma Thurman) puts the guests, including Batman (George Clooney) and Robin (Chris O'Donnell), under a spell using pheromone powder (what she calls her "love dust"). Batman and Robin battle over Ivy while under her charms, exposing the dangerous power of lust. For Batman and Robin, this is also a power struggle. They want to feed their sexual appetites while claiming possession over the female body. This film shows the ways the male gaze can leave the city vulnerable and have dangerous repercussions. Infatuation with Ivy becomes paralyzing and even deadly for men who succumb to her charms. Ivy says, "I really am to die for" as she kisses and kills Mr. Freeze's prison guards (Schumacher 1997). Ivy's sex appeal serves to be an effective weapon that empowers her and makes men appear weak.

As previously mentioned, Catwoman also uses her sexual prowess to gain the upper hand over Batman. In *Catwoman* #4, she manipulates and asserts power over Batman. At one point, Catwoman argues with Batman about the proper way of handling criminals. She sees Batman as aligned with the police, whom she does not trust. Batman says, "So it's to be a war between us," to which Catwoman replies, "It's always a war between the sexes." When Batman asks her, "And who will draw first blood?" she responds, "Me?" and kisses him (Newell, Birch, and Bair 1989b). Like Poison Ivy's methods of seduction, the kiss serves as a distraction so that Catwoman can then punch Batman. She catches him off guard by seducing him and then uses this advantage to attack. Catwoman then calls Batman "just another cop" and says, "I don't do cops" (Newell, Birch, and Bair 1989b). She may seduce Batman but will not take things any further with him sexually because the battle is more important to her. This declaration also allows Catwoman to assert her choice in how her romantic or sexual relationships progress. She is in complete control, manipulating Batman—whom she aligns with the criminal justice system—in order to subvert that system and continue her criminal activity. Catwoman heightens the sociocultural threat and power of a woman's sexual agency.

Supervillainesses frequently use their sex appeal and sexual behavior to gain criminal advantage. But sexual violence in the Batman franchise often occurs where women are the victims. In Alan

Moore and Brian Bolland's ([1988] 2008) *The Killing Joke*, the Joker shoots Barbara Gordon, which results in paralysis and confinement to a wheelchair. He also takes photos of her to torture her father. Barbara is simultaneously desexualized and hypersexualized in these photos. On one hand, the Joker's photographing is a violation of Barbara, putting her naked, wounded body on display, making her into an object to fulfill his sadistic purposes. She becomes a model for sexualized violence; the photos zoom in on different body parts and are displayed as part of a carnival ride where the Joker shows them to Gordon in efforts to drive him mad. But since Barbara is on the brink of death, the violence to her body also desexualizes her and makes her into a graphic display of pain and suffering. With either reading, the Joker wants to draw the voyeuristic male gaze to Barbara's battered body.

Women also commit acts of sexual violence toward women. In *Batwoman* #34, after learning Batwoman's identity, Natalia Mitternacht—a vampire who goes by Nocturna—enters her residence at night and uses her powers to assume the appearance of Kate's ex-girlfriend Maggie. The sight of a former lover arouses sexual desire in Kate, which Nocturna uses to overpower her (Andreyko, Moritat, and Haun 2014). Later, in *Batwoman* #36, Kate and Natalia are in a relationship, but Kate's lapses in memory make her unable to recall Natalia biting her and taking advantage of her sexually (Andreyko and Jeanty 2015a). Kate remains under Natalia's hypnosis for several issues. Critics have found parallels between Natalia's actions and rape. Mey Rude (2014) criticizes *Batwoman*'s creative team for including this plot to make the comic "sexy." She finds that "the way Kate and Nocturna are drawn both in issue #34 and in #36 in Kate's flashback is catering to the male gaze. And that makes this even more insidious" (Rude 2014). The criticism asserts that men would enjoy and be aroused by having an intimate view of the violent vampire-human lesbian relationship. In the final image of *Batwoman* #34, Nocturna bites Kate while Kate leans back, eyes closed, mouth open, stroking Nocturna's hair. Kate's body is positioned as if experiencing sexual pleasure in the moment that she is bitten (Andreyko, Moritat, and Haun 2014). The illustration draws the reader's eye to the sexualized bodies.

While Nocturna's behavior is certainly sexual manipulation and could be considered rape, this depiction may also be regarded as a progressive approach against traditional gender roles. The graphic nature of the lesbian relationship and the female attacker showcase sexual dominance in women. However, Rude (2014) criticizes the creative team and the editors at DC because the story does not address rape as a problem; instead, she claims that the comics glamorize it. She argues that *Batwoman* is "simply showing it off and using it to titillate and create drama." Rape is used "as a gimmick to sell comics, and unfortunately, to abuse one of their best characters and perpetuate rape culture" (Rude 2014). The comics illustrate a relevant and frequently occurring problem in the lesbian community. The Centers for Disease Control and Prevention's (CDC) (n.d.) National Intimate Partner and Sexual Violence Survey (NISVS) reported results from 2010 data that 44 percent of lesbian women "experienced rape, physical violence, and/or stalking by an intimate partner in their lifetime," and "approximately 1 in 8 lesbian women (13%) ... have been raped in their lifetime." The glamorization of rape would be counterproductive to trying to reduce the occurrences of rape in this subculture and also in society in general. Instead, rape becomes a voyeuristic opportunity. In *Batwoman* #36, one panel depicts Kate and Nocturna wearing only their undergarments, passionately kissing. Kate is covered in blood (Andreyko and Jeanty 2015a). The illustration combines passion with violence, essentially romanticizing the rape, and providing a voyeuristic opportunity for the reader. Kate reacts in horror when she has the flashback, but she does not understand what she has seen. Her blackouts make her ignorant to the sexual manipulation. The passion that the panel exudes shows how powerful Nocturna is at contrivance. She has developed an unconventional method of rape where the victim is unaware that she is being exploited and thus consents to sex. Nocturna not only takes advantage of Kate sexually, she also uses Batwoman as a puppet because she manipulates her mind.

Aside from the biting, this would be considered a nonviolent rape that has the appearance of being consensual but only because Kate has been deceived—hypnotized to thinking that the woman who initially approached her was Maggie. The nonviolence of the rape makes it terrifying because Kate physically has the ability to fight back, but since she is under hypnosis, she cannot use her strength and skills. The manipulation is so deep that she is not even aware that she is being taken advantage of. In *Rethinking Rape*, Ann J. Cahill (2001, 8) finds that "feminist theories of the body will approach rape as a crime not limited to an assault on a woman's sexuality, but as an assault on various but fundamental aspects of her embodied selfhood." In manipulating Kate into a relationship with her, Nocturna disrupts Kate's sense of self. Kate thinks she is a consenting member of a healthy relationship, not realizing that she is actually a victim of mental and sexual exploitation.

The comics, in making the rape visible, may also be interpreted as publicizing rape. Tanya Horeck (2004, 1) defines "public rape" as "an unusual but powerful way of thinking about how sexual violation circulates in the public domain as a culturally invested issue. It provokes and horrifies, but also engages and fascinates." The reaction to these *Batwoman* comics exhibits these binaries within a culture that is simultaneously repulsed and fascinated by rape. Since Nocturna is a supervillainess, her behavior is unacceptable and assumedly for selfish gains. She wants to be able to control Batwoman like a puppet. But the eroticism of the illustrations suggests an irresistibility to hypnotic lesbian vampire mind control. This raises tensions as to whether the comics are publicly sanctioning lesbian rape in displaying it so erotically or whether they are raising public awareness to a less visible kind of rape that even a superheroine can fall victim to.

Public rape includes "representations of rape that serve as cultural fantasies of power and domination, gender and sexuality, and class and ethnicity" (Horeck 2004, 3). Nocturna is inhuman, so the rapist is an Other, a creature who creates the image of human desire. She is terrifying and dangerous because she can replicate and then exploit an individual's deepest desires, which makes Kate vulnerable. When Nocturna breaks into Kate's apartment, she approaches Kate when she is in bed and says, "Who do you **want** me to be?" (Andreyko, Moritat, and Haun 2014). This makes the interaction entirely about Kate's sexual desires. Kate's love and lust for Maggie become her weakness, which stimulates her to consent, completely ignorant to the truth behind the façade. The rape is successful because of the fantasy that Nocturna creates.

This story arc dispels the popular rape myth that "only certain types of women become victims of rape, and they are responsible for their victimization" (Garland, Branch, and Grimes 2015, 3). Kate's experience shows that anyone, even a superheroine, can be a rape victim. *Batwoman* also dispels the rape myth that "men of a certain age, education level, race, class, etc., always rape women" (Garland, Branch, and Grimes 2015, 3). Nocturna is female and possesses supernatural powers that make her undefinable in terms of social stratifications such as race and class. In addition, "one of the most common myths surrounding rape is that rapes are violent and/or involve a weapon or use of force" (Garland, Branch, and Grimes 2015, 12). Nocturna uses hypnosis and maintains an extended relationship with Kate. The comics do not reinforce most rape myths and therefore expose and warn against alternative methods of sexual exploitation. They also show the frightening reality that anyone can be a victim of rape, even one who seems as strong and indestructible as a superheroine.

These comics are not about male dominance but about the exploitive powers of a female. Nocturna controls the seduction and the relationship both physically and mentally. The cover of *Batwoman* #34 illustrates Nocturna in a physically dominant position over Batwoman (Andreyko, Moritat, and Haun 2014). The rapist's superior power is made visible and continues through the sexual acts. In biting Kate, Nocturna exerts her nonhuman power and combines violence and eroticism. Kate temporarily develops fangs when she gets angry, which means that Kate's rape is not just taking advantage of her body but turning her into something other than human. In *Batwoman* #38, Kate and Natalia get into a fight, and then Natalia slams Kate against the wall, yelling, "Enough **talk**! Just show me you **love** me" (Andreyko and Ryp 2015). Kate tilts her head back and groans while Natalia licks her neck. The moment quickly moves from tense to violent to erotic. Natalia makes demands of Kate, forcing her to physically prove a brainwashed "love." The power struggles become a matter of claimed ownership as well. In *Batwoman* #36, Natalia tells Kate, "You're **mine**" (Andreyko and Jeanty 2015a). Even here, Kate does not realize that she is a victim holding little power in the relationship. Natalia also makes their relationship public instead of concealing it. In doing so, she creates a façade of a consensual relationship for the rest of Gotham to witness. Her manipulation, hypnotizing powers, and sexual exploitations remain hidden. Maggie criticizes Kate since Natalia is a known criminal but is not privy to the deceit that led Kate into this situation.

Rape is simultaneously an attack on the body and on the identity of the victim. Ann J. Cahill (2001, 10) argues that we need to "understand rape as an act charged with political and bodily meanings, as a threat to the possibility of the bodily integrity of women, and therefore as a threat to her status as a person." Kate's chronic rape threatens who she is as both herself and Batwoman. The hypnosis blurs reality and disrupts her social interactions with others. She also loses credibility. The rape creates a fantasy—confounding her own sense of self and the world around her.

Blame in rape cases is often a sensitive matter. Carine M. Mardorossian (2002, 753) argues that there is a public "expectation that women should now know better than to let themselves get raped." Tammy S. Garland, Kathryn A. Branch, and Mackenzie Grimes (2015, 10) echo this point and find victim blaming the result of a rape myth:

> Blaming victims revolves around the myth that an individual is able to prevent a rape and that a "real rape" is often characterized by fighting back. Therefore, if a victim fails to "fight back" she or he is blamed for the victimization, because it is perceived that she or he could have prevented the act if she or he had chosen to do so.

Kate certainly could have fought back, but she was unaware that she was being exploited. In *Batwoman* #40, Natalia confesses to Kate, "You were just so easy to snare. All your broken-hearted martyr-complex self-loathing … it was like a neon sign flashing, '**over here!**'" Natalia also denies being a rapist, saying that Kate desired her: "You wanted something raw, a lesbian **Sid and Nancy** thing. Kinky, yes? But that was all **yours**. Remember what your sister said: hypnosis can't make you do anything you don't really want to do" (Andreyko and Jeanty 2015b). Rape fantasy is the idea that women actually fantasize about being raped—that they want to be violated (Horeck 2004, 4). Natalia uses this excuse to argue that she is not actually a rapist. However, since she assumed the appearance of Maggie in their first sexual encounter, Kate's desire was initially due to pretense. Once sexually exploited, Kate became Natalia's possession and perpetually under her influence. In blaming Kate, Natalia deflects responsibility to the victim. Mardorossian (2002, 756) argues that "the responsibility of the rapist is seen as inherently linked to the victim's behavior and as a result often gets erased. Whether it is because she did not fight back physically or verbally, somehow rape always comes to be grounded in the victim's behavioral or emotional dynamics rather than in the perpetrator's actions." Kate's behavior is consensual only because she does not realize that she is being victimized. According to the Bureau of Justice Statistics, from 2005 to 2010, 64 percent of rape or sexual assault victimizations went unreported to the police (United States Department of Justice 2013). While survey responders gave a variety of reasons for not reporting, the survey did not have an option linked to victim blaming, which could certainly contribute to the number of victimizations.

Abuse to women in the Batman franchise extends to Catwoman as well. Newell, Birch, and Bair's *Catwoman* miniseries depicts Selina as someone who reaches a breaking point and then acquires autonomy. On the cover of issue #1, Selina lies unconscious on the ground, her body contorted. She wears high heels, fishnet stockings, garter clips, and a slinky, torn red dress. Above her body rises the figure of Catwoman. The statement, "In the Ruins of Innocence, the BATMAN'S Enemy is Born ..." appears on the cover (Newell, Birch, and Bair 1989a). This depiction of Selina posits that the loss of innocence suffered as a prostitute encourages and even empowers her to become a supervillainess. The issue opens with another visual perspective of Selina's battered body, her torn dress hardly covering her breasts. As a prostitute, Selina embodies the commodification of sexualized violence, but when her pimp, Stan, beats her, her battered body becomes a visible display of the brutalization of an object of sex. Selina has to change the way that she uses her body in order to survive and thrive in Gotham City.

The miniseries also illustrates how prostitutes are viewed as a lower class than other citizens of Gotham. Flannery, of Gotham Vice, questions Selina and tells her that she could charge her attacker with rape (Newell, Birch, and Bair 1989a). He says, "Even whores got rights," implying a prostitute holds inferior status to other citizens of Gotham but is still human and therefore eligible for the benefits of the law. Later, when Captain Strunk attacks Selina's friend Holly,

Selina reports the crime to Flannery. Selina says, "Holly's not a liar," and Flannery replies, "She's a whore" (Newell, Birch, and Bair 1989b). The male concludes that a female who sells her body has sacrificed any credibility. Once sex is commodified, a woman in Gotham is considered inferior, but the violent attacker gets away with abuse because his job holds respectability. Ultimately, Batman assures Catwoman that Strunk will be prosecuted, but Catwoman doubts the legitimacy of the criminal justice system. She feels a jury will not believe a prostitute over an officer because of the embedded class and gender disparities.

Selina's loss of innocence, her transformation from product to independent woman, ironically occurs through a sexualized object intended for her to use to please others. Selina's pimp, Stan, gives her a cat costume and wants her to wear it for a customer (Newell, Birch, and Bair 1989a). Stan sexualizes the cat costume that Selina eventually repurposes when she frees herself from him and becomes an autonomous figure. She realizes that Batman uses his costume as a tool and that she can also be empowered by hers. Selina uses the sexualized costume to rid herself of her prostitute identity. What was intended to turn Selina into a sexualized object of the male gaze becomes a suit of arms. Instead of assuming the role prescribed to her, she rewrites it, though for criminal purposes.[3]

Instead of suppressing sexuality, DC creators have used sex as a tool of empowerment for women—though often for criminal gains. However, there are no longer restrictions to the ways in which the female body is depicted. Women can dress provocatively, and their curves do not need to be downsized. With such a wide readership and viewer base, fans will continue to have mixed reactions to the ways in which characters—particularly women—are represented. Sex and sexuality are delicate topics for creative distribution. While creators have often been sensitive to the outcries of fans, it is impossible to please everyone since what is offensive to one person may feel liberating to another. Creators have the ongoing difficult task in negotiating how to represent sex and violence in ways that will reach twenty-first-century readers and audiences. The comic book industry has to adapt its content to stay relevant in a society where views regarding sexual expression and sexual representation constantly shift.

Putting Pressure on Heteronormativity

The early comics within the Batman franchise created several love interests for Bruce/Batman, but his chosen career made it difficult to maintain a serious relationship. The comics often show initial attraction, dating, and imagining a relationship that ultimately cannot be realized. Julie Madison was Bruce Wayne's first love interest, appearing in *Detective Comics* #31 as his fiancé (Fox, Kane, and Moldoff 1939b). They later break up in *Detective Comics* #49 (Finger and Kane 1941d) after Bruce refuses Julie's request that he find himself a serious career. In *Batman* #1 (Finger and Kane 1940a), Catwoman ("The Cat") makes her first appearance. After Batman captures her, she tries to seduce him, wrapping her arms around his neck and saying, "Why don't you come in as a partner with me! You and I <u>together!</u> You and I … King and Queen of Crime!" Catwoman's ideal relationship is unrealistic for Batman but plants the suggestion for romance. Later, Batman allows her to escape and muses, "Lovely girl! … What eyes! … Maybe I'll bump into her again sometime." The comics repeatedly tease the potential for a relationship between Batman and Catwoman. Batman expresses interest in her and is often vulnerable to her sexual advances where he lowers his guard and allows her to escape capture. In the final panel of *Batman* #3 (Finger and Kane 1940d), The Cat muses, "I sort of wish the Batman were driving this car—and I were sitting beside him… .and we were just another boy and girl out for a ride on a moonlight night. That would be sort of … of … <u>nice</u>!!" Catwoman imagines herself with Batman in a romantic setting as if on a date. Here, the panel suggests romantic possibilities for Batman and Catwoman, but throughout the franchise, their relationship is often complicated.[4] Bruce also dates Linda Page in the early 1940s and, later, Vicki Vale (first appearance, *Batman* #49 in 1948). He cannot commit to a serious relationship due to his vigilantism, but that does not stop him from casual dating.

Despite Bruce's heterosexual dating and relationships, Dr. Fredric Wertham ([1954] 2004) presented evidence to make an argument in *Seduction of the Innocent* for gay subtexts between Batman and Robin. He defines the Batman comics as "psychologically homosexual" (189) and states that Batman and Robin's daily life and activities in Wayne

Manor are "like a wish dream of two homosexuals living together" (190). Travis Langley (2012, 209) remarks that Wertham was not concerned that Batman endangered a child (Robin) but that Batman rescuing Robin from villains was a sexual act. Wertham's ([1954] 2004, 191) focus remains on the relationship between Batman and Robin, which he claims provided the visible potential for the arousal of gay fantasies in readers. Andrew Wheeler (2012), too, finds the comics as containing gay undertones: "The gayness of Batman was not just a joke about sidekicks, it was a scrap of identification for a starved gay audience. Robin established Batman as an early totem for a nascent and repressed gay subculture." During the 1950s, this raised concerns for the influence on the adolescent male reader base. Wertham ([1954] 2004, 189) argues that young male readers may experience sexual anxieties after reading comic books:

> Many adolescents go through periods of vague fears that they might be homosexual. Such fears may become a source of great mental anguish and these boys usually have no one in whom they feel they can confide. In a number of cases I have found this sequence of events: At an early age these boys become addicted to the homoerotically tinged type of comic book. During and after comic-book reading they indulged in fantasies which became severely repressed. Life experiences, either those drawing their attention to the great taboo on homosexuality or just the opposite—experiences providing any kind of temptation—raise feelings of doubt, guilt, shame and sexual malorientation.

Wertham finds that comic books have the powerful potential to stimulate sexual fantasies that leave young readers uneasy and uncertain about their own sexuality. He warns that readers of Batman comics could find homoeroticism between Batman and Robin, which could create sexual confusion.

Will Brooker (2001, 102) argues that Wertham does not express homophobia but "concern" for young male readers. Wertham "understands that in a climate where homosexuality is a great taboo, gay fantasies might be a source of worry for young men" (Brooker 2001, 111). Through Brooker's perspective, Wertham had the social interests of the readership in mind. Batman creators may have not intentionally created gay characters, but for Wertham and the Comics Code Authority (CCA), consideration of the social impact of different interpretations was critical. Brooker (2001, 141) finds "that there was more than enough material in the Batman comics of the early 1950s to provide a gay reader, viewing the texts through his cultural understanding of 'gayness' during that period, with fantasies of homosexual romance and stylised echoes of his own situation." With the opportunity for such an impact on a reader, the Comics Code of 1954 (Comics Magazine Association of America, Inc. 1954) included rules alluding to the representation of sexuality: "Illicit sex relations are neither to be hinted at nor portrayed. Violent love scenes as well as sexual abnormalities are unacceptable," and "sex perversion or any inference to same is strictly forbidden." The code also states, "The treatment of live-romance stories shall emphasize the value of the home and the sanctity of marriage." The attempt was to preserve social norms for the 1950s, which were based on heterosexual normativity. The code aligns gayness with violence and perversion, and the regulatory measures sought to eliminate public exposure to anything that violated domesticated heteronormativity.

Since the content of the Batman comics could be interpreted as displaying or fostering gay subtexts, DC introduced Kathy Kane (Batwoman) in 1956 to reaffirm Batman's heterosexuality. Her role also combatted Wertham's ([1954] 2004, 191) claim that "in [Batman] stories there are practically no decent, attractive, successful women … The atmosphere is homosexual and anti-feminine. If the girl is good-looking she is undoubtedly the villainess." It seems Wertham would only find attractiveness combined with moral stability as the components of femininity. Batwoman was created to refute Wertham's claims about the comics. She was "a sultry crime-fighter in a leotard and sporting a utility belt holding scant but lipstick, perfume, and bobby pins. Batwoman's role was to serve as a lust-interest for the, clearly, hetero Batman" (Devore 2017, 195). Creators had to avoid hypersexualizing Batwoman (to abide by the code) but make her enticing enough to Batman to affirm his heterosexuality.

Batwoman embodied femininity to realign sexual normativity in the comics. Batman could be viewed as embodying masculinity; thus, Batwoman and Batman were, theoretically, an ideal heterosexual match. However, Wheeler (2012) finds that the subcontext of Batman and the paths the comics have taken culturally throughout history permanently mark a gay association with his character: "Batman will always have his gayness, however straight they write him." Batman can be simultaneously read as gay and straight, as every iteration allows for multiple interpretations of his character. Brooker (2001, 127) argues that "the critics who attempt to 'prove' that Batman is heterosexual are doing the character a disservice by denying his availability to multiple readings." Even with the presence of female love interests, Batman still has the potential to be read as gay or capable of arousing gay fantasies in readers.

Batwoman disappeared from the comics in 1964. She made some appearances in the 1970s and 1980s, but her big comeback did not come until the twenty-first century. After the Infinite Crisis, in New Earth, Kate Kane appeared in *52* #7 but not intended to be a potential love interest for Batman (Johns et al. 2006). In the twenty-first century, her character no longer needed to disprove something about Batman's character. Batwoman could now stand alone and be her own, independent woman. Ironically, the new iteration of her character has been used to illustrate gayness as acceptable in Gotham rather than refute it. Kate Kane was introduced to readers as a lesbian who does not struggle with her sexual identity. In fact, that is one part of herself that she is confident about. Instead, Kate struggles to find a purpose for herself—one where she can help others. Greg Rucka and J. H. Williams III explore this in *Batwoman: Elegy* (which contains *Detective Comics* #854–60 from 2009 to 2010), where Kate is dismissed from the US Army for her sexuality and needs to find a new way to serve society.

Rucka and Williams III (2010a) open *Detective Comics* #859 by thanking 1LT Daniel Choi (USMA 2003) "for his generous assistance in research for this issue." Dan Choi was an infantry officer in the US Army whose service included time in Iraq from 2006 to 2007. The Federal Recognition Board recommended that he be discharged for "moral and professional dereliction" after he came out as gay on *The Rachel Maddow Show* in 2009 (Ireland 2009). Choi fought the military's "Don't Ask, Don't Tell" policy.[5] In having Kate experience similar prejudice, and in thanking Choi, Rucka draws social awareness to a relevant American problem where an institution's code becomes an inhibitor to social realities. Paul Petrovic (2011, 71) finds that Rucka's acknowledgment of Choi "highlights the military's exclusionary practices and makes explicit the damage inflicted on real-life minorities in the name of heteronormative ideology, all the while suggesting the political interrogation that comics can offer as they retrace and therefore out the censored scenario of gay rights in the military." Before even becoming Batwoman, Kate is a role model for social justice. Kate does not deny her sexuality in order to appease a system. The *Elegy* comics put pressure on the systemic American practice of silencing. As cultural artifacts, they expose discriminatory institutional practices to their readers in efforts to redirect society's priorities and perspectives regarding gender and sexuality.

In a flashback in *Elegy* (*Detective Comics* #859), Colonel Reyes asks to see Kate, who is a cadet in the US Army. He tells her that she has been accused of violating Article 125 of the Uniform Code of Military Justice. He then says, "I have some **discretion** in this matter, however," and "You can tell me right now that this is a **mistake**. That it's some joke, that you were goofing around. That it's a simple **misunderstanding**. And that it will **never** happen **again**." If Kate does so, she will be disciplined but be allowed to remain in the Army. Kate says that as a cadet, she "cannot **lie**, cheat or steal, nor suffer others to do so" (Rucka and Williams III 2010a). Kate will not be silenced in order to stay in an organization that denies her sexuality; she will not treat her sexual identity as a joke. Petrovic (2011, 75) argues that Kate resists "heterosexual and assimilationist hegemony." Kate's refusal to sacrifice her identity to go along with the system shows a firm understanding of herself and her values. The comics take a stance against oppression and silencing of gay individuals in America.

Elegy critiques the oppressive practice of silencing that demands performance and denies identity. In her seminal work *The Epistemology of the Closet*, Eve Kosofsky Sedgwick (1990, 3) theorizes that "'closetedness' itself is a performance initiated as such by the speech act of a silence—not a particular silence, but a silence that accrues particularity by fits and starts, in relation to the discourse that surrounds and differentially constitutes it." In Kate's case, Colonel Reyes gives her an opportunity to remain in the military if she stays in the closet, performing silence by lying about who she is. Reyes wants to encourage silence in order to conform to the military's code. Their exchange exposes the code as a construct to maintain the appearance of heteronormativity. It is a rule book for performance that denies truth. Kate realizes this but will not perform silence and lie about who she is to appease an exclusionary system.

Honesty regarding self is a very important value for Kate. Later on, when dating Renee Montoya, Kate criticizes Renee for keeping her sexuality secret: "At least I'm not **pretending** to be something I'm **not!**," and "You're afraid you cop-buddies will find out you're **queer!**" (Rucka and Williams III 2010a). Kate finds weakness in Renee for her silence. She accuses Renee of pretending, essentially performing one identity at work while her true self remains suppressed and hidden. Renee performs silence in her work environment and remains closeted as she fears how others will treat her upon learning about her sexuality. Fear has the power to dictate her daily performance of her identity, whereas Kate does not perform silence because she does not care about the opinions of others.

Ironically, when Kate becomes Batwoman, her new role is a performance. Kate, like most superheroes, treats her street self and Batwoman as two separate identities. Using Sedgwick's rhetoric, Andréa Gilroy (2015, 23) finds that "superheroes are subject to an epistemology of the phone booth wherein any superheroic identity is necessarily broken into several identities, each determined by the secrets they must keep." While Kate does not perform silence regarding her sexuality since she values openness and honesty about who she is, in donning the cape and cowl, she needs—as a protective measure—to perform silence about her secret identity as Batwoman. She remains an out lesbian but a closeted vigilante.

When Kate is discharged from the army, she struggles to find her place and a way to continue public service outside of the military. She realizes that she can no longer defend others as Kate, due to systemic rejection, but Batwoman is a persona that she can assume to protect and defend the citizens of Gotham City. As Batwoman, she also does not have a superior, and Gotham does not have a strict code regarding sexual identity by which she must abide. "No person or, more importantly, political administration here wields the power to subordinate or close down her queer identity" (Petrovic 2011, 73). Batwoman makes her own agenda and her own rules. Becoming Batwoman is the only way that Kate can simultaneously serve others and be a queer woman in Gotham City. While the identities coexist in one body, they must remain disassociated in the public eye. Thus, Kate can live without restrictions as a lesbian while Batwoman can fight crime to protect the people.

In everyday clothes, Kate is social and open with her sexuality. At a Gotham socialite fundraiser, she wears a tuxedo to the frustration of her stepmother, who utters, "You couldn't wear something more **appropriate**?" (Rucka and Williams III 2009b). Kate's attire is certainly appropriate for such a formal event, but her stepmother is concerned about the social implications of a woman wearing attire that is socially gendered as male. She tells Kate, "Not that I don't **approve,** it's your life, of course. I just don't think it's **appropriate** for a **formal** event. It's like you're trying to draw **attention** to yourself." Kate's stepmother finds the openness of Kate's sexuality, which is manifested in her clothing, as ill-suited for public social settings. She would prefer Kate wear attire gendered female because it would draw less attention and, in doing so, essentially closet Kate. Kate's stepmother wants to silence her sexuality through her clothing choices in public space. However, Kate "asserts herself as queer, manifesting the visibility of oppositional difference and consequently affirming its centrality to her personage. She cannot be read as woman without the foregrounding that she is a gay woman" (Petrovic 2011, 73). Part of Kate's conviction to live openly as a gay woman (though closeted as Batwoman) is to avoid repressing an aspect of herself at the demands of others. She chooses to perform silence about her vigilantism, whereas a superior tells her to treat her sexual identity as a joke. And concealing her identity as Batwoman serves as a form of protection for her family and friends from criminals and supervillains, whereas concealing her queer identity in the army denies her personal identity. GCPD Captain Maggie Sawyer also arrives at the ball in a tuxedo and asks Kate to dance. Maggie mentions Gordon's zero-tolerance discrimination policy, which has allowed her to be comfortably out in the workplace. This policy shows how in Gotham, a work environment need not suppress, deny, or silence identity.

Other media within the Batman franchise have also mainstreamed gay characters. In the third season of Bruno Heller's TV series *Gotham* (2014–19), Oswald Cobblepot falls in love with his good friend, Edward Nygma. The series does not focus the story line on his queer identity but on him being in love. *Gotham* does not ultimately grant Oswald a relationship with Edward because doing so would humanize the villain. Oswald's love is a selfish love—he murders an innocent woman in efforts to have Edward for himself. *Gotham* does not deny gay relationships because of sexuality; it simply does not permit villainous behavior to result in happiness and consumation. No supervillains in *Gotham* can maintain romantic relationships. In Season 1, Edward murders Kristen Kringle's ex-boyfriend in the name of love (Stephens 2015), just as in Season 3, Oswald orders the murder of Edward's girlfriend Isabella in an attempt to have Edward for himself (Chun 2016). In Season 2, Edward also kills Kristen (though unintentionally; Cutter 2015). The supervillains of *Gotham* are too concerned with themselves and fulfilling their own desires and passions that they cannot be loyal and devoted partners to others. *Gotham* shows that love is love, but villains are villains, and love will not change their selfish, unethical, and criminal tendencies.

Problematic Relationships

The challenge of balancing love and villainy is also seen in *Batman: The Animated Series* in the episode "Heart of Ice" (Dini 1992a). Victor Fries's wife is plagued with a deadly, incurable disease and is cryogenically frozen while Victor searches for a cure. Love fuels Fries, but when he is told he needs to shut down his experiment, he gets into an altercation that leaves his body in a fragile state and motivates him to become the supervillain Mr. Freeze. Lost love is the trigger for a turn toward villainy. A similar scenario occurs with Harvey Dent in Nolan's (2008) film *The Dark Knight*. Dent murders those whose actions contributed to his girlfriend Rachel's death. The pain he suffers after losing her is so crushing that it stimulates the transformation from a hero of the city into one of its supervillains. Dent becomes Two-Face because he cannot cope with his loss. For several supervillains, love is problematic but powerful and a strong motivator for action.

In Gotham City, relationships are rarely sustainable or healthy even for the heroes. Frank Miller and David Mazzucchelli's ([1987]

2005) *Batman: Year One* shows Commissioner Gordon cheating on his pregnant wife. In *Batwoman* #34, Kate leaves her girlfriend Maggie so that Maggie's ex-husband will drop the custody battle for their child (Andreyko, Moritat, and Haun 2014). Bruce tries to open up to various love interests in Burton's *Batman* (1989) and *Batman Returns* (1992) and Schumacher's (1995) *Batman Forever*, but these relationships do not exist beyond the containment of the films. In Nolan's (2008) *The Dark Knight*, Bruce's love for Rachel goes unreciprocated. At the end of *The Dark Knight Rises* (Nolan 2012), Bruce and Selina are together, but this is outside of Gotham City. Bruce can only have a healthy relationship with a woman when he is no longer Batman and no longer in Gotham. As Batman, he is too tied to his commitment as a hero, and Gotham is too ravaged by supervillains for Batman to focus on a relationship. This has also been an argument for his heterosexuality. In an interview, Frank Miller said that Batman is not gay and that "his sexual urges are so drastically sublimated into crime-fighting that there's no room for any other emotional activity" (qtd. in Sharrett 2015). Batman's attempts for relationships may illustrate heterosexual attraction and desire, but he lacks the ability to serve the role of a romantic partner. His vigilante responsibilities demand too much attention of him.

In *Batman* #214, mobsters try to get Batman married. One says that women are the greatest weapon against Batman because if he gets married, his wife would not let him out every night (Robbins and Novick 1969c). In 2017, Tom King proposed that Bruce does not need to be a bachelor to serve the city as Batman. In *Batman* Vol. 3 #24 (King et al. 2017), Bruce proposes to Selina, and she says yes in *Batman* Vol. 3 #32 (King and Janín 2017b). Bruce and Selina prepare for their wedding in *Batman* #50 (King 2018). The issue juxtaposes letters from Bruce and Selina to one another where both write specifically about each other's eyes. Bruce writes that his mask contains white slits for the eyes so no one can see his actual eyes: "I want them to see the bat, not the man. I want to be the bat, not the man." Bruce finds that his eyes are the humanizing aspect of himself. Selina comments that Batman's lack of eyes makes him "a man impossible to understand. A man of pure anger. A bat. An animal." However, the man may separate himself from the animal through his marriage to Selina. Selina's friend Holly observes that Batman is now happy. She says, "He always seemed to need his misery y'know. Like it was how he did what he did." At the end of her letter, Selina remarks that if she helps Bruce with his pain, then she would be killing Batman. She says she needs to sacrifice her love and him because she cannot destroy the hero (King 2018). Rather than Bruce realizing he needs to be single to continue as Batman, Selina perceives that the defense of the city is at stake. In the twenty-first century, Batman still cannot be granted a healthy marriage. He needs to remain the animal and deny the man the relationship that he craves. Just as the villains struggle to achieve healthy, happy relationships, Batman cannot have one either. His role is too important to the city to be able to successfully balance both.

* * *

While the Batman franchise has evolved over time in accordance with shifts in American cultural perceptions and principles, it has still gone under scrutiny for its portrayal of sexuality. The reader or audience member may reflect on the comics and films in terms of his/her personal values and sexual identity, which may not align with the interpretation and significance that others take from them. Sexualization, sexual violence, and sexuality can be delicate subjects to address artistically, but they are deeply rooted aspects of the social fabric of American cities. Gotham City, as a microcosm of urban America, continues to house relevant representations of sexuality and its relationship with power, identity, and socialization.

4

Pluralism and Identity Formation: Race and Ethnicity in Gotham City

Critics and fans alike have vocalized accusations of racial blindness in the Batman comics. The hyper-white appearance of the Batman comics offers commentary on contemporary social dynamics and reflects upon social progress, stagnation, or regression regarding urban racial relations in America. Racial and ethnic diversity has been present in Gotham City to some extent over the years, but in an industry that must meet consumer demands, the readers are a strong determinant of content—whether for inclusion or not. The CCA also previously maintained strict regulations over content, specifically to avoid the promotion of prejudiced thinking. Ultimately, the representations of race and ethnicity in Gotham City may reflect popular sentiments of contemporary readers while also trying to shape a particular image of urban America. When the comics address racial and ethnic conflicts in the urban environment, they demonstrate the problems inherent to prejudiced racial formation. Society, time, and space all inform racial formation and influence popular perspectives. The Batman franchise has been socially aware of the potential for detrimental effects resulting from prejudiced racialized identity formation and subsequently has sent messages to promote social change.

This chapter turns to theories of racial formation to analyze social constructs of identity as represented in Batman comics. Through a close analysis of specific comics, this chapter argues that the Batman comics have not historically encouraged stereotyping; rather, they have discouraged prejudiced thinking and promoted equality and inclusivity. Racial and ethnic representation in the comics has aimed to promote a positive social agenda. In the twenty-first century, such representation also reflects extant social concerns in the real world, further illustrating Gotham City as a microcosm of urban America.

Racial Formation

Many critics, academic and fans alike, find that the whitewashing of comics and the select, infrequent depictions of nonwhite individuals perpetuate stereotypes within a white hegemonic society. Marc Singer (2002, 107) argues that superhero comics "have proven fertile ground for stereotyped depictions of race." Singer makes a strong argument regarding stereotyping in superhero comics: "Comics rely upon visually codified representations in which characters are continually reduced to the appearances ... This system of visual typology combines with the superhero genre's long history of excluding, trivializing, or 'tokenizing' minorities to create numerous minority superheroes who are marked purely for their race" (107). He finds that race and ethnicity are contingencies of identification and that comics perpetuate stereotyping. According to Facciani, Warren, and Vendemia (2015, 2), prior to the Modern Age, "the normative portrayal of women and minorities in comic books has tended to reflect simplified, exaggerated, and immature view of gender norms and race relations." They conducted a content analysis of Modern Age comics to examine how creative teams approached race, gender, and class in their comics. The authors conclude, "While modern day comics may not be as blatantly racist as earlier ages, our data shows that Black characters are still disproportionally portrayed as lower class and possessing less agency than white characters" (11). However, this study does not cross-examine statistics regarding race and class in the real world to see whether the comics are actually reflective of the demographics of the people in America.

Critics and fans may find stereotyping and prejudice visible in various forms within popular culture. When creators choose to diversify representation of individuals rather than include only white characters, they have the challenge in determining how to include diversity in ways that are inclusive rather than discriminatory. If Batman creative teams include non-white characters as criminals, this could spark further social controversy and backlash. On the one hand, neglecting to include Black criminals could contribute to whitewashing, but including them could be interpreted as racist. With the need to tread carefully, creative teams are faced with the challenge of how to include nonwhite characters in a way that is inoffensive to fans. Phillip Lamarr Cunningham (2015) suggests that neglecting to include Black villains in fear of appearing prejudiced is by no means progressive:

> As a result of movements by the likes of activists such as Jesse Jackson and the NAACP, over the course of the last three decades, popular media has overcompensated for its lengthy history of negative depictions of Black folks by either greatly limiting or outright eliminating roles in which Black men and women portray villains. However, ... what appears to some as altruism is more akin to an inability (or refusal) to develop complex black characters.

The Batman franchise has not repeatedly created negative depictions as Cunningham describes in the history of popular media. But it does have a history of keeping most of its characters white. This was done not because of discriminatory practices but to avoid perpetuating prejudices. As far as Cunningham's argument about the neglect "to develop complex black characters," the Comics Code of 1954 (Comics Magazine Association of America, Inc. 1954) states, "Crimes shall never be presented in such a way as to create sympathy for the criminal, to promote distrust of the forces of law and justice, or to inspire others with a desire to imitate criminals." With these requirements, a criminal could never be given the complexity that Cunningham suggests would be more socially progressive than the typical neglect of inclusion altogether. Criminals, instead, were often mere plot objects used to highlight the goodness of the superhero. If readers were given access to the hardships that drove the characters to crime, then they could achieve the same complexity and depth of character. However, the existence of the Comics Code and DC's adherence to it demonstrates a sentiment where people feared the consequences of indecent exposure. The perception was that the comic books could influence young boys to commit crime and therefore had to be tailored to avoid such a danger. Publishers used their comics to try to shape a society and raise the youth of America according to the CCA's values. Essentially, then, the Batman comics reflected the stressed values of the people even if they did not necessarily reflect the complexities of the criminal characters or even racial profiling of police—who had to be depicted in a positive light. This has changed greatly since the code was amended in 1971 and 1989, and especially after DC dropped the code in 2011.

While there have been very few Black characters given detailed interiorities and backstories, twenty-first-century Batman comics have made some moves to raise awareness to some of the recent social issues regarding racial profiling and the tensions between urban groups. Spencer Ackerman (2015) finds a push driven by the readers for comics creators to engage with contemporary social issues:

> Much as a new black protest movement is forcing the US to confront the implications of racialized policing, vocal comics readers are prompting publishers to confront the implications of showing mostly white characters written by mostly white creators—particularly when heroes motivated by justice have nothing to say about collective pushes for social justice.

The demands of readers often drive the comic book industry, which then makes the content even more reflective of contemporary social moments. Despite the limited occurrences of racial representation in the Batman comics, there are some that speak profoundly to the contemporary social mindset of urban Americans regarding race and racial relations. They effectively serve as cultural artifacts during a time when readership has expanded and comics have more freedoms with their content. Thus, I find that Batman comics do contain racial discourse and discourage prejudiced perspectives in urban America.

Theories of race, which provide rhetoric for how individuals may be identified, can facilitate discussion on urban racial relations offered by the Batman franchise. In *Racial Formation in the United States*, Michael Omi and Howard Winant (2015, 106) define race as "a social construction" that is in fact "a master category—a fundamental concept that has profoundly shaped, and continues to shape, the history, polity, economic structure, and culture of the United States." Since race is constructed, racial relations reflect the collective perceptions that individuals have of others. As a "master category," race has a powerful influence in defining American culture. Robyn Wiegman (1995, 24) also comments on race as a construct, calling it "a fiction" because it is "a profound ordering of difference instantiated at the sight of the body." Race is a visual term that speaks to conceptual ideas about socialization, urban development, and collective perspectives. Despite race being a visual signifier, it is associated with assumptions deeply rooted in history. Race as a concept, then, is also shaped by time and place. Omi and Winant argue, "As social beings, we must categorize people so as to be able to 'navigate' in the world," and these categories are "subject to enormous variation over historical time and space" (2015, 105). Thus, a significant relationship exists between time, space, and racial formation. When race is represented in the comics, it creates the visual signifier of extant social dynamics.

As a construct, race is imagined and prescribed. It signifies identity that stems from popular assumptions. Ethnicity also affects the social relations of individuals in America. Omi and Winant (2015, 21) find ethnicity theory as "an approach to race that affords primacy to cultural variables." Surveying the Batman comics allows us to see how race and ethnicity have been identified, defined, and represented in America. The few occurrences of racial tensions in Gotham City in the Batman comics, especially those from the twenty-first century, provide commentary to social concerns in the urban environment regarding the ways that individuals are racially or ethnically identified. The comics are not only a reflection of the popular mindsets of a particular era, but they may also continue to shape the perspectives of the readers. Thus, the comics may be read as sociohistorical artifacts of racial and ethnic relations in urban America. However, we must also keep in mind the target audience for the comics. Young white male readers were the prevalent market for the early comic books. Facciani, Warren, and Vendemia (2015, 10) use this point to explain the results of their study: "This predominance of white males as consumers, may reflect their overrepresentation in comic books." Therefore, racial formation that occurs in Batman evolves from a predominantly white industry targeting predominantly white readers. For Joshua Ostroff (2016), "the pale, maleness of comic book creation is a state of affairs that goes back to the beginning as the industry was developed by white males for white males because that's who could afford to buy their wares." Even as urban racial pluralism expanded throughout history, DC Comics maintained a cast of heroes that reflected its white male readership and continued this trend since it was successful. Their intentions may not have been to exacerbate stereotypes or neglect individuals of nonwhite races but to present what the publishers felt would sell. From this standpoint, the consumeristic agenda defines race through its products in a way that may not be consistent with the self-defining of members of a nonwhite race who are perhaps just trying to be themselves rather than sell themselves. Therefore, the industry becomes illustrative of the white perspective of racial formation. Wiegman (1995, 31) finds, "The move from the visible epidermal terrain to the articulation of the interior structure of human bodies thus extrapolated in both broader and more distinct terms the parameters of white supremacy giving it a logic lodged fully in the body." Urban racial relations that reflect social hierarchies based on race combined with a consumer-driven industry create a product that appears to be rooted in white hegemonic capitalistic practices. The publishers were catering to a specific market but over the years have created content to increase inclusivity.

Regulating Content

When the Batman comics were first published, the Black population in American cities was very low. The percentage of Blacks in New York City, according to the 1940 census, was 6.1 percent (United States Census Bureau n.d.d) and in Chicago was 8.2 percent (United States Census Bureau n.d.c). Few Black characters appeared on the comic book pages, which accurately reflects the makeup of the cities during this time. But racial tensions still existed throughout the country. DC was aware of the racial climate in the United States at the time and published a public service announcement (PSA) comic in 1950 titled "Batman and Robin Stand Up for Sportsmanship!" where Batman tries to teach some boys about racial acceptance. On this page, Batman and Robin mediate a crisis regarding the lack of acceptance of a Black boy on a football team. Batman preaches against discrimination and prejudice in defining what it means to be an American. Batman is the voice of a social acceptance agenda that does not maintain racial categories but identifies all individuals as American. He offers the message that everyone here is American except for those who exclude others. He also says, "Don't believe those crackpot lies about people who worship differently, or whose skin is of a different color, or whose parents come from another country. Remember our American heritage of freedom and equality!" ("Batman and Robin Stand Up for Sportsmanship!" 1950). Batman discourages prejudiced thinking in his discussion with the boys. He does not need to resort to his methods for handling criminals or incite fear in the boys but merely speaks to them calmly. Because they are young and influential, there is still hope for a change for acceptance and equal treatment inspired merely through a conversation with Batman and Robin rather than through an attack or incarceration.

In 1950, this PSA was a progressive approach to changing prejudiced attitudes prior to the civil rights movement. This particular announcement demonstrates awareness of prejudice and inequality even if the publishers were not yet ready to adapt this mindset and these problems to full-length comics issues. This PSA, then, shows that prejudiced behavior was certainly occurring during the 1940s, and it encourages its target audience (young white males) to change their attitudes and perceptions and treat everyone equally. Batman is a powerful spokesperson for this effort because his young white fans admire and respect him. The effort to change popular prejudiced perspectives through the PSA promotes social inclusivity. While the infrequency of comics with these themes may suggest that this particular social change was not a priority, publishers had a consumer-based prerogative to entertain young boys, which may have overshadowed reform agendas for the most part.[1]

As soon as the comic book industry was regulated, representations of racial relations diminished further. The omission of Blacks and racial commentary during the civil rights movement can perhaps be attributed to Wertham's ([1954] 2004) *Seduction of the Innocent* and the subsequent passing of the Comics Code by the CCA. While not a complete whitewashing, the comics of this time certainly lack the cultural pluralism of the US population during the civil rights era. The absence illustrates a perspective of urban America where racial relations are fine; the problem, instead, is rampant criminality. The threats to humanity are supervillains not racial difference (or indifference). Concern about crime exists but none that is specifically racially motivated, which seems to be a direct response to the voices regulating what is appropriate for publication. However, the monochromatic appearance of society was not an attempt to be neglectful but an effort to avoid perpetuating prejudices altogether.

Regarding the potential for comics to influence readers' perspectives regarding race, Wertham's ([1954] 2004, 50) *Seduction of the Innocent* preaches that comic books "expose children's minds to an endless stream of prejudice-producing images." He further contends, "When a child is shown a comic book that he has not read and is asked to pick out the bad man, he will unhesitatingly pick out types according to the stereotyped conceptions of race prejudice, and tell you the reason for his choice. 'Is he an American?' 'No!'" (51). Wertham bases his criticism of the influence of comics on how they highlight specific criteria to identify an individual as American. He finds that race connotes otherness, which will exacerbate prejudices in young boys. Wertham also believes that older children will act out on their prejudices that have been formed and perpetuated through comic books (51). The subsequent whitewashing of comics, especially in Batman comics, appears to be a response to avoid such potential opportunities for negative influence. Arguably, then, publishers had a positive social agenda. They did not intend to be exclusionary but to promote acceptance by avoiding the opportunity for prejudiced thoughts to develop. While the publishers may have been attending to a predominantly white readership, they were socially conscious in aiming to prevent the proliferation of prejudice that Wertham warns against.

Regarding race specifically, the 1954 (Comics Magazine Association of America, Inc. 1954) and 1971 (Comics Magazine Association of America, Inc. 1971) codes state, "Ridicule or attack on any religious or racial group is never permissible." The code was trying to imbue nondiscriminatory perceptions on its young readers. The 1989 code (Comics Magazine Association of America, Inc. 1989) revised its language but kept the same message: "In general recognizable national, social, political, cultural, ethnic and racial groups, religious institutions, law enforcement authorities will be portrayed in a positive light," and "references to physical handicaps, illnesses, ethnic backgrounds, sexual preferences, religious beliefs, and race, when presented in a derogatory manner for dramatic purposes, will be shown to be unacceptable." Through omission, the code presents a value system that discourages prejudiced and discriminatory beliefs and practices. But this also meant that the comics could not tackle topics related to real-world racial tensions. While whitewashing comics may seem exclusionary, it was deliberate in order to avoid breaking the code's standards of propriety. The intentions of the comics were to decrease prejudiced mentalities and encourage the youth of America to refrain from exclusionary thinking. This could be especially effective given that comics are a visual medium. Wiegman (1995, 37) argues that "what the eye sees is not a neutral moment of reception but an arbitrary and disciplinary operation, one in which experience is actually produced in the subject." In excluding race from the comics, the publishers were attempting a disciplinary visible practice that teaches the readers not to associate prejudiced thinking with visual racial difference.

In following the code, the comics within the Batman franchise historically imagined an American city where racial tensions essentially did not exist, thus making Gotham City an idealistic social setting. However, given Gotham's inherent criminality, violence, and disrupted peace, it seems it would be an appropriate place to address racial conflicts in the real world—which finally does occur in the 2000s. Before then, Gotham subverts its attempt to accurately reflect urban America when neglecting relevant social issues plaguing the real world. The Batman comics' social consciousness thus seems at odds with reality, and Gotham City appears, to some, to be stagnated rather than progressive. While whitewashing has drawn criticism, the comics do attempt to achieve a social utopia and influence social perspectives of readers simply by being inactive. Despite Cunningham's (2015) argument to the contrary, it is essentially a progressive agenda. The intentions are to eliminate prejudiced racial formation in the minds of the readers through omission. This is still problematic, though, as Cunningham argues that such treatment of race is actually misguided. Providing complexity to Black characters would instead be much more of an equalizer. However, the franchise made other attempts to be more socially progressive.

The 1950 PSA was an attempt for the comics to use their influence on racial relations and social perspectives of Americans. Years later, at the end of the civil rights movement, the TV series *Batman* made a notable decision to cast Eartha Kitt, an African American woman, as Catwoman (Kitt replaced Julie Newmar, who played the role previously). Kitt's Catwoman appeared in the third—and final—season of the series, which ran from 1967 to 1968. Kitt's casting was pivotal because it provided a new type of role to a Black woman: "Kitt's performance stood in contest to the roles available to Black women on television, insofar as she did not fit the proverbial mammy, Jezebel, tragic mulatta, and sapphire stereotypes that were abundant on television and in the cinema at this time" (Whaley 2011, 9). Instead, she served as a worthy foe to match wits with one of America's most renowned superheroes. She did not embody a stereotype and instead illustrated the ways Black actresses could approach the complexity of a role such as Catwoman.

Deborah Elizabeth Whaley (2011, 9) also notes that while Newmar's Catwoman was sexualized, Kitt's version was not allowed to incite romance with Batman due to her race. The casting choice itself was a progressive step for African American actresses and for the representation of this community on screen through a powerful figure. But such social progress in the film industry and comic book culture still had its limitations. It seems the show's writers felt that America was not yet ready to witness or accept an on-screen romance between a white male and a Black female.[2] Catwoman could be a strong, bold woman, but any indication of sexual energy between her and Batman would be socially taboo.

Whaley (2011, 4) argues that a Black Catwoman speaks to the shifting social and cultural genetics of America:

> In her television and feature film premier from the mid-twentieth century to the twenty-first century, Catwoman became a dubious mixture of 1960s civil rights protest, racial inclusion, and post-racial

cultural politics. The alchemy, or fabrication of postracialism that creators of the character place her to embody, rubs up against the realities of how race—specifically Blackness—shapes production, perception, and interest among a wide variety of fans, and the cultural and political implications of this process.

A Black Catwoman signifies American social progress regarding race, but it also is a construct, a deliberate choice of creators. Fans who firmly believe that characters from superhero comics cannot be reimagined as a different race may influence a consumer-driven agenda of comics culture. On the other hand, fans who accept a Black Catwoman show that comics and media need not be whitewashed to still achieve the creative team's intended effects. Kitt displays a powerful Catwoman; she demonstrates depth of acting rather than prescribed or stereotyped role-playing. However, the character's change in race did not incite a canonical revision in the Batman franchise. Catwoman's race has typically remained white in the comics, and subsequent films have cast white women in the role of Selina Kyle.[3] This will change in 2022 as Zoë Kravitz, whose parents are mixed race, has been cast as Catwoman in the upcoming film *The Batman* directed by Matt Reeves. But Kitt's Catwoman, despite the limitations regarding romance, was progressive for the 1960s and offered an opportunity for fans to embrace the pluralistic representation of an iconic character.

Ethnic Relations in Gotham City

Despite some critics' claims to the contrary, the Batman comics have historically paid attention to assumptions based on race and ethnicity—though only in a select number of issues. When they do, though, the comics reflect the present perspectives of individuals, expose problems inherent to prejudice and stereotyping, and encourage acceptance. Much of the ways that the comics address social perceptions of individuals is based on "othering," which creates hierarchies of difference (Omi and Winant 2015, 105). Early comics preach against this, and later comics make visible the devastation occurring in America due to the fear, hatred, and violence that come from stereotyping. Identities are formed based on "otherness" and assumptions that go along with difference. The comics also show the relationship between racial formation and space—where space itself also becomes racialized.

Even though the 1940 census reported low Asian population percentages in American cities—0.2 percent in New York City (United States Census Bureau n.d.d) and 0.1 percent in Chicago (United States Census Bureau n.d.c)—Chinese communities make several appearances in early Batman comics. This may be due to an association with New York City's Chinatown, which developed during the middle of the nineteenth century. In *Detective Comics* #39 (Finger and Kane 1940g), Batman battles Chinese villains in Chinatown, and the main criminal is referred to as "the Chinaman" and "Fatty." This tong leader assumes "the police would probably hunt for white gangsters and never suspect a Chinese of kidnapping." Here, the Chinese character presumes to know the social perspectives of others. He uses his ethnicity as a disguise, claiming that his actions are not in line with the identity that whites associate with Chinese people. A static ethnic inscription does not exist because characters such as this criminal disrupt preconceived notions of ethnic identity. The ironic double standard is that in purporting to know what whites think of the Chinese, he is making his own potentially false assumptions about white people.

In *Detective Comics* #52 (Finger and Kane 1941e), Batman heads to Chinatown to stop Chinese criminals and says to an elderly Chinese man, "Finally your people can walk free again as all men should." Batman is the voice of acceptance and equality fighting against those who suppress others. While some Batman comics present crime in Chinatown, they do not provide much commentary on the perception of Asians. Crime is simply rampant in all parts of Gotham—Chinatown included. Will Brooker (2001, 93) finds that "the portrayal of 'Orientals' in Batman during the opening months of the 1940s—a time when … Chinese and Japanese were frequently conflated in an anti-Asian discourse—is relatively subtle on closer inspection, and clearly avoids pathologising the villains purely on the grounds of race." The comics do not lean toward a particular prejudiced perspective of others. Instead, they actually align prejudiced behaviors with the criminals. In *Detective Comics* #35 (Finger, Kane, and Moldoff 1940), the criminal

Sheldon Lenox disguises himself as a Chinese man in yellow gloves and face makeup, but since this is again a criminal engaging in racist practices, the issue posits that making assumptions based on race is associated with criminality and therefore found within immoral individuals, not model citizens.

Detective Comics #627 (Wolfman and Aparo 1991) addresses stereotyping within the comic to provide commentary on the unjustness of assuming that foreigners are terrorists. This stems from the fears of the foreign other and results in the mislabeling of good people. It also exposes the unequal treatment toward foreigners who are assumed to be subpar compared to Americans. In Wolfman and Aparo's (1991) issue, an Iranian cab driver exposes the false assumptions Americans have made about him and how difficult that has made his life in America:

> *This* country is no easier, you know? *Iran*, that is *hard* … very hard. I thought, ahh—America. United States, now that is the country, you know. But when I came here, *no* jobs … not for Iranian, no way. I was *teacher* in Tehran … teach *math*. Here? What do I do? Drive stinking *cab*. Went to university six *years*. I drive stinking cab here. This *fair*? I am Iranian. I am *evil*. They tell me not good to teach. Just good enough to drive stinking cab.

The driver knows that he is a qualified educator but finds that prejudice and false assumptions prevent him from attaining a teaching job in America. The driver is identified for being Iranian, not for his previous experience or qualifications to teach. When the supervillain Pesticyde attacks the cab, he asks, "Why you killing me? Is because I am Iranian? I—I'm *not* a terrorist" (Wolfman and Aparo 1991). The driver immediately assumes he is targeted because of his ethnicity since he has only experienced unfair treatment in America. He knows the common practice of identity formation—in this case, ethnicity associated with terrorism—that has plagued him in America. Driven by their distrust in the foreign other, Americans have shaped their prejudices based on this fear.

In drawing awareness to the cultural pluralism of twenty-first-century Gotham City, *Batman: Orpheus Rising*, a miniseries by Alex Simmons and Dwayne Turner published from October 2001 through

February 2002, also exposes fear as a stimulus for the formation of identity and imagined threats. The narrator asks:

> What defines a culture? Status? Antiquity? Academia? The Lockner Street Market is rich with cultures. Once Irish, then Jewish, it is now a potpourri of nations mingling names, languages, and ideals. Every day, cultures are tested, challenged, lost and found. Sometimes, someone feels threatened by the ideals of another. Then that fear, or confusion, strikes out at the perceived threat ... or a symbol of that authority. (Simmons and Turner 2001a)

This part of the city is defined by its cultural makeup—its identity formed through the interrelation of cultures. When people with different values occupy the same space, otherness is more visible, which instigates fear. Cultural conflict, then, is relational—derived specifically from the notable differences of groups that occupy the same space. The assertion of cultural identity also becomes a struggle for power within space. Orpheus, a Black vigilante, thinks, "Purgatory's gates overflowing. Gotham drowning in a thick, infectious pool of hatred" (Simmons and Turner 2002a). In comparing this space to purgatory, the narration suggests that a pluralistic space is stagnant. Progress seems unlikely, and the individuals are trapped, unable to move out of the tense environment. Hatred of the other keeps the people stuck in this space. When one person's race or ethnicity is pitted against someone else's in this version of Gotham, the response is not toward acceptance, understanding, or progress but toward hatred, violence, and destruction.

Orpheus also fears regression due to social tensions between different groups. When a showdown occurs where gangs from different communities are at odds, "Orpheus feels a shudder run through him. Surrounded by so many signs of social advancement ... the crowd looked more like a force of nature. One wrong move and all forms of civility will be stripped away, leaving only primal anger unleashed ... and perhaps, unstoppable" (Simmons and Turner 2002b). The language here suggests an atavistic condition. Difference and otherness are perceived as a threat that has the potential to drive social progress into a primitive state. To prevent this from happening, the city needs acceptance, tolerance, and undivided community.

By illustrating cultural conflict, the miniseries speaks to the public regarding such social needs.

The 1998 "Ragman" arc by Doug Moench and Kelley Jones also illustrates the destructive power of hate that is rooted in racializing others. In *Batman* #551, Batman hunts for the murderer of Benjamin Mizrahi, who was shot outside the Temple of Beth Israel. Batman questions whether a suspect—who has a swastika tattoo with "HITLER YOUTH" etched below it—is a member of the Aryan Reich. The young man confesses to the murder, saying he hated Mizrahi because he was Jewish, and "Jews take over **everything**—even this stinkin' slum! … It's time the **pure man** stood up to them! It's time they were **stomped!**" (Moench and Jones 1998a). These sentiments further draw awareness to the association between identity and space. The perspective of the young man illustrates a constructed identity of Jewish people based on perceived acquisition of space. Batman's narration provides some civil wisdom: "When a man possesses **hate**, he loses everything else." The comic demonstrates the ways in which prejudiced thinking manipulates one's mentality to construct racialized identities of others. The rabbi talks about the Aryan Reich group that formed in Blackgate Prison, declaring that released prisoners bring their hate out of prison with them, "a disease to infect others." This makes racialized identity formation an epidemic of false perceptions based on collective hatred. The comic also includes narration of a radio segment where Vesper Fairchild interviews hate crimes expert Dr. David Levy. Dr. Levy describes the history of anti-Semitism, which he finds a result of xenophobia. He contends that Judaism is very "insular," where for Jews, "it is everyone else who is 'different.'" In this way, those who construct identity are also constructs; everyone is always already an other in the eyes of a different other. Dr. Levy also states that hate crimes are "perhaps the **greatest evil of all**." Thus, evil is not embodied in a villain but in the minds of those who act on hatred. When crime is fueled by hate, it is a result of identity formation, where the criminal has imagined the identity of another person or group and lashes out due to hatred of the constructed identity. Racial and ethnic formation can be a dangerous practice, then, especially when it manipulates the perspectives of individuals, distorts the true identities of individuals, and disrupts opportunities for sound social structures.

Rory Regan, a Jewish descendant of a line of Ragman vigilantes, emerges self-proclaimed as "defender of the **weak** and **oppressed—punisher of evil**" (Moench and Jones 1998a). Like Orpheus, he represents the underrepresented. Ragman descended from a long history of avengers of evil that goes back to the creation of Golem by a rabbi in Prague in the sixteenth century, which marks the historical precedence of intolerance. Ragman's suit is composed of rags that have been empowered by the souls of dead evil people. In this two-part story, Regan loses control of the rags that want to kill the members of the Aryan Reich. The comics preach anti-violence, with efforts made to stop the rags from killing. In the second part, *Batman* #552, Rabbi Luria urges Regan to "use the **power** of evil to do **good**" (Moench and Jones 1998b). Rather than hate evil, the rabbi tells Rory that he must love God and love the victims. The rabbi then teaches Rory about the Kabbalah and the relationship between God, man, and the universe, saying, "We are all part of the 'world soul' … God is the one, and we are all part of the one. Seek and find God **everywhere**, even in evil—and evil's power will wither before God." This argument does not isolate particular spaces to particular groups and, instead, posits that all people are a part of all space. The comics encourage individuals to look within themselves to combat inner hatred and adopt a mindset of acceptance.

Black Lives in Twenty-First-Century Gotham

The 1989 revisions to the Comics Code and DC dropping the code altogether in 2011 have both allowed the Batman comics to expose readers to racial and ethnic tensions and concerns directly rather than ignore them in hopes that silence would deter prejudiced thinking and actions. While not a frequent occurrence, these specific comics still serve as cultural artifacts of racial and ethnic identity formation in twenty-first-century urban America. The comics address real-world social issues and reflect a Gotham City that is much more diverse than in the earlier comics. Twenty-first-century Batman comics illustrate the growing diversity seen in American cities, as the 2010 census reported the percentage of Blacks in New York City at 25.2 percent (United States Census Bureau n.d.b) and at 34 percent in Chicago (United States Census Bureau n.d.a)—up considerably from 6.1 percent and 8.2 percent in 1940. They also effectively demonstrate violence, including police brutality perpetuated by racial assumptions, and the potential detriments of gentrification. When the comics aim to portray extant conditions regarding race and ethnicity in American cities, they encourage social change rather than ignore the problems in fear of inappropriateness and negative influence.

The 2007 "Grotesk" story arc directly discusses race and identity formation with specific commentary on Blackness as defined through the contrast with whiteness. Wayne Franklin, a successful plastic surgeon, kills mobsters and criminals under the name Grotesk and justifies his actions by claiming that he is destroying bad people (Ostrander and Mandrake 2007b). Early in the story, his date, Jaqui Tremayne, says, "There are some who call you the black Bruce Wayne!" He responds, "Really? Why shouldn't they call *him* the pale Wayne Franklin?" (Ostrander and Mandrake 2007a). Franklin does not want to be identified as the Black version of someone else. His impressive career should be distinctly tied to his identity rather than have someone else's projected onto him. When race is attached to the men, it denies Franklin another aspect of his identity. He is not only another version of another man, but he is a Black version of a white man. Franklin loses his individuality and becomes disempowered when Tremayne makes this comment. She effectively forms race as a contrast, an other in a white hegemonic society.

Race as an identifier extends to physical space and intangible concepts in this story arc as well. In a flashback, Franklin's father—who was a criminal—says, "I'm not doing black man's time in a white man's prison!" and turns his gun to Franklin, planning on killing both his children before Franklin pushes the gun back toward his father, where he shoots himself in the head (Ostrander and Mandrake 2007c). Franklin's father thinks that his children are only safe from the injustice of the world if they are dead. Franklin repeats his father's rhetoric later on: "I won't do black man's time in a white man's jail—or in a white man's asylum" (Ostrander and Mandrake 2007c). The idea that space can be imbued with whiteness suggests that the city is composed of spaces that are racially inscribed. Space takes on its own race and thus the assumptions projected on that particular race. Time, too—specifically, a prison sentence—is definable through race. These men's comments argue that there are Black spaces and white spaces and Black time and white time. The concepts are only understood in contrast to the racialized other. The "Grotesk" issues deliberately challenge racialization and racial formation by exposing it and questioning it, demonstrating the inequalities and injustice that emerge when people, spaces, or things are racially defined.

Prior to "Grotesk," Alex Simmons and Dwayne Turner's *Batman: Orpheus Rising* (2001–2) brought a Black superhero into Gotham to make the case that Batman's whiteness limits his communal reach. Gavin King becomes the vigilante Orpheus to provide the city a much-needed Black superhero. Pointing to his own face, Orpheus says, Batman can't "represent my people" (Simmons and Turner 2001b). He recognizes that racial formation has constructed particular group dynamics. As a Black vigilante, he can simultaneously work to make the city safer and more inclusive. Orpheus finds that the Black youth need a hero that Batman, as a white man, physically cannot be: "They may see heroes, humans and aliens … but they don't see themselves. They don't see their people defending the streets, the country, or the planet, so many don't believe they're a part of the solution—especially the kids. They don't realize we can make a difference, too" (Simmons and Turner 2001b). Here, King emphasizes the importance of the visual aspect of race. King wants to be a hero for the Black youth of America—a role model for those who have been underrepresented (or perhaps not represented at all). King makes the argument that people inherently identify with those who share a race, "their people." In becoming Orpheus, he has to share the city with Batman, and he is aware that Black and white have to coexist in order to serve their purpose as superheroes. Orpheus says, "Hello Gotham. Now there's a darker knight in town" (Simmons and Turner 2002b). This pun demonstrates the way in which Orpheus is in some ways an image of Batman, but he is also what Batman is not and cannot be: a physical embodiment of hope and inspiration for the Black youth of Gotham City.

The miniseries grapples with tensions between groups within the city. Orpheus speaks to the leader of The Deacons gang, who explains that a few years before, "the man didn't care about me, or community, or nuthin' 'round here." The Deacons were a community that took care of one another. He observes that during No Man's Land, "some rich white boy gets lost in the city and the media's all over it! Even the president! But not for none of us!" (Simmons and Turner 2002a). The gang leader finds his identity with his gang. He accuses society for its white hegemonic practices and argues that the only place to find community is with those who share a race and neighborhood. The narrator asks, "What is a community? It's conflict, history, joy, cooperation, and misunderstandings ... all stirred with the potential for despair and greatness" (Simmons and Turner 2002b). Because community is so delicate, it is potentially on the brink of devastation. But it has the capacity for greatness so long as the individuals within the community do not drive it into ruin.

Conflicts within a community are also exacerbated by the police. In issue #1, police officers have an altercation with The Deacons, and there are suggestions of racial profiling. Police Commissioner Michael Akins meets with community members in Four Points, a point of convergence of many of Gotham's minority neighborhoods, where individuals express their discontentment with the police department's actions toward these groups. Because the commissioner is Black, one person shouts, "You've chosen blue over black!" (Simmons and Turner 2001a). The minority groups feel targeted rather than protected by the police. The outburst demonstrates the way that identity has been formed in Gotham City. Even though blue associates with a profession and Black is biological, the colors demonstrate conflicts of interest. Since the commissioner is both blue and Black—again pointing to Wiegman's (1995) comment regarding the disciplinary influence of arbitrary visual signifiers (37)—the citizen's cries accuse him of prioritizing his police identity over his biological race. The feeling is that Akins cannot be part of the Black community if he puts his job before the Black people. As the police search for the serial killer gunning down officers, the public outcry of racial profiling remains high. One picketer's sign reads, "What are you checking ... gang colors or skin colors?" (Simmons and Turner 2001b). Identification is further complicated here with the accusation that officers look at skin color as an identifier of criminality. Real-world conflicts between police and race spilled onto the pages of the comics, reflecting racial profiling incidents of the 1990s, such as the attack on Rodney King and the subsequent Los Angeles riots. Clearly, the comics have transitioned from their previous silence to openly presenting extant issues in urban America.

Ultimately, the storyline reveals that a few corrupt cops instigated the tensions between gangs. These cops also killed the officers and made it appear that they were murdered by gang members. Orpheus describes, "Shoot down cops to tick off your boys in blue and panic the city fathers ... stir up the racial thing to keep the community off balance, sic the gangs and mobsters on each other for bloodletting" (Simmons and Turner 2002b). The corruption of the police shows the power that individuals can have to affect public perceptions and stimulate violence. The ringleader of the corrupt cops, Karl Esterhaus, says, "I don't care what color you are. I'm talking about any leeches sucking the life's blood from this city. The foreign criminal garbage that's washing up on our shores ..." (Simmons and Turner 2002b). Esterhaus denies race as a motivator for his actions, but he admits to fearing the foreign other. He finds criminality in difference and perpetuates such a belief through staged attacks.

DC could not represent the police in such a way prior to the 1989 amendment of the Comics Code because it was forbidden for law enforcement to be depicted in a negative light. The Comics Code of 1954 (Comics Magazine Association of America, Inc. 1954) states, "Policemen, judges, Government officials and respected institutions shall never be presented in such a way as to create disrespect for established authority." This was also included in the 1971 Code (Comics Magazine Association of America, Inc. 1971), with the addition, "If any of these is depicted committing an illegal act, it must be declared as an exceptional case and that the culprit pay the legal price." The 1989 Code does not mention any standards for the portrayal of police, and *Orpheus Rising* was approved by the CCA. To suggest that the police were guilty of racial profiling prior to the 1989 Code would risk denial for publication, further demonstrating the CCA's power over content in order to push its social agenda of tolerance by eliminating exposure. The ultimate message of *Orpheus Rising* is to promote acceptance and inclusion and discourage prejudice and assumption. Orpheus fears that "whatever progress or tolerance that's been achieved will fall twenty steps back" (Simmons and Turner 2002a) due to the police murders and subsequent suspicion of minorities.

The visible exposure to racial profiling provides readers access to familiar occurrences and offers a different method for shaping values and perceptions of others.

Similarly illustrating racial profiling by police and the potential for fatal effects of such discrimination, Scott Snyder, Brian Azzarello, and Jock's (2015) *Batman* Vol. 2 #44 reflects social tensions between Black lives and blue lives, making the comic book a cultural artifact of contemporary urban America. *Batman* Vol. 2 #44 exposes the problems on urban streets that Batman cannot fix because they are embedded in the social assumptions of individuals. It also presents a moment when Batman becomes socially aware of the way that he inadvertently perpetuates racial inequalities as Bruce Wayne. He learns that his idea of what is best for economic progress can be detrimental to social progress and realizes that as Batman, he can intervene and try to reach the poor Black youth of Gotham City.

The issue begins with a visual signifier of identity as Batman shows Gordon a Black teenager's body. When Gordon asks for the boy's I.D., Batman replies, "I can *see* his I.D." (Snyder, Azzarello, and Jock 2015). The victim, Peter Duggio, was from the Corner, a part of the Narrows section of Gotham City. The issue's narration discusses the history of police encounters with those who live in the Corner. Many officers have been shot, and many officers have also shot unarmed young Black men and have been getting away with these shootings. Batman's inner narration states, "It's too much to bear." This overlays a piece of an article called "The Problem with Authority," which provides statistics of the past two years' officer-related shootings. Most of the victims, thirty-seven of forty-five, were Black. Clearly, this part of Gotham is suffering, where not just criminal and authority face off, but criminality is also projected upon Blackness. Such a form of racial formation results in racially motivated police brutality. When racial identity is constructed in such a way, it can be devastating to wider culture.

The concurrent occurrences of Black and blue shootings speak to both the Black Lives Matter and the Blue Lives Matter movements in America. In 2013, #BlackLivesMatter sparked a justice movement for Black communities after the acquittal of George Zimmerman for shooting and killing Black teenager Treyvon Martin. Part of the mission of Black Lives Matter is to work "for a world where Black lives are no longer systematically targeted for demise" (Black Lives Matter n.d.). The shooting of Blacks in the Corner of Gotham City illustrates such targeting that this movement addresses. The comic simultaneously draws attention to the Blue Lives Matter organization, "America's largest law enforcement support community" (Berg 2017), which began following the 2014 killings of two police officers. According to Reuters reporter Sarah N. Lynch (2016), the movement "advocates tougher hate-crime sentences for the murder of police officers." The targeting of police officers, according to the organization, stems from "the false narrative of Black Lives Matter" (Berg 2017). The two organizations are much at odds with one another, and *Batman* Vol. 2 #44 illustrates such tensions. The comic does not deny the existence of prejudice, whether Black or blue. Instead, it shows an urban setting where both sides are victims of unjust targeting and killing. Yet, the focus is much more predominantly on the victimization of Blacks. In the issue, Batman encounters Officer Ned Howler, who is quick to draw his weapon, which seems to be a reactionary response. Howler tells Batman about "the firepower on the streets these days" (Snyder, Azzarello, and Jock 2015). Therefore, he finds using his weapon justifiable. But Batman's mind turns to the high numbers of unarmed Black men who have been shot by police in this neighborhood. Like *Orpheus Rising*, this comic illustrates a Gotham City where crime and corruption are not reserved to street criminals but also exist within the very institutions meant to uphold the law. When the crimes appear to be racially motivated, social unrest ensues, as innocent people are unjustly targeted. The targeting may occur from both sides, showing how assumptions can turn deadly, perpetuate social division, and create a hostile, dangerous environment. Regardless of the interpretation, though, *Batman* Vol. 2 #44 illustrates social problems and asks readers to consider the factors that exacerbate such tensions.

Batman Vol. 2 #44 also addresses racialized spaces and the problems involved when space is racially formed. A segment of a news article visible on one page discusses the history of protests against segregation in Gotham City. It refers to the ways that poor slums are created due to racial segregation (Snyder, Azzarello, and Jock 2015). But nothing ever came out of the protests except for violence against the demonstrators. The comic book draws attention to the ways in which space and identity overlap, where sections of the city become identifiable with those who live there. However, this is forced upon people when the occupants are only living in the space due to segregation. The attempt to gentrify the Corner upheaves the current residents. A portion of an article reads, "While some think an infusion of capital is needed, others question whether private developments—even ones like Wayne Apartments, designed to provide upscale living conditions for lower-middle class families in the Corner—might drive up property values and force out longtime residents." The comic exposes the ways in which the upper class can hurt poor Black urban communities, making Bruce Wayne complicit in racializing space.

Batman Vol. 2 #44 calls for action that requires consideration of the pitfalls of gentrification. Scott Snyder says, "If we were going to do an issue that dealt with potent problems that people face in cities that are reflected fictitiously in Gotham, then we want to really put our money where our mouth was and explore something that's extremely resonant right now, and, I think, tricky, murky waters" (qtd. in Ackerman 2015). The issue asks for more social and racial awareness in city planning. The Black criminals turned to crime due to their environment; the city simply failed to provide for them. The problems associated with gentrification in *Batman* Vol. 2 #44 reflect similar circumstances happening in twenty-first-century American cities. This version of Gotham is recognizable. It does not gloss over problems or avoid them completely as during the time of the strict Comics Code in hopes that readers would not be prejudiced if they did not read about prejudice. When interviewed, Brian Azzarello, who is from Chicago, stated that when the Cabrini-Green's housing projects were redeveloped in 2011, residents were left "scattered all over the city, just uprooting them, and they had no choice in the matter because they had no money. And if you have no money, you have no voice" (qtd. in Ackerman 2015). This incident is reflected in *Batman* Vol. 2 #44 as individuals in Gotham are defined by their race and class. They are unseen and unheard if they are not among the white elite. By the end of the issue, Batman realizes that his shortcoming as Bruce Wayne has been his failure to see and hear the individuals in his city who live in dire circumstances. This issue calls to Americans to pay attention to what is happening in their cities because what may appear as social progress may actually result in regression. When doing so, the readers can better view the characters as real people in real-world America.

Tracing the way race and ethnicity have historically been represented in the Batman comics illustrates a slow, gradually shifting perspective of the handling of urban social problems. More significantly, though, the comics demonstrate the ways that social perspectives are created and perpetuated. The intentions of the comics under the code were to encourage a community of acceptance. Unfortunately, this came at the cost of whitewashing and apparent neglect. The twenty-first-century comics have made urban racial and ethnic tensions more visible and confronted them in search of solutions. The comics of any decade, then, are cultural artifacts reflective of popular perspectives and intentions of individuals in America.

5

From the Slums to the Manors: Gotham City's Class Disparity

The Batman franchise has provided readers and audiences access to all corners of Gotham City. We have been invited to fancy galas and toured alleyways that scream of destitution. The spectrum of social class difference not only is visible in Gotham City but also provides commentary on class disparity. Criminal activity, though, seems to have no limitations as creators show both the money-motivated crimes of the poor and the power-driven crimes of the wealthy. The Batman franchise actually needs class disparity to fuel both its criminals and its number one vigilante. Any negative perspective on class that the franchise provides would seem to be an attack on capitalism in America. However, no alternative social structure is presented as an option, and, instead, Gotham continues to exist as it always has. While capitalistic society is often illustrated as a destructive force where hegemonic financial influence reinforces divisiveness, order cannot be restored to the city—even if momentarily—without Batman. Ironically, Batman is the embodiment of the social elite and cannot exist without his wealth. The city, therefore, depends on class disparity to combat class disparity—a vicious cycle with no end in sight because it keeps the franchise going.

Looking at the Batman franchise through the lens of Marxism can help us develop an understanding of class formation and disparity in the real world. Such a perspective allows us to consider the ways that Batman comments on the socioeconomic structures that make up American society. This chapter considers the role that class plays on urban development. It approaches problems in Gotham City as a way to think about class in urban America. While the franchise may appear to critique capitalism and class-based society (and certainly a Marxist perspective supports such criticism), ultimately, Gotham City cannot exist as a classless society and relies upon capitalism for its survival. Gotham City simultaneously shows the problems of wealth disparity and the need for it. The city's only hope to dissolving class inequality is a man who is a member of the upper class while also a vigilante who depends upon his wealth to fund his crime-fighting efforts. While the class issues in Gotham seem to be paradoxical and cyclical in nature, the franchise only ever offers Batman as a viable solution to class-related problems. Thus, class disparity must continue to exist, but the hope is that Batman's efforts can help decrease the crime rates and help maintain social order and peace.

Batman's energy is not aimed solely toward lower-class criminals, though. The franchise also depicts white-collar criminals and organized crime syndicates, illustrating how anyone of any social standing may turn to crime. Ultimately, the franchise argues that any person can become a criminal for a variety of reasons (or for no explainable reason at all). While we can certainly analyze the social structures of Gotham, and specifically in this chapter look at the frequent depictions of socioeconomic difference, ultimately, both classlessness and a class-based society have social problems that may lead to violence and crime.

Marxism and Social Conflict

Karl Marx and Friedrich Engels's ([1848] 1969) renowned pamphlet *The Communist Manifesto* makes broad claims about society, critiquing the social infrastructure of hierarchies, and provides the basis for Marxist criticism. When people are put into roles based on economic power, the result, Marx and Engels argue, is problematic and dangerous. The first chapter of *The Communist Manifesto* begins, "The history of all hitherto existing society is the history of class struggles." In looking to history to see the trends in social oppression between the classes, Marx and Engels argue against a traditional social structure and encourage radical change. Their observation, though, makes for relevant material for adapting urban social structure into fiction. Gotham City has its own history and social development and follows a historical tradition of class struggles.

For Marx and Engels ([1848] 1969), though, class struggles have not been mitigated through the growth and development of society through the ages. The "modern" time when their pamphlet was published (1848) has found that with the development of new classes have come "new conditions of oppression" and "new forms of struggle." Marx and Engels focus on the bourgeoisie and the proletariat classes and specifically how the means of production contribute to class divisiveness. They accuse "too much civilisation, too much means of subsistence, too much industry, [and] too much commerce" for destroying society. This perspective accuses commodity as having the power to influence social hierarchies. Gotham City mirrors the historical tradition, and it never finds a way to quell class conflict. Money certainly does seem to hold power in Gotham City, but its corruptive influence may be questionable depending on the motivations of both the wealthy and the poor.

Bruce Wayne, member of the upper-class elite, puts on a façade of conforming to typical high-class trends and behaviors while actually using his wealth to serve a greater purpose than personal gain. Brian Cronin (2015) has identified comics where Bruce's wealth is discussed. Cronin notes that Bruce is described as a socialite in the earliest comics and then described as a "spendthrift society playboy" in *Batman* #3 (Finger and Kane 1940d). *Batman* #19 (Samachson and Sprang 1943) refers to him as a millionaire, and then, over fifty years later, *Legends of the Dark Knight* #61 (O'Neil and Barreto 1994) uses the word "billionaire." *Batman: Year One* (Miller and Mazzucchelli [1987] 2005) calls Bruce "the richest man in Gotham City." Despite Bruce's social standing, though, Matthew Joseph Wolf-Meyer (2006) finds that Batman cannot be classed because of his position as a superhero and due to his relationship with Robin. He argues that "children exist outside of class" (191), so Robin's presence in Batman's life would further contribute to a classless identity. Wolf-Meyer argues that the superhero is in a unique position of ur-class: "untouched by the law and oblivious to the constraints of hegemonic capitalism (while simultaneously enforcing both)" (191). With this argument, Batman would then exist outside of class but unable to unclass all of society. In fact, his existence shows the need for laws and social structures even though they may not apply to him. For Wolf-Meyer, " 'ur-class' is that of existing within a class system but without class—superheroes are neither upper, middle or lower class, but rather something other. They exist as a member of a hyper-class, able to affect the class system (in some way) but being untouched by the class system" (203–4). This argument places Batman outside of class, making it seem as though being a member of ur-class gives him more power. The superhero needs power to try to quell problems associated with hegemony—so, if he holds power outside of class, then what would a classless society even look like? He is also above the law, so classlessness may be associated with lawlessness—even though his intentions are in the interest of protecting the people. The paradox is that lawlessness exists both in a class-based society and under the cowl of classlessness.

Gotham City cannot exist without class conflict because that would defeat the purpose of and need for Batman. Ironically, Bruce Wayne, who illustrates one end of the spectrum of class divisiveness in the city, is the hero the city begs to restore order. Bruce cannot be Batman without his money, though, so Batman's existence necessitates extreme class disparity in the form of a billionaire playboy. Batman's purpose is to maintain order in a chaotic city, but the franchise will never allow him to be completely successful. The dissolution of class in Gotham would also mean the loss of Batman. This also cannot happen because the motivations of the supervillains are not necessarily related to class disparity. Thus, a classless Gotham would still have crime.

Batman reinforces the need for class because he relies on the Wayne wealth for his own existence. In *Detective Comics* #105 (Cameron and Mortimer 1945), the treasurer of Bruce Wayne's motor firm steals investor money, and Bruce has to pay it all back to the investors. This leaves Batman and Robin without any funds. The issue shows how the crime-fighting duo continue to successfully fight crime even if they have to get creative in finding ways to earn money. By the end, the treasurer is captured, and the money is returned.

While Batman and Robin typically rely on the Wayne wealth, without access to large funds in this issue, their skills are enough to combat crime. However, money is still a necessity; it is just the means of earning that money that is different in this issue. And the return of the wealth at the end of the issue is the restoration of order. Batman and Robin need funding, and even though they are successful in finding ways to get by temporarily, the franchise needs them fully financed to continue their crusade.

While Bruce Wayne actually reinforces the notion that the upper class can use wealth for noble purposes, the franchise shows the challenges that poverty has caused for many of Gotham's people. Marx and Engels's ([1848] 1969) theories involve looking at the effect of society on the individual. For the proletariat, Marx and Engels find that the workman has become dehumanized and exists essentially as "an appendage of the machine." This point takes a group of people and illustrates the loss of humanity that occurs as a result of the machinization of the class. The depiction of lower-class individuals as in- or sub-human can be seen in examples where they are oppressed. In the episode "The Underdwellers" (Ruegger 1992) of *Batman: The Animated Series*, a group of children live in the sewers in a community run by the Sewer King. The Sewer King sends the children to the streets to be pickpockets. He claims that he provides and cares for the children and knows what is good for them, but they all wear tattered clothing, are forbidden from speaking, and are punished by being locked in a room with a bright light. When Batman finds the underdwellers, he says that the children will now be treated as human beings. The Sewer King says to Batman about the children, "I feed them. I clothe them. I discipline them. And I teach them a trade." The Sewer King positions himself as a ruler over an oppressed class of individuals—children nonetheless. They lose their basic human rights and are forced to contrive ways to acquire money for the Sewer King. Meanwhile, he reaps the benefits of their efforts, feasting on a meal while forcing the children to watch him eat. In denying the children permission to speak, they lose any opportunities for social relationships and self-expression, which further dehumanizes them. Despite his claim to the contrary, it would seem that he does not provide for the children's basic needs. This episode illustrates the dangers of social oppression and the distorted rationale of someone who has claimed hierarchical authority.

Identification based on class can also be seen in *Nightwing* Vol. 3 #8 (Higgins and Barrows 2012), which flashes back to Gotham City of 1910. William Cobb, a child during this time, says that he was not "a child of Gotham City" because "such a thing would have required [his] father to be a member of Gotham's high society." Instead, his father was an ironworker who built bridges for the city's "powerful families." Despite growing up in the city, Cobb's class does not allow him to identify as being a member of Gotham. He is an outcast, a social other whose class is meant to provide for people higher on the social ladder. The members of the lower class are dehumanized in a similar fashion to Marx and Engels's ([1848] 1969) description because they are not afforded recognition as part of the city. This issue also shows the historical tradition of class inequality, providing a glimpse into the social structures that both literally and figuratively built the city. Cobb feels like an outsider in his own city, as he describes his childhood: "Juggling for pennies while surrounded by the 'extravagance' of Gotham. How much more hopeless can one feel?" (Higgins and Barrows 2012). Survival becomes a struggle for him that is emotionally exacerbated by the lavish society around him. He does not belong to the elite that seems to be the identifier of membership into or even identification with the city. It is not enough to live in Gotham; to feel a sense of belonging, one must have wealth. Early-twentieth-century Dutch criminologist Willem Bonger ([1916] 1969, 436) argues, "Poverty ... kills the social sentiments in man, destroys in fact all relations between men. He who is abandoned by all can no longer have any feelings for those who have left him to his fate." Bonger dwells on the effect that hopelessness has on humanity. In his argument, class division destroys the opportunity for man to establish social relationships. He also places the blame of this outcome on the upper class for neglecting the lower class. Cobb's feelings in *Nightwing* Vol. 3 #8 reflect this sentiment. As he gets older, despite getting off the city's streets and joining the circus to make a living, Cobb is not able to climb the social ladder high enough to marry the woman he loves. Ultimately, he becomes an assassin for the Court of Owls. Cobb's journey illustrates the path toward violence and crime that are arguably a result of class disparity—another Marxist critique of the effects of class inequality.

The Communist Manifesto (Marx and Engels [1848] 1969) also critiques the effects of classing due to dehumanization. Marx and Engels's theories in this regard lay the groundwork for theories of conflict, specifically the social conflict theory. In retaliation for their position, the members of the proletariat class, according to Marx and Engels, violently attack the instruments of production. The authors "traced the more or less veiled civil war, raging within existing society, up to the point where that war breaks out into open revolution, and where the violent overthrow of the bourgeoisie lays the foundation for the sway of the proletariat" (Marx and Engels [1848] 1969). Here, Marx and Engels argue that unequal social classes bring forth violence, which is precisely the point of interest for a class analysis of Gotham City, particularly when the franchise has made much use of crime plots of the poor against the wealthy.

Marx and Engels ([1848] 1969) do not use the term "social conflict" specifically in their pamphlet, but their arguments have fueled what has become known as social conflict theory.[1] For Erik Olin Wright (2005, 28),

> One of the standard claims about Marxist class analysis that [*sic*] it foregrounds conflict within class relations ... The distinctive feature of the Marxist account of class relations in these terms ["conflict theory"] is not simply that it gives prominence to class conflict, but that it understands conflict as generated by *inherent properties of those relations* rather than simply contingent factors.

The social conflict theory finds that class relationships are essentially built for unavoidable contention between classes. Harmony cannot exist in a system based on dominance and oppression. Wright also finds a relationship between exploitation and domination that exists within class-based society (25). Conflict that arises due to class discrepancies, therefore, may be linked to the treatment from upper class to lower class. The Batman franchise has shown that both classes may hold the other in disdain.

Early Batman comics have illustrated such social conflict where the wealthy are the targets of criminal activity. In *Detective Comics* #42 (Finger and Kane 1940h), an artist paints portraits of Gotham's wealthy class. The portraits are defaced with bullet wounds or other murderous prophecies, and later, the individuals are murdered in the same fashion. It turns out the killer's motive was money. He targeted victims who represented that which he desires: wealth. Likewise, in *Batman* #98 (Hamilton and Moldoff 1956a), criminals target a group of millionaires and hold them hostage for ransom. The economic disparity between the classes causes financially motivated crimes that attack the wealthy for their complicity and reinforcement of capitalistic hegemony.

In the episode "Appointment in Crime Alley" (Conway 1992) of *Batman: The Animated Series*, a news reporter discusses Gotham's Park Row, a formerly glamorous neighborhood that has declined into what is now known as Crime Alley. In this episode, Roland Daggett wants to gentrify Crime Alley, a plan that is under protest by the neighborhood's current residents. Daggett loses his appeal to the zoning board, so he plans to blow up several buildings for what one of his men calls "urban development." Daggett argues, "We cannot allow the underclass to hinder us from building a better tomorrow." He sees the lower-class population as preventing urban growth and development. He does not respect the residents of this part of the city and is dismissive of human life in planting explosives. This perspective illustrates how Daggett's social standing affords him the power to neglect and even eliminate those below him on the socioeconomic hierarchy, just as Marx and Engels ([1848] 1969) describe the bourgeoisie oppressing the proletariat. However, it takes a member of the elite to stop the crimes of another member of the elite as Batman saves the lives of the residents and disarms most of the explosives.

The Park Row/Crime Alley section of the city made its first appearance in *Detective Comics* #457 (O'Neil and Giordano 1976). It is where Thomas and Martha Wayne were murdered, which marked a turning point for this part of the city from fashionable to decayed. The cover page reads, "One night, two brutal slayings occurred signaling the beginning of the end." Murder in an upscale part of the city triggered a downward spiral into a place renowned for its criminal activity. This used to be where the rich found "laughter" and "pleasure," while now, "only the forlorn and the desperate walk these streets." This narration claims that pleasure is associated with wealth, which suggests that the poor cannot enjoy their lives. Crime

Alley is a space that associates crime directly with class. Throughout the franchise, this area is often depicted as a breeding ground for crime. However, both "Appointment in Crime Alley" (Conway 1992) and *Detective Comics* #457 show that there are still good people who live in this part of the city. *Detective Comics* #457 also offers a positive outlook, as Batman tells Leslie Thompkins that people like her are "the hope of Crime Alley." Toward the end of the issue, the narration reads, "At last, the long night is over ... and the rising sun brightens Crime Alley and the haunts of the rich alike" (O'Neil and Giordano 1976). The sun does not distinguish class, indicating that nature has not formed class. Class disparity is a man-made, social creation, and the inherent conflicts would seemingly also only be able to be dealt with by man.

A constant visual signifier of the upper class throughout the Batman franchise is Martha Wayne's pearl necklace. In the various depictions of Batman's origin story, the necklace is always present during Thomas and Martha Wayne's murders. *Batman* #1 (Finger and Kane 1940c) provided readers with Batman's origin story for the first time. A man approaches Thomas, Martha, and Bruce with a gun and says, "I'll take that necklace you're wearing lady!" While it is unclear whether this version of the necklace is made of pearls, in Frank Miller and Klaus Janson's ([1986] 2002) *The Dark Knight Returns*, Martha's necklace is clearly comprised of pearls. Brian Cronin (2019b) notices that in subsequent iterations of the murders, the necklace breaks, spilling pearls all over the ground. However, Cronin argues that a pearl necklace would never break in such a way because there would be knots tied between each pearl. Cronin doubts that Martha's pearls were intended to be fake and that the pearls dropping is intended to be "an artistic flourish." But Cronin (2019a) has also noted that Grant Morrison's (2010) series *The Return of Bruce Wayne* and Greg Rucka and Klaus Janson's (2004) *Batman: Death and the Maidens* #4 both suggest that Martha's pearls were fake. Martha's necklace is supposed to be the symbol of wealth that causes the family to be targeted. When Joe Chill murders the Waynes because of resistance to him taking Martha's necklace, he demonstrates the dangers of greed and desperation. However, if the pearls are fake, then the tragic irony is that Thomas and Martha, though members of the aristocracy, were killed for something entirely worthless. The spilling of the pearls marks the breakdown of the aristocracy by a symbol of wealth that is actually meaningless. Since the incident sparks the rise of the Batman, the sacrifice of wealthy bodies serves to birth a crusader who will repurpose his wealth to protect innocent people against violence.

Sometimes, though, lower-class crime is committed not as an attack against the wealthy but as a means for survival or to help those in need. Such examples are not indicative of the social conflict theory, but they do illustrate poverty leading to desperation, which can lead to crime. In *Batman* #5's "The Case of the Honest Crook" (Finger and Kane 1941a), a man steals money to save his sick wife after the mafia had framed him. In *Batman* #239 (O'Neil and Novick 1972), a man named Tim attacks Santa Clauses and steals their charity collection money. It turns out that Tim was laid off from his job with the promise of being rehired—which never happened. He lives in "Gotham's worst slum," trying to raise his niece Betsy and pay her medical bills. Tim's turn to petty crime is a desperate measure to help his ill niece. Tim eventually plans to murder his former boss—an attack on the individual guilty of domination, as Wright (2005) would term. However, he ultimately saves his former boss's life. Tim's hopelessness may have led him to contemplate committing murder, but in the end, his moral character prevails, showing his compassion for mankind. He is not a criminal at heart and only turned to crime in desperation. In this scenario, his poverty may be argued as the fuel for criminal motivation, but the issue also teaches the lesson that a man can rise above his dire situations and act heroically.

The Batman franchise establishes Gotham City as a place with visible class disparity. *Batman* #307 (Wein and Calnan 1979) describes the executive offices of the Wayne Foundation as the place where "the fortunes of others are made and ruined, the economies of nations are transformed." Clearly, the Wayne Foundation holds economic power not only within Gotham but also globally. The same issue also describes a poor area of Gotham: "The slum-ridden lower west side of Gotham City, where the sun rarely shines to begin with …" (Wein and Calnan 1979). Unlike *Detective Comics* #457 (O'Neil and Giordano 1976), this description suggests that the natural world actually discriminates against the lower-class part of the city. The lack of sunshine would also suggest a lack of hope to this area. This description, then, may be a figurative means to portray the bleak living conditions of the poor. Socioeconomic disparity is unavoidable in Gotham. Batman cannot change the class structures because he relies on them. So, instead, he focuses on crime reduction and trying to defend the people of Gotham.

Capitalistic Hegemony

Despite any Marxist argument about class fueling violence and conflict, ultimately, the franchise illustrates the necessity of the upper class. Batman's need for his gadgets, vehicles, and hi-tech gear could not be met without Bruce Wayne's wealth. Since he is not a superhero with superpowers, his money is essential to his survival as a vigilante. Wolf-Meyer (2006, 193) argues, "Bruce Wayne's originating event, the killing of his parents over a necklace (a symbol of upper class status) by a criminal (a member of the lower class), grounds Bruce Wayne's motivations in the preservation of hegemonic order, and particularly one based upon class hierarchies and the privilege of power. The superhero is meant to enforce the status quo." Despite crime being associated with the lower class, Batman does not ever try to achieve a classless society because he knows that this would not eliminate criminality. Instead, he tries to prevent ongoing destructive behaviors and morally educate individuals to dissuade them from turning to crime.[2] Gotham City in any iteration is consistently a place under threat. The perpetuation of crime necessitates Batman's existence. However, the complete dissolution of crime would also destroy Batman's purpose and the franchise itself. The status quo of Gotham is actually a dilapidated state, which must be maintained. Wolf-Meyer (2006, 203) argues further, "Capitalistic hegemony depends on economic constraints to limit the potential of its citizens, but if one finds ways out of the traditional economic and cultural system of control by acting ethically, by acting in the selfless defense of the social (if not the law itself), then one defies the control of the system." Since Bruce uses his wealth to save lives, he does not follow traditional hegemonic hierarchies where wealth is mostly equated to control and ownership of land and goods. While Bruce has this kind of power in his day clothes, Batman is not a figure who is part of the hegemonic order even though his existence depends upon it. In Christopher Nolan's (2008) *The Dark Knight*, Batman develops surveillance technology that provides access to all corners of the city. Lucius Fox criticizes the database, calling it "unethical," "dangerous," and "too much power for one person." Batman likely felt the same, as he had programmed the system to self destruct after Fox used it to find the Joker. Even when dealing with something as unethical as "spying on thirty million people," Batman uses his wealth solely to capture a supervillain, not for any personal gain or advantage.

In Christopher Nolan's (2005) *Batman Begins*, before Bruce Wayne becomes Batman, his friend Rachel Dawes takes him on a tour of the dilapidated areas of Gotham City. She notes mafia boss Carmine Falcone's influence in driving others to crime—including Joe Chill, who murdered Bruce's parents: "This city is rotting. They talk about the Depression as if it's history; and it's not. Things are worse than ever down here. Falcone floods our streets with crime and drugs, preying on the desperate, creating new Joe Chills every day." Rachel compares the state of the city to an earlier depression, arguing that there has not been relief from the destitution in the city; criminals continue to breed and influence one another and, in doing so, maintain an appearance that the city is decaying. Such a relationship is also visible in Todd Phillips's (2019) film *Joker*. When Arthur Fleck kills three young men who work for Wayne Enterprises, he inspires protests against the wealthy. The protesters wear clown masks, suggesting that the Joker represents the unrepresented in Gotham—the lower class that seems to be disregarded by the wealthy. Phillips's film makes a connection between the lower class and the supervillain as if he can lead their crusade against capitalistic hegemony. Ironically, a wealthy crusader is what will be needed to help the people.

Nolan's (2012) *The Dark Knight Rises* illustrates the need for capitalism and the dangers of trying to disrupt that system. Bane tries to destroy capitalistic hegemony by first going to the roots of class disparity—the money. He attacks a stock exchange with the agenda of bankrupting Bruce Wayne. He then declares that he and his men are "liberators" with a plan "to return control of this city to the people." In the film, class and politics overlap through a critique on power. For Slavoj Žižek (2012, 50), *The Dark Knight Rises* exposes the threat of a totalitarian agenda using the Occupy Wall Street movement and the idea of a "People's Republic of Gotham City," which he describes as "a dictatorship of the proletariat in Manhattan." The comparison of the film's plot to Occupy Wall Street, though, has faced a lot of criticism. A peaceful protest movement that began in 2001, Occupy Wall Street's intentions have been "fighting back against the corrosive power of major banks and multinational corporations over the democratic process, and the role of Wall Street in creating an economic collapse that has caused the greatest recession in generations" (Occupy Wall Street, n.d.a). The Occupy Wall Street movement preaches, "We Are The 99% that will no longer tolerate the greed and corruption of the 1%" (Occupy Wall Street, n.d.b). However, Bruce Wayne/Batman cannot be described in such a way. Batman's "main animus, if not his methods, is defined by the ideals of philanthropy and a simplistic sense of justice: a selfless billionaire by day who strives to protect the defenceless people of Gotham by night – the 1% fighting for the 99%" (Kelly 2011). Batman uses fear to defeat enemies and quell criminal activity. But Batman bloggers have noted that fear is ingrained in the people of the city as well: "The lower and middle class fear the power that the upper class have and the the [sic] upper class fears the overwhelming numbers of the lower classes and the [sic] fear of losing what they have" (Dan 2012). Regardless of class, according to this perspective, all people experience fear; however, their fears are deeply motivated by class-related issues. Additionally, "fear is used as a weapon to reorganize society according to an ideological and utopian vision (a vision that is impossible to achieve if history is any guide)" (Kerrigan 2011). S. J. Kerrigan's argument here notes that a classless society is impossible; however, the people will still be intrigued by its potential to be a place where their current fears will no longer exist.

While both the film and the Occupy Wall Street protesters oppose the wealthy class, Bane uses terroristic methods to achieve his agenda, which has prompted critics to argue that the comparison is poorly aligned. Reviewer and protester Harrison Schultz (2012) argues that Bane and his men "in no way resemble the comparatively impoverished, peace-seeking protesters who armed themselves with signs, sleeping bags, tents, and iPhones at best in their attempts to fight for social justice." From a personal standpoint, Schultz comments, "The occupation gave many of us the support and confidence we needed in order to end the isolation we've felt obliged to impose upon ourselves in order to avoid the stigma, guilt, and shame that perpetually broke, debt-ridden people tend to experience from living in the most crassly materialistic society ever designed by human beings." Schultz argues that the protest was an opportunity for those who felt oppressed to unite and unify against a common enemy and collectively critique and stand up against a social system that has enabled class disparity and divisiveness. This is not Bane's approach. Rather, much of his true agenda remains hidden for the bulk of the film. He is not actually trying to unify the people but to make the people fear one another. His methods arguably cause more divisiveness than already existed.

Žižek (2012) thinks even further about the intentions of the film in associating the Occupy Wall Street agenda with that of a terrorist's plans: "Why does [a Hollywood blockbuster] even fantasise about OWS exploding into a violent takeover? The obvious answer—that it does so to taint OWS with the accusation that it harbours a terrorist or totalitarian potential—is not enough to account for the strange attraction exerted by the prospect of 'people power.'" Certainly the Occupy Wall Street protesters, as Schultz (2012) argues, have always intended for a peaceful protest. The film seems to be commenting about the dissolution of capitalism through literally destructive means and the rise of the people to be equals. But the film, then, would seem to be in favor of capitalism since the efforts for economic equality seem only possible at the cost of human life. Žižek (2012) notices this "strange attraction" for classlessness, as it teases a utopian vision for America. However, capitalism has endured in America because it has been the root of American growth and prosperity. A classless Gotham City would require a momentous event (such as Bane's nuclear bomb) to even become a reality. After the loss of human life, there is no guarantee that the city would thrive or that any depraved living conditions would improve. Supervillains—who are not reliant upon wealth—could still terrorize the city, but Bruce Wayne could not fund his vigilantism, so the city would likely still be rampant with problems.

Nolan's films also visually nod to symbols of wealth and development and include recognizable settings as reminders to audiences that Gotham City represents urban America. Nolan filmed *The Dark Knight* mostly in Chicago. In one scene, Batman perches atop Willis Tower, which, at the time of filming, was America's tallest building, a recognizably iconic symbol of American growth and prosperity. Batman and the Joker's final battle occurs at Trump Tower, representative of expansion, development, and prosperity through real estate that the villains threaten to disrupt. *The Dark Knight Rises*, though predominantly filmed in New York City, also includes scenes that were filmed in Pittsburgh, which offers a visual entry point into the historical foundations of American industrialization. Nolan includes PPG Place (PPG was founded in 1883 as Pittsburgh Plate Glass Company, the United States' first successful manufacturer of plate glass, which has grown into a Fortune 500 company) and the US Steel Tower, and with these landmarks in the film, Bane infiltrates a city that represents the roots of American prosperity through the industries that developed the country. Bane and Batman's final battle in the film takes place on the steps of a building at Carnegie Mellon University, an institution known for its research and technology. Thus, the supervillain infiltrates the American city to destroy the urban infrastructure, and the film warns of the threat to prosperity through visual signifiers of industrial and technological growth and development. For Bane's attack on the stock exchange, though, Nolan filmed at 23 Wall Street, formerly owned by J. P. Morgan & Co., in the heart of New York City's financial district, tapping into anxieties related to capital gain and financial corruption in the recognizable space of America's financial sector. These filming locations are also historically linked: in 1901, Andrew Carnegie's Carnegie Steel merged with other steel corporations to become US Steel, which was brokered by J. P. Morgan. Nolan's juxtaposition of shots from Pittsburgh and New York City, especially the scenes that alternate between the two cities during Bane's initial takeover and the final battle, demonstrates that Gotham is at once both, and, in fact, all American cities. The audience may recognize the landmarks of American progress and see how the supervillain threatens to destroy posterity in a city that represents ideologies of the American populace and the development and growth of America afforded under capitalism.

Bruno Heller's television series *Gotham* also provides a look at capitalism in urban America. Critic Ceren Mert (2019) argues that the show provides commentary on global capitalism rather than just America's system. He also looks specifically at the set of the show and how space used for commodification has transitioned into space used for crime:

> As global capitalism became more sophisticated in its production and distribution channels, some of the old warehouses, which were initially intended for storing large quantities of products, turned into dark, underground spaces for criminal activities such as illegal negotiation, trading of contraband, and homicide. In Gotham, these warehouses are the shadowy and clandestine underbelly of the postindustrial city, with its glamorous and flashy lights. (Mert 2019)

The physical infrastructure of the city has been repurposed, and the space formerly representing industry is now aligned with criminality. The city has grown and developed, though, so it seems as though the criminals do not reflect a problem caused by capitalism. Rather, they have nowhere else to go but to fill empty space in the city. As society advances, the criminals are left with the remains of a time from which the city has evolved into its current postindustrialist existence. The warehouses may remind audiences of the industrialization that built the city, but the buildings' repurposing for criminal activity also reminds audiences that society has advanced beyond the need for such spaces.

Mert (2019) identifies visible examples of disparity in the show: "The contrast between Ivy Pepper's streets and Barbara's penthouse exposes the stark disparities of two social worlds in a global city." Gotham's criminals also seem to have their own visible class range based on wealth. Selina lives on the streets, but she also gains access to the wealthy criminal organizations of Fish Mooney and later Barbara Kean. Criminality affords individuals to rise in the ranks of criminal hierarchy—an independent class system that does not follow the rules of society. Selina coexists as both criminal and noncriminal and survives both when she is poor and when adopted into a wealthy criminal syndicate. If criminals also have hierarchies based on wealth, then are they a product of an unjust class system or reinforcers of it? Perhaps they just realize that this is their best means for survival.

However, the supervillains typically are not financially motivated. For critic Martin Fradley (2012, 22) regarding Nolan's (2008) *The Dark Knight*, "[Heath] Ledger's Joker makes manifest the cruelty and contradictions of neoliberal capitalism, his actions literalizing the symbolic violence of Gotham's rigid class system." In the film, the Joker burns a mountain of money. Financial gain is not a motivating factor for the Joker. He would rather expose Gotham's people to the inherent problems that money creates. He burns money[3] to show them that it is meaningless, but in doing so, he also knows that he will incite a chaotic response. The Joker is intrigued by the obsessed mind, and, therefore, popular obsession with money fuels his desires to create panic. The Joker says to a man working for him, "All you care about is money. This town deserves a better class of criminal, and I'm gonna give it to them" (Nolan 2008). The Joker finds that crime that is financially motivated essentially shows weakness. Satisfaction with money gathered from criminal activity also does not fulfill a greater purpose. The Joker is an artist and master of crime. He does not commit crime to fulfill a basic need. Instead, his schemes have a greater agenda. The Joker says, "It's not about money; it's about sending a message. Everything burns." He wants to arouse chaos, but he also desires exposing the futility of the people's preoccupation with money. Their world as they know it can come crumbling down because "everything burns," not just money. Paper money is a tangible but combustible representation of the fragility of the city itself.

While most renditions of Gotham City show a spectrum of class through the population and geography of the city, there have also been examples of a Gotham City that is difficult to compare with class-based, capitalistic societies. In the "No Man's Land" story arc—a crossover event that spanned eighty-seven issues and ran from March 1999 to February 2000—a devastating earthquake has ravaged Gotham City. The city appears to be on the brink of complete decimation, so the US government deems the city unfit for residents. It declares Gotham a No Man's Land and orders complete evacuation. Yet, many people remain—the poor, the destitute, and illegal immigrants all feel that they must stay. Criminals and supervillains stay to gain power through the acquisition of space, and the police remain to try to maintain order and protect people. Those remaining in Gotham focus their energy on survival and territorial occupation. Corporate power does not exist. Gotham has been brought back to its primitive roots where power comes in the form of space occupancy and possession of goods. Battles for territory ensue, and the city is constantly remapped. Hegemonic power still exists, just not in modern form rooted in wealth. Monetary wealth is an obsolete concept in No Man's Land. Instead, objects and space hold power. While class has dissolved, though, the individuals do not have a socialist perspective of their lives. Ownership of objects provides power, but the greed for possession comes out of desperation for survival. For example, in Bob Gale and Alex Maleev's (1999) *Batman: No Man's Land* Vol. 1 #1, people frequently steal food out of the hands of others. Those who have more moral grounding will trade commodities, as an apple is first traded for three cans of beans and two cans of soup, then traded again for a flashlight with batteries, and then traded for a box of ammo. The trading of goods establishes a capitalistic foundation in a land where the class system has crumbled. When the Penguin acquires the apple, he auctions it off but takes a bite out of it as his commission, showing that the man who holds the commodity holds power and dictates rules. The group dynamics in No Man's Land are based on give and take. As "tribes" develop, individuals seek to join by offering their skills. People who have a trade, such as a mechanic and a seamstress, are deemed valuable. The tribal communities create a sense of classlessness, but it may also be that No Man's Land has created a redistribution of valuable assets. Marx and Engels's ([1848] 1969) criticism of the bourgeoisie lies in overproduction, which, they argue, has caused society to revert to "a state of momentary barbarism." The image of reversion to a state of barbarism can certainly be compared to Gotham City—a place that is frequently in a state of disarray.

In Miller and Janson's ([1986] 2002) *The Dark Knight Returns*, a gang called the Mutants terrorizes the city and even claims ownership of Gotham. The gang's crimes have no clear motivation other than accruing additional power. In this version of Gotham, class seems insignificant and perhaps just a memory of an older version of the city. Gordon muses, "I see a high-priced car, gleaming like new in the streetlight, once a symbol of wealth and power, now just another target in a city of victims." The object's signification has shifted from that of product of upper-class consumerism to casualty of the pitfalls of excess. Gordon realizes that the commodities that make capitalism visible in Gotham have ceased to exist, as capitalism seems to have lost its organizing power. Gordon also says about a liquor merchant, "I wonder how many men he's had to kill, just to stay in business." In this Gotham, business does not succeed through capitalistic methods but through brute force. Life in Gotham, as in No Man's Land, appears to have reverted to more primitive means, heavily focused on survival.

Wolf-Meyer (2006, 199) argues, though, that "*The Dark Knight Returns* (1986) emphasizes the growing disparities of class masked by the myth of classlessness in the post-industrial Gotham City." He finds class disparity still exists under the surface. Yet, definitive class delineations are hard to describe as depravity and survival have formed a relationship. In Gotham, which is rampant with criminality, drives for survival can come in many forms, and Batman's efforts are to protect people who may not have the means or abilities to successfully defend themselves. While he may seem to exist in a class of his own—or no class at all—he reinforces the need for class while trying to combat dangers that may arise in a society with stark class disparity.

Wealth, Power, and White-Collar Crime

Every creative iteration of Batman requires a criminal element. The franchise has successfully diversified the types of criminals and criminal behaviors to keep the Bat Family in constant opposition to threatening forces. While the comics and films often depict low-class criminals and dangerous neighborhoods, they have also included white-collar crime, which Batman must also contend against. Essentially, anyone in Gotham City can be a criminal, regardless of class.

American criminologist and sociologist Edwin H. Sutherland (1940), a pioneer in the field of criminology, coined the term "white-collar crime" and developed the theory of differential association. Sutherland argued against theories of criminologists who claimed that poverty and social characteristics of lower-class individuals cause criminal behavior (1–2). For Sutherland, "a description of white-collar criminality in general terms will be also a description of the criminality of the lower class. The respects in which the crimes of the two classes differ are the incidentals rather than the essentials of criminality" (7). His concern was in essentializing criminality as a condition rather than differentiating based on the means. To do so, he had to define white-collar crime; this was intended so others would be less dismissive of such criminals or treat them with privilege.

Tim Burton's (1992) film *Batman Returns* introduces Max Shreck, a rich, powerful business owner who plans on building a power plant under the guise that it will provide the city with additional power. In reality, he plans on storing the power for his own personal control. Cory A. Reed (1995, 43) notes that Shreck, named after the actor who played Dracula in F. W. Murnau's 1922 film *Nosferatu*, "is, in effect, a vampire who preys on Gotham City, whose giant capacitor will drain the city of its electrical power, literally sucking Gotham's life blood." Shreck is an industrialized monster who needs the city to satiate his lust for power by feeding on the energy of Gotham's infrastructure. Shreck owns a department store, too, so his villainy is also a critique of capitalistic consumerism. When Catwoman blows up Shreck's store, she is attacking capitalistic power that, for her, also represents oppression and murder. Shreck, her former boss, silences her role as his assistant embarrassingly in front of others and also privately when he attempts to kill her. Selina's relationship with Shreck illustrates Sutherland's (1940, 9) description of the exhibition of power: "White-collar criminality flourishes at points where powerful business and professional men come in contact with persons who are weak. In this respect, it is similar to stealing candy from a baby." Selina is an obedient employee in a submissive role—essentially a coffee girl even though her title is "assistant." Ironically, though, her lack of status and power does not prevent her from learning the truth behind Shreck's plans for the power plant. She is not as ignorant as Shreck assumes, so he resorts to physical force over her. This attempted murder actually gives rise to Catwoman. As Catwoman, Selina can subvert the parasitic, power-hungry male power. She gains the skills and confidence to fight back against both the destructive system and male dominance.

Reed (1995, 48) argues that *Batman Returns* can give audience members a glimpse into the potential dangers of a capitalistic society:

> Burton's millennial worldview appears to condemn ineffective government and the extremes of uncontrolled capitalism, portraying a decadent end-of-century society that glorifies industry and corporate profits while the common people live in abject poverty and crime runs rampant. The Max Shrecks of the world amass their personal fortunes by preying on a society that lives in fear of death and lawlessness.

He finds that the people of this Gotham celebrate capitalistic extremism. However, since Shreck is a villain in the film, the audience witnesses the dangers of such a society. Even though Catwoman is intended to be a supervillainess in the film, she fights against corrupt corporate power. For DiPaolo (2011, 67), Catwoman "understands far better than Bruce Wayne does that white-collar, corporate criminals are the most dangerous after all, and the most in need of being brought to justice by any means necessary." She realizes the widespread effect of Shreck's plans on all the citizens of the city. The audience can now reflect on corporate power and unchecked capitalistic hegemony.

Batman as a cultural reference made direct commentary on real-world white-collar crime when *New York Magazine* (2009) published a Jokerized photo of Bernie Madoff on its cover. Madoff was a hedge fund investment manager who operated a forty-year-long Ponzi scheme where investors ultimately lost billions of dollars. The cover of *New York Magazine* (2009) shows Madoff's photo altered to the appearance of wearing white makeup across his face and black makeup around his eyes. A long, thin red smirk stretches across his face, and the roots of his hair have been slightly tinted green. His suit jacket is colored a dark shade of green, and his tie is tinged purple. The headline reads, "Bernie Madoff, Monster." This image directly associates a real-world white-collar criminal with the activities of a supervillain. The message to readers is that white-collar crime is just as barbaric as that of a crazed fictional character—one of the greatest and most iconic supervillains. Ironically, the magazine chose a supervillain who is not actually a white-collar criminal. The emphasis is on monstrosity rather than the type of crime. Such analogies do not make such an impact with lower-class criminals. There exists a kind of prestige associated with this example, as Madoff was a former chairman of the National Association of Securities Dealers Automated Quotations (NASDAQ) and such a powerful figure in American investing. Someone with so much influence and wealth took advantage of the trust his investors had in him. Sutherland (1940, 5) argues that the great detriment of white-collar crime is the risk that it places on social ties and networks: "The financial loss from white-collar crime, great as it is, is less important than the damage to social relations. White-collar crimes violate trust and therefore create distrust, which lowers social morale and produces social disorganization on a large scale. Other crimes produce relatively little effect on social institutions or social organization." Madoff's sons Mark and Andrew turned their father in to authorities when they learned of the Ponzi scheme. Madoff pled guilty to multiple counts of criminal activity, but the family name was ruined as a result. In the aftermath, Mark committed suicide. Two other individuals who lost big investments due to Madoff also killed themselves. Madoff's scheme caused charitable organizations, including the Elie Wiesel Foundation for Humanity and the Gift of Life Bone Marrow Foundation, to lose significant amounts of money (Menza 2009). Madoff's schemes and the subsequent aftermath are illustrative of Sutherland's (1940) argument that white-collar crime disrupts many layers of society. Associating Madoff with a supervillain also shows just how deep the Batman franchise is ingrained in American society. Readers can look at the magazine cover and understand the depths and real-world social impact of Madoff's villainous behavior.

The franchise has made efforts to expose the corruption of the criminal or immoral upper class and teach lessons about valuing humanity and society. In Season 4 Episode 9 "Let Them Eat Pie" (Sosa 2017) of the show *Gotham*, the supervillain Professor Pyg cooks meat pies out of the poor people of Gotham. At a fundraiser dinner of Gotham's wealthy citizens, he orders them to eat the pies, saying, "You have all fed upon the poor of Gotham for years. Now you are going to know what they taste like." Even though Professor Pyg is the villain in this episode, he exposes Gotham's wealthy for their immoral behavior toward Gotham's lower-class citizens. While we are not made privy to white-collar crimes specifically, Pyg's attack seems to generalize the wealthy with corruption and taking from the poor, as Sutherland (1940, 9) defines through his "stealing candy from a baby" analogy. Pyg uses rhetoric of consuming, criticizing capitalism at its core. He blames the wealthy for taking from the poor and decides to punish them by forcing them to literally eat human meat.

The Batman franchise has also made efforts to teach lessons about the abuse of wealth and power. "A Christmas Peril" in *Batman* #27 (Cameron and Robinson 1945) is an adaptation of Charles Dickens's 1843 classic *A Christmas Carol* that focuses on economic generosity. In the issue, racketeers target the Christmas tree industry. They demand sellers raise their prices and pay them the difference. Once Batman and Robin hear of the scheme, they go after the racketeers. Batman says, "Hogging the Christmas tree market through terrorism isn't respectable!" The Dynamic Duo learn that millionaire Scranton Loring is backing the racketeers. Loring, "the richest boy in the world" after inheriting the fortune of his uncle—who was known as "Old Scrooge"—is proud to declare that he is called "Young Scrooge." The inheritance of criminality is fitting of Sutherland's (1940, 10) theory of differential association, which hypothesizes "that white-collar criminality, just as other systematic criminality, is learned; that it is learned in direct or indirect association with those who already practice the behavior." Loring has followed his uncle proudly, stating, "While others throw their money away, I'm making a quarter-million dollars by cornering all Christmas trees in town and quadrupling prices!" (Cameron and Robinson 1945). Batman and Robin, in the manner of the spirits, arrive and whisk Loring away to show him the devastating results of his scheme. The journey exposes Loring to extreme poverty and associated misery. Loring's experience allows him to find value in life as superior to money. Loring learns "the secret of real happiness" and decides to spend his time and money "spreading cheer" to others by using his money for good. Following the Dickensian model, this tale shows the potential exploitive power of wealth but also offers hope for mankind, suggesting that we are not inherently power-hungry savages but that man has humanity, sympathy, and compassion for others.

Other comics have offered similar lessons about wealth. Through a modernized adaptation of Greek mythology, "Money

Can't Buy Happiness" in *Detective Comics* #47 (Finger and Kane 1941c) teaches that money will not solve problems. In the issue, rich Midas and his wife are so preoccupied with their wealth that they neglect their children. The Midases force their daughter against her desires to marry a European count who turns out to be corrupt. Meanwhile, their son gets involved with criminals. Through the help of Batman and Robin, Mr. and Mrs. Midas learn that money cannot actually buy happiness. The issue also teaches that money can be the root of misery—even for the wealthy—as all of the problems in the Midas family are directly related to their wealth. Rewriting the Greek myth of King Midas, Finger and Kane tap into a traditional lesson about the dangers of obsession with wealth. Using Dickensian or mythological tradition to teach lessons about misapplied wealth and/or priorities allows readers to see the relevance of such messages today.

Likewise, *Batman* #19 (Samachson and Sprang 1943) supports the capitalistic path where one works to earn his or her wealth. When distraught siblings try to kill themselves because they lost their fortune, Batman advises them, "Why don't you try to earn your own living?" This issue supports and encourages the capitalistic tradition of working for one's money. In the same issue, the criminal Ali has filled a prison with wealthy captives, which he has named Millionaire Row. Ali hires actors to take the place of the prisoners to try to gain some of their money. Ali's gripe with his prisoners is that they are too rich. He complains that one never gives away any of his money and says of another, "Never give a poor fellow a break, that's your motto!" Later, after Batman and Robin free the captives and capture Ali, the millionaires say that they will be more generous with their wealth from now on. Bruce says that they have "reformed" due to Ali's schemes. Consequently, the only way to change the greedy perspectives of Gotham City's millionaires is to put their wealth at risk. This issue does not suggest that a breakdown of the capitalistic system is necessary but that greed can lead to preoccupation and the neglect of others and oneself. Batman's involvement in lessons about wealth shows a need to reassess values and behavior but not the entire socioeconomic infrastructure of the city.

While the Batman franchise certainly makes socioeconomic differences visible in the comics and films, it also shows that America depends on a capitalistic society. However, several examples expose the fragility of such a structure and the dangers of hegemonic extremism. In creating both lower-class and white-collar criminals, the franchise shows that immoral people will turn to crime regardless of their socioeconomic status. Batman will continue to fight any criminals and villains he is faced against and attempt to restore capitalistic order to Gotham City.

6

Criminal Productivity: Gotham City's Most Wanted and Most Needed

Crime in Gotham City ranges from petty to terroristic while the Bat Family works to quell any threats to humanity. Throughout the franchise, Gotham City has always been a place that houses the constant, cyclical recurrence of threat and temporary relief. The criminals will never completely destroy the city, nor will Batman ever completely restore order. Due to these fluctuations, the city maintains a state that is just bad enough to necessitate a superhero but not good enough to be free of crime. The dilapidated conditions of the city foster the breeding of new criminals and recycling of old ones. The supervillains are supposed to be the "bad guys" who threaten the peace of society. However, since Gotham is never at peace, the supervillains are not so much a threat but an intrinsic aspect of the city's genetic makeup. In fact, since the supervillains are bred by Gotham, they are not actually enemies of the city; rather, they do the city's bidding of maintaining a condition of depravity. The Joker, as Batman's most iconic foe, especially excels at maintaining chaos in the city. Gotham actually thrives on being perpetually rogue-infested. While the superheroes offer temporary relief, the actual agenda of the city and the maintenance of the Batman franchise both depend on Gotham continuing to house its miscreants. Thus, those whom

Batman targets and takes down are those whom Gotham actually needs the most.

The mere existence of Batman ironically ensures the perpetual resurgence of adversaries. Although Batman's intentions are to defend justice and protect the people, some supervillains make it their mission to target him (e.g., the Joker and the Riddler), committing destructive crimes or murders along the way, craving his pursuit. Batman uses the attention the supervillains pay him to his advantage. In *Batman* Vol. 2 #33 (Snyder and Capullo 2014), Batman says, "In the city today, Alfred, **now** more than ever, evil men, sick men, they step from the shadows to kill and terrify, and **Batman** will draw their fire. He will be the lightning rod." Batman knows that he has the power to attract the rogues who want the challenge of facing the Dark Knight. By turning their attention to Batman, his hope is that the supervillains will not harm innocent civilians.

In donning his cowl, Batman had the intention to instill fear in Gotham's miscreants to mitigate their criminal tendencies. However, the mere existence of Batman may encourage supervillains who want a worthy competitor. The *Batman: The Animated Series* episode "Trial" (Dini and Timm 1994b) addresses this concern as several supervillains put Batman on trial for creating criminals. Ultimately, though, Batman is found innocent according to the argument that the rogues would still exist even if he did not. Questions of purpose also emerge in Tim Burton's (1989) film *Batman*, specifically revolving around the hero/villain influence on character origination. Batman says to the Joker, "I made you. You made me first." The "making" of the supervillain is the depraved city's propensity for genesis. Peter Coogan (2006, 110) argues, "Supervillains are created in reaction to the hero's ability to defeat ordinary criminals in order to create narrative tension." He quotes Gordon in Nolan's (2005) *Batman Begins* to illustrate how Batman "pushes criminals to heighten their attacks" (Coogan 2006, 110). Such an argument suggests that there is a symbiotic relationship between Batman and supervillains. Since Batman is also born of the city, the relationship between the setting and character is again blurred as the city creates a figure that may stimulate heightened criminal activity.

In Nolan's (2005) film *The Dark Knight*, the Joker enjoys the challenge of his adversary, saying, "I won't kill you because you're just too much fun. I think you and I are destined to do this forever." The Joker finds much pleasure in wreaking havoc that will draw Batman toward him. In never killing Batman, he can ensure that they will continue to battle one another, to play the game that he sadistically enjoys. Brian Azzarello and Lee Bermejo's (2008) graphic novel *Joker* demonstrates the incessant nature of the clown prince's criminality through a disease metaphor: "There will always be a Joker. Because there's no cure for him. No cure at all. Just a Batman." The existence of Batman ensures the existence of the Joker. From a franchise standpoint, Batman's supervillains certainly are created to provide him adversaries and regular battles in order to perpetuate the continuation and the growth of the Batman multiverse. But from an interior perspective, the city itself is guilty of breeding and maintaining criminality.

Batman's own origins and perpetual existence—along with that of the entire Bat Family—also raise controversy as to the effectiveness of the criminal justice system in Gotham. Defining Batman's role and motives is also complicated when considering how criminologists have conceptualized vigilantism in America. Gotham necessitates a hero who is actually a criminal himself. This chapter turns to various theories of criminality to consider the roots of crime in Gotham City. It examines the methods and motivations of various types of criminals, including Batman's vigilantism. Ultimately, though, I argue that the city itself is an organism that has an innate propensity for breeding and fostering criminality. This is perpetual, as Batman's existence requires criminals. In Gotham, crime is normalized and purposeful for the continuation of the franchise.

The Birthplace of Batman's Adversaries

Gotham City was a passive setting for many years, initially serving as a backdrop for crime and vigilantism. Batman was conceived as a detective who solves mysteries, so the early comics were plot driven. The setting was not as significant as the focus on intricate crimes and Batman's pathways to solving them. When *The Dark Knight Returns* (Miller and Janson [1986] 2002) and *Batman: Year One* (Miller and Mazzucchelli [1987] 2005) were released, Gotham

City came to life as a Gothic organism. The city was no longer merely a canvas for crimes, it was—and has remained—a breeding ground for criminality. This approach to Gotham bled into film and TV adaptations. Tim Burton's (1989 and 1992) films imagined a Gotham with pronounced contours of buildings that reach endlessly high. The supervillains become part of the cityscape, as Catwoman perches on buildings, and the Penguin's rotundity and sharp, pointed nose mirror the various shapes of the buildings. Christopher Nolan's films aimed to depict the twenty-first-century American city, filming in real cities rather than on sets and showing the ways that the city has become infested with crime. *Batman: The Animated Series* created its own aesthetic, envisioned by Eric Radomski, which was called "Dark Deco." Radomski says, "As dark as I can do the show, this is the way I would play it. I'd love to have characters moving in the shadows. At night, you only see elements; you fill in the gaps. Kind of the perfect approach to Gotham City" ("Batman: The Legacy Continues" 2005). Radomski created a world of darkness to evoke the terrors that fuel Gotham City and show that anything can emerge from the shadows.

In the comics, the city is also often described with organic rhetoric, further displaying its vitality as a producer of criminals. In the "No Man's Land" arc, after the earthquake and subsequent evacuation, the city is physically dilapidated, and the remaining occupants revert to survival instincts and brute force. In its ailing condition, the city is described as "a bleeding urban ulcer" (Hama and Deodato 1999) and "amputated from the body of society and left to rot" (Klink and Davis 1999). Gotham is also in a mental state of decay. Scarecrow thinks, "Gotham is insane … and terrified!" (Grayson and Eaglesham 1999). While the language suggests that the city is dying, the deteriorating state fuels criminality. The organic nature of the city maintains its intrinsic criminality, and the destroyed status perpetuates it further. Supervillains and gang members battle for the acquisition of territory. They want to control land in Gotham, which serves as a source of power. Brett Chandler Patterson (2008, 42) observes that "No Man's Land" evokes a Hobbesian philosophy that "human beings in their natural state are inclined to war and distrust. When the structures of social order are challenged by large-scale disasters, this 'natural state' rears its ugly head again, forcing representatives of that social order to step in and fight to reclaim the social contract." Batman and his cohorts try to restore the city from its various threats; however, the natural state, being an apocalyptic state, has become the norm. Therefore, a restored state can only be imagined as an antithesis to the normalized dilapidated status, which is not actually achievable.

Gotham City—especially since the late 1980s—is an organism that propagates criminality. Sociologists and psychologists have long offered theories regarding the causes of criminality. In *The Pathology of Mind*, nineteenth-century British psychiatrist Henry Maudsley (1880) presents a classification of criminal types that allows for the consideration of the root of criminality. His first class includes individuals "who, not being really criminally disposed, have fallen in consequence of the extraordinary pressure of exceptionally adverse circumstances" (104). Mr. Freeze falls under this category in the episode "Heart of Ice" (Dini 1992a) in *Batman: The Animated Series*. Gothcorp researcher Victor Fries cryogenically froze his terminally ill wife Nora to buy time to find a cure for her. A surveillance tape shows, after Fries's research funding was cut, the CEO, Boyle, demanding that the freezing chamber be disconnected. Fries, taking desperate measures to protect his wife, grabs a security guard's gun and points it at Boyle, crying, "Stay away from her! Murderer!" When Fries lowers the weapon in submission to talk, Boyle kicks Fries into a table of chemicals. The final image of the tape shows Fries's hands sliding across the glass of the chamber as he cries, "Nora! Nora!" Mr. Freeze, the legendary supervillain, emerges from the event. Fries turns supervillain specifically as a result of extreme circumstance. In fact, his desperation is the result of deep love for his wife. Aligned with Maudsley's description, Fries is not a criminal by nature but transforms due to this experience. He seems a good man with noble intentions but suffers a great loss, which reorients his moral compass.

Many of Gotham's criminals do not show a good side turned bad. Instead, they may fit Maudsley's (1880) other classifications. His second class of criminals are "those who, having some degree of criminal disposition, might still have been saved from crime had they had the advantages of a fair education and of propitious conditions of life, instead of the disadvantages of an evil education and of criminal surroundings" (104). These are the circumstances that Batman finds in the slums in *Batman* #3 (Finger and Kane 1940e), in Crime Alley in

Batman #408 (Collins and Andru 1987) and #409 (Collins and Warner 1987), and in the project the Narrows in *Batman* Vol. 2 #44 (Snyder, Azzarello, and Jock 2015). In each of these locations, children are at risk for falling victim to its criminal influences. Batman's positive influence on the boys who live in these rough sections of Gotham aims to remove them from the corrupt and immoral influences stemming from the city's innate criminality.

Finally, Maudsley's (1880, 104) third class are "born criminals, whose instincts urge them blindly into criminal activity, whatever their circumstances of life, and whom neither kindness, nor instruction, nor punishment will reform, they returning naturally to crime when their sentences are expired" (104). The repeated lack of success to rehabilitate inmates from Gotham State Penitentiary, Blackgate Penitentiary, or the psychiatric hospital Arkham Asylum demonstrates the inability of reform efforts to quell the innate criminal nature of many of Gotham's criminals and supervillains. Grant Morrison and Dave McKean's (1989) graphic novel *Arkham Asylum: A Serious House on Serious Earth* provides journal entries of Amadeus Arkham, the institution's creator. In one entry, Arkham writes, "Madness is born in the blood. It is my birthright." Referring to madness as a birthright suggests privilege in being born mad. The hospital's architect understands madness because he suffers from it himself. Unfortunately, his institution repeatedly fails to rehabilitate its patients. In Paul Dini and Bruce Timm's (1994a) *Batman Adventures: Mad Love*, a flashback shows psychologist Dr. Harleen Quinzel acquire a job at Arkham. As she holds therapy sessions with the Joker, she gradually falls in love with him. By the end of several weeks, Dr. Quinzel ends up on the couch while the Joker sits in the chair with pencil and pad in hand, illustrating a doctor-patient role reversal. Dr. Quinzel's love for the Joker causes her to break the Joker out of Arkham and join him on his criminal escapades under the name Harley Quinn. Arguably, Harley may have been born of circumstances rather than innate propensity; however, Amanda Conner and Jimmy Palmiotti's (2014) *Harley Quinn* series shows an independent Harley who is free of the Joker (and even moves away to New York City) but still driven toward excessive violence, which suggests that she actually may have an innate compulsion for violence and chaos. The Joker, I argue, is the epitome of a born criminal because the franchise repeatedly refuses to canonize an origin story, allowing the Joker as criminal to be an association that always already exists in any iteration of his character (or at least is expected to emerge in the instances where an origination is offered). The therapy efforts for the Joker fail to rehabilitate him and, instead, actually create a new supervillain (Harley Quinn). Even Batman does not feel that Arkham can successfully rehabilitate its patients. In *Arkham Asylum* he says, "It's hard to imagine this place being conducive to **anyone's** mental health" (Morrison and McKean 1989). Arkham is merely a confined space for holding the chaos that typically runs loose throughout Gotham City.

Inmates frequently escape from or take control of Arkham Asylum, Blackgate Penitentiary, and Gotham State Penitentiary throughout the franchise. In *Batman* #400 (Moench 1986), Ra's al Ghul orchestrates a massive breakout of both Gotham State and Arkham. In *Detective Comics* #489 (Kupperberg and Novick 1980), the prisoners at Gotham State start a riot and take over the facility. The spaces intended for discipline cannot control the chaos inherent to the criminals that they hold—but neither can Gotham City. In *Arkham Asylum*, when Batman and the Joker part ways, leaving Arkham, the Joker says, "Enjoy yourself out there. In the asylum. Just don't forget—if it ever gets too tough … there's always a place for you here [at Arkham]" (Morrison and McKean 1989). The Joker perceives that Gotham City houses madness rather than the asylum. The video game *Arkham City* (Warner Bros. Interactive Entertainment 2011) literalizes the Joker's comment, as it presents Gotham City as a madhouse by enclosing supervillains and criminals within designated parts of the city. Neither the city nor the disciplinary institutions can rehab their criminals. They are an extension of Gotham's depravity and necessary to the continuation of the franchise.

Maudsley (1880) argues that committing crime, for the third class, is instinctual, whereas criminal behavior for the first two classes is related to environmental influence. An urban setting festering with criminality, like Gotham City, effectively combines Maudsley's distinctions as it is a city that is an organism capable of breeding criminals. Not only is there an effect of environmental influences, but when authors use rhetoric that gives the city organic agency, a blurred distinction between biologically and environmentally inherited traits also develops. The Joker perceives this somewhat lucidly in *The*

Dark Knight (Nolan 2008) when he wants to show that "even the best of us" are corruptible. The Joker says to Batman about the people of Gotham: "See, their morals, their code, it's a bad joke dropped at the first sign of trouble. They're only as good as the world allows them to be. I'll show ya. When the chips are down, these, uh, these civilized people, they'll eat each other. See I'm not a monster. I'm just ahead of the curve." The Joker acknowledges the organic agency of the environment in maintaining a particular state and his role in facilitating moral decline.

The fictional city may be viewed as a character with prescribed agency that is a construct of particular times, but the development of Gotham City and its subsequent relationships with its characters allow it to maintain its nature of cyclical depravity well beyond physical publication or theatrical release. In a rare glimpse at the conception of Gotham City, "The Destroyer" miniseries shows Gotham City inspired by Bruce Wayne's ancestor, Justice Solomon Wayne, as a space designed to keep crime out. He argues, "For what *is* a city, gentlemen? A sanctuary! A stronghold! A fortress! A bulwark against the godlessness of the wilds—wherein we may nurture the gifts of Christian civilization—and be protected from all the savagery which lurks in untamed nature" (O'Neil and Sprouse 1992). Solomon seeks protection from the rampant immorality and criminality that exist in the natural world. Evil preexists the city as an inherent part of the ground that Gotham is ultimately built upon. Solomon hires architect Cyrus Pinkney, who shares his vision, viewing "Gotham as an organic whole—almost a living being that would itself fight against evil" (Grant and Aparo 1992). Pinkney ascribes life and agency to the city; however, the Gotham City that evolves from this original conception actually encourages evil rather than dispelling it. Its organic nature is grim and corrupt; therefore, it cannot serve as a fortress. Instead, the city becomes a space that encourages depravity, deviance, and destruction because it prefers to be a criminal breeding ground rather than a sanctuary. Gotham's agentive status and its ability to resist being known also make it a dangerous space. In "The Court of Owls" story arc, Harvey Bullock says, "When it comes to Gotham, you don't know it, brother. It knows you. And the moment you think otherwise, the moment you get too comfortable … that's when it stabs you right in the back" (Snyder and Capullo 2011). Gotham's foul mystique is maintained by its unpredictability and fluctuating condition, which is especially visible when considering collected works within the multiverse. The city cannot be trusted or truly known, especially through varying depictions, as it is an agent of chaos, an infernal organism that perpetually breeds criminality.

In 2006, DC offered an alternate explanation of Gotham's criminal nature. The series *Shadowpact* introduces Dr. Gotham, an evil warlock living underground, below the city, who believes his spirit has influenced Gotham's criminal condition (Willingham and Scott 2006). This plot further blurs origin certainty while suggesting that a supervillain supernaturally influenced the city's criminal nature. It offers an explanation for the city's consistently depraved condition and the feasibility for the frequent creation and resurgence of criminals and supervillains. In Azzarello and Bermejo's (2008) graphic novel *Joker*, the Joker is repeatedly described as a carrier of a communicable disease: "One that has been around longer than Gotham, the city infected. A disease that's older than any city. Hell, it's probably the same disease that built the first one." Suggesting that cities spawn from infection, *Joker* argues that evil preexists physical infrastructure. Additionally, presenting the supervillain as a carrier further establishes the relationship between setting and character and the way in which a supervillain may provide for the city by propagating its depravity. In Mark Sable and Jesus Saiz's (2009) "Two-Face: Year One," the police commissioner says, "Vice is a part of Gotham." While *Shadowpact* offers its backstory of Gotham City to counter the idea of spontaneous evil, here, the police commissioner's observation is applicable to all representations of Gotham City, whether its villainy is explained or not. The city cannot be without its criminals; they are a part of its iconic sustainability.

Sociologist Émile Durkheim ([1895] 2014) argues from a social perspective that crime is normal and that society needs criminals because crime actually clarifies moral boundaries. Crime, for Durkheim, is "an integrative element in any healthy society" because criminals will allow society to morally progress (61). Following a Durkheimian perspective allows us to accept the normality of urban crime. However, in the Batman franchise, there is not necessarily a moral agenda at stake. Crime is normal because it is intrinsic to the corrupt condition of the city and because the franchise needs it.

Even though the "good guys" may unite in their attempts to combat evil, the city's wanton agenda does not actually encourage morality. It allows for good to fight evil so the evil cannot have excessive power and completely destroy the city, but it also encourages miscreant resurgence to preserve its depravity. Regarding Burton's (1992) *Batman Returns*, Julie Salamon (1992, A14) says, "Evil is simply part of the fun house," suggesting that Gotham City is a space that contains evil as part of its intrinsic makeup. Gotham City regarded as a carnival speaks to Mikhail Bakhtin's (1984) analysis of the degradation made visible through grotesque realism, which "knows no other lower level; it is the fruitful earth and the womb. It is always conceiving" (21).[1] Such a condition and Batman's inability to completely eradicate crime allows the supervillains to repeatedly come back to unleash new destructive machinations and further fuel the franchise.

Contrary to Durkheim's ([1895] 2014) theories that deviance promotes positive social change in real cities, society does not progress in Gotham City so much as it maintains a status quo. In "The Night of the Owls" story arc in *Birds of Prey*, the Talon remarks that from 1842 to the present day, "Gotham's streets are the same. The blood flows in the gutters just the same. The crimes, the wicked acts, the atrocities … all the same" (Swierczynski and Foreman 2012). The static nature is largely due to the criminals who maintain the city's depraved status. The reader/audience has expectations for crime in Gotham, knowing that the criminals and supervillains will perpetuate crime and devastation in the city.

While the city breeds criminals to satisfy a need for crime, in offering a space for criminal activity and the fulfillment of passionate impulses, the city provides the criminal with the means for pleasure. Thus, a mutualistic relationship exists between the criminal and the metropolis that has hedonistic and often sadistic underpinnings. In *The Dark Knight* (Nolan 2008), Alfred tells Bruce a story from his past about a thief who stole jewels and threw them away "because he thought it was good sport, because some men aren't looking for anything logical like money. They can't be bought, bullied, reasoned, or negotiated with. Some men just want to watch the world burn." Many of Gotham City's criminals and supervillains take sadistic pleasure in causing destruction. When this occurs, materialist motivations cannot be applied. Enjoyment is the unrestrained motivator, and pleasure proves to be satisfied by the feasibility for criminal activity in the city. Later in the film, the officer guarding the Joker's cell says to him, "I know the difference between punks who need a little lesson in manners and the freaks like you who just enjoy it" (Nolan 2008). The officer is aware that the Joker cannot be disciplined because his criminality is the result of passion fulfillment. He is not just uncivilized but enjoys being uncivilized, and, therefore, he is difficult if not impossible to tame. Gotham City, which rejects discipline, offers the Joker a space to fulfill his criminalistic sadism.

The root of the mutualistic relationship between criminal and city provides the nexus of birth/generation and regeneration. Jimmy Stamp (2009) questions the nature of urban crime and, in doing so, suggests that it is indiscernible: "So what came first, the city or the crime? the hero or the villain? The architect or the city?" The cycling of supervillains in the city prevents linear reduction and suggests that both always already exist. The city may breed criminals, but that is only to maintain urban crime. Architectural questions may be raised as to whether the city were built to prevent existing criminal behavior or whether the city's layout actually encourages crime. Certainly Solomon Wayne, in conceiving Gotham City, intended for a space free from criminal activity, but Gotham became a breeding ground for criminals and supervillains.

Ambiguous criminal origination occurs as well, especially with the Joker's character, ultimately suggesting that backstory narrative does not matter so long as he serves his purpose of perpetuating crime and causing devastation in Gotham City. Because of different continuities and the various origin stories of supervillains that are frequently rewritten and reimagined, we cannot actually pinpoint the roots of their criminality either. The Joker's backstory in Alan Moore and Brian Bolland's ([1988] 2008) graphic novel *The Killing Joke* suggests that a combination of family tragedy and a chemical reaction turned a regular man into a crazed supervillain. In providing an origin story, the novel presents "the attempt to make sense out of a senseless world" (Phillips and Strobl 2013, 35). An ordinary citizen became the Joker in this context because he felt betrayed by the world and lost his sense of place within it. Peter Coogan (2006, 87) argues along a similar line of thinking: "For the Joker, the mania that drives the supervillain is a reasonable and understandable reaction to the universe—it is an attempt to impose meaning on the void, a god-like act emerging out of an ego folded in on itself in an attempt to defend its sovereignty against injury." However, in *The Killing Joke*, though the Joker remembers what "made" him what he is, he says, "Sometimes I remember it one way, sometimes another ... If I'm going to have a past, I prefer it to be multiple choice!" (Moore and Bolland [1988] 2008). This admission may nullify the provided backstory. If the backstory panels have been read as the Joker's memory (the faded colors do suggest flashback), then with this comment, the Joker has duped readers who believe that the memories are his actual past. If the memories are not actual memories, then we cannot know the Joker's true motivation to become a supervillain. There is no longer a meaningful explanation, and therefore, the Joker's relationship to his environment is unclear. Nolan (2008) also does not provide his Joker with clear origins in *The Dark Knight*. The Joker's facial scars serve as physical indicators of a past event that he repeatedly refers to, but he tells several different stories about the cause of his scars. The film suggests that the truth of the Joker's origins does not matter. As the most iconic Batman villain, the Joker always already exists in the minds of the audience as an intrinsic part of Gotham City.

The Joker in *The Dark Knight* cannot be easily defined, and a lack of origin story makes it harder to rationalize his actions. Anthony J. Kolenic (2009, 1025) argues, "The Joker denies a narrative or an easily identifiable defect to blame for the creation of his identity. Instead, the film turns the conflict between order and chaos back on the audience by keeping the Joker anonymous, and by keeping him anything but neutralized." The Joker merely exists and foils any attempt for anyone, including the audience, to really know who he is. For Eric Garneau (2015, 34), "the Joker depends on having a mutable identity, one full of 'blurred borderlines' that ignore 'chronology and sequence.'" Kolenic (2009, 1027) also observes that *The Dark Knight*'s Joker, with his clown makeup, is "alluding to an identity behind an identity that is covered and inaccessible." In his first appearance in the film, the Joker wears a clown mask over his makeup, adding another layer to his intangible identity where "under the surface there's only more Joker" (Langley 2012, 22). Likewise, in the New 52 reboot, the Joker invites the Dollmaker to cut off the skin of his face and then proceeds to wear it as a mask (Daniel and Winn 2011). Since his own actual face becomes a mask, there is no way of truly knowing the Joker. Clown masks also serve as a symbol of protest against the wealthy in Todd Phillips's (2019) film *Joker*. This film provides the iconic supervillain with an origin story as Arthur Fleck (Joaquin Phoenix) and suggests that the Joker's supervillainy emerges out of a combination of mental disorder and a resurgence of childhood trauma. However, as in *The Killing Joke*, even the audience cannot be certain what they see is real. Several scenes end up being delusions imagined in Arthur's mind. While refuted by documented paperwork, the notion that Arthur could be Thomas Wayne's biological son suggests that the Wayne genes contain strong dispositional power. *Joker* reminds us that while we crave explanation, the root of supervillainy is not always clearly definable.

When identity is in flux, the supervillains become unpredictable and uncontrollable. But at the same time, they are always recognizable to the audience. The audience knows certain accepted rules about the supervillains, especially physical characteristics that tend to be maintained through different iterations in the franchise. Even with that consistency, part of the appeal of the supervillains is their unpredictable behavior. Paul Dini, a writer for *Batman: The Animated Series*, feels that for the Joker, the show "struck a nice balance between the clown and the killer" ("Batman: The Legacy Continues" 2005). Since neither the clown nor the killer can be completely knowable, the Joker remains a mystery. The audience expects his volatility, but his behaviors are not bound or controlled by any particular code of conduct.

Criminal Types

Within the Batman franchise, the rogues make visible and exacerbate real-world anxieties. While they may be colorful, gimmicky, and exaggerated versions of petty criminals, supervillains also allow for analysis of the root of criminality. Nickie D. Phillips and Staci Strobl (2013, 83) argue, "Villains become important cultural artifacts in understanding popular ideas about why individuals engage in criminal behavior." Likewise, Marc DiPaolo (2011) tracks the changes in the

Joker throughout multiple iterations in different media. He likens the early Joker of the 1940s to a violent "Moriarty figure," who, in the 1950s and 1960s, "softened into a Mad Hatteresque figure" (59). Then, in the 1970s and 1980s, "the Joker was re-imagined ... in response to the emergence of celebrity serial killers such as Charles Manson and the Zodiac Killer" (60). The Joker appears to shift with the changing conditions of the real world. DiPaolo describes the Joker of *The Dark Knight* (Heath Ledger) as more "realistic" than Jack Nicholson's version in *Batman* (60). Ledger's Joker has also been literalized in comparison to real-world criminality. The 2009 Jokerized Bernie Madoff cover of *New York Magazine* demonstrates the ways in which fiction and culture regularly bleed into one another and how the supervillain figure is reflective of real-world anxieties regarding corruption. Supervillains fuel the metropolis through their constant surges of bedlam. DiPaolo (2011, 60) describes Ledger's Joker as "more of a force of nature than a mere man—an agent of chaos." As "a force of nature," the Joker embodies an essence of chaos provided by Gotham City. Disorder and disruption are the norm in the city, and the Joker is the epitome of controlled chaos.

The supervillains of Gotham range from those who want to enact social or political change (Anarky, the Court of Owls, etc.) to those who have physical deformations (Killer Croc, Man-Bat, Mr. Freeze, etc.) to those who just seem to find pleasure in crime (the Joker, the Riddler, etc.). Terrorism also plagues Gotham, as Bane, Ra's al Ghul, and the League of Assassins all believe that cleansing is an effective way to eliminate that which they dislike in the city. In *Batman Begins* (Nolan 2005), Ra's al Ghul (Liam Neeson) says, "Crime. Despair. This is not how man was supposed to live. The League of Shadows has been a check against human corruption for thousands of years. We sacked Rome, loaded tradeships with plague rats, burned London to the ground. Every time a civilization reaches the pinnacle of its decadence, we return to restore the balance." Ra's orchestrates the release of a toxin that puts the citizens into irrational panic so they will destroy themselves, which he thinks will allow for the city to be reborn void of criminality and depravity. However, his plan would purge the city of both criminals and innocent people, making his restoration plan an act of terroristic liquidation. Phillips and Strobl (2013, 78) find such actions common in comic books, where "this cycle of cleansing in order to save is reflective of apocalypticism." They further observe that such "nihilistic solutions, such as those perpetuated by comic supervillains, echo the tactics of real-life cults and terrorist groups" (78). *Batman Begins* was released in 2005, which was during a time where post-9/11 anxieties ran high in America. The anthrax attacks, which occurred one week after 9/11, perpetuated fears of bioterrorism. Letters with anthrax spores were mailed to journalists and politicians, resulting in thirty thousand people at risk of exposure, twenty-two infected individuals, and five deaths. This incident caused the US government to drastically increase its spending on biodefense: "The NIAID [National Institute of Allergy and Infectious Diseases] budget for biodefense research has grown from $200 million in 2001 to an annual average of $1.6 billion since 2004" (Cole 2012). The anthrax attacks illustrate the dangers of widespread exposure and contamination to a chemical threat that *Batman Begins* again brings to the audience's attention to demonstrate the constant need for protection against bioterrorism.

Pathological terrorism allows Gotham to remain in an apocalyptic state that is fueled by its criminals and the devastation that they create. In the 1996 "Contagion" story arc, the Order of St. Dumas infects Gotham with a rapidly mutating, deadly strain of the Ebola virus. No one is allowed to leave Gotham, which results in the inhabitants panicking and rioting. In its 1996 sequel series, "Legacy," Gotham is threatened by the return of the plague. In both cases, the virus is brought into the city by a bioterrorist trying to commit widespread destruction of human life. The two story arcs demonstrate the instability of the city but not its complete destruction. Commissioner Gordon says, "The mood of the city is ugly. It's ready to plunge back into panic and anarchy at any excuse" (Grant and Taylor 1996). Fear of the plague causes a reversion in behavior because the city's condition is anarchic. Pathology, then, may be viewed as a threat, but the larger threat is that an urban condition where disease runs rampant is normal. This contrasts with Foucauldian theory that "the plague-stricken town ... is the utopia of the perfectly governed city" (Foucault [1975] 1995, 198). Rather, the spread of the disease is also a means for spreading chaos. Strong discipline or control over the abject population does not exist in the apocalyptic environment. Batman's surveillance and vigilantism try to control the criminal population, but the constant resurgence of miscreants thwarts achieving a utopian vision of a "perfectly governed" state. A disciplined and well-ordered environment would disrupt the city's organic criminal nature, which thrives on chaotic forces, such as disease, rather than progress and development.

In the video game *Batman: Arkham Origins* (Warner Bros. Interactive Entertainment 2013), Anarky, a social activist, uses terroristic practices to attempt to cleanse the city, declaring, "Oppressed citizens of Gotham, your cries for help have been heard! I am Anarky—voice of the people—here to save you from the plague of corruption that now infests this once proud city!" Anarky plants three bombs throughout Gotham, one of which he places behind the Gotham City Police Department (GCPD) building. In targeting police officers, Anarky taps into a potential mistrust of law enforcement that has been exacerbated in recent history regarding police brutality. Anarky, then, would serve as the embodiment of some individuals' frustrations with corruption in a criminal justice system that is supposed to protect others. Players could align such a sentiment with media outlets that highlight police brutality—a topic that became widespread through the Rodney King incident of 1991 and has continued to be a part of media conversation today.

Gotham City also notoriously houses several corrupt mayors and policemen. In Miller and Mazzucchelli's ([1987] 2005) *Batman: Year One*, Police Commissioner Gillian B. Loeb has ties to mafia boss Carmine Falcone, bribes James Gordon, and arranges for the kidnapping of Gordon's infant son. Internal corruption helps fuel the depravity of the city from all areas. This is especially dangerous when it involves individuals who have pledged to uphold the law. Likewise, those involved with political corruption encourage distrust or at least wariness of government. In *Detective Comics* #472 (Englehart and Rogers 1977), Rupert Thorne, a corrupt Gotham City councilman, makes it his mission to uncover Batman's identity with no regard to the cost of such efforts, including murdering Hugo Strange. Another example of political corruption is seen in "No Man's Land" when Lex Luthor, using his political power, contrives a criminal plot to take over Gotham City.[2] A quest for land acquisition and control serves to be a driving motivator for Luthor, who puts on the front of philanthropically helping with the recovery process of the city. Luthor's potential takeover of the city demonstrates the expanse that a villain's reach can extend. In Gotham City, those whom the city's citizens entrust to maintain order and keep them safe cannot always be trusted. As reflective of urban America, Gotham City suggests a level of mistrust that Americans may have of those who hold power. At the very least, the comics show the feasibility of corruption and the effects of such behaviors.

Sutherland's (1940) theories of criminal activity and differential association posit that crime is learned behavior. He suggests that crime is learned through communication and "within intimate personal groups." His theory of differential association argues, "Crime is rooted in the social organization and is an expression of that social organization." Thus, crime can be learned behavior through the social interactions with other criminals. Gotham provides ample opportunity for such interactions and associations. Even Gotham's authority figures encourage putting people in situations that foster criminal behavior. In "Legacy," a city councilman advocates for quarantining all those who could become reinfected with the Ebola virus. The mayor says such a suggestion would be putting sick people in "prison camps." Gordon responds that such an environment would be detrimental to humanity: "I know **crime** better than almost any man in this city. **Criminalize** people, and they'll **act** like criminals. **Tell** them they're killers, they'll **become** killers" (Grant and Taylor 1996). Thus, innocent individuals may turn to crime through spatial positioning. Gordon externalizes criminal culpability on space and systems rather than individuals. He sees how people in Gotham City may be corrupted as a result of the edicts put in place by decision makers. Quarantine could turn the space into a crime- and disease-infested area. For Sutherland (1940, 6), "when persons become criminal, they do so because of contacts with criminal patterns and also because of isolation from anti-criminal patterns." Gordon's position follows this theory, as his experiences have shown that individuals can be criminalized when forced into such dire situations. This argument would not align with an innate propensity toward crime; but I argue that Gotham City, as an organic environment, fosters criminal behavior and the spawn of criminals. Gotham enables differential association to occur.

The councilman's suggestion for quarantine and Gordon's response foreshadow the events of "No Man's Land." After the US government has abandoned Gotham City, gang violence runs rampant in the city, and individuals and groups battle for territory. The inhabitants look to gain power and control by acquiring physical space. Gangs establish a system of rule and relegate commodity distribution within their territories. Throughout the Batman franchise, gang violence aggravates opportunities for peace in the city. Such groups include the Mutants, the Gorilla Gang, the Red Hood Gang, the Royal Flush Gang, the Wonderland Gang, and others. The gangs have their own gimmicks or costumes that make them recognizable, and they terrorize the city to fulfill particular agendas for power or control. In Miller and Janson's ([1986] 2002) *The Dark Knight Returns*, the Mutants' leader says, "Don't call us a gang. Don't call us criminals. We are the law. We are the future. Gotham City belongs to the Mutants. Soon the world will be ours." Though made up of teenagers, this gang uses crime and murder to stake their claim of spatial dominance. They see their version of law as the way of the future. Like Lex Luthor in "No Man's Land," they want to own the city. Criminals in Gotham clearly have a strong relationship with the city. They are fueled by their environment and assume that in controlling Gotham, they will be unstoppable. The city enables and even encourages the gangs because they contribute to its depravity, which allows the cyclical nature of both the city's condition (from destruction to temporary restoration to devastation again) and criminal activity (as Batman defeats one threat, a new one emerges). Batman and friends will never allow for Gotham to be completely overrun or destroyed, but the franchise will never allow Gotham to be completely restored or crime-free either.

Gotham's organized criminals, including Black Mask, Sal Maroni, Carmine Falcone, Rex Calsbrese, Squid, Erin McKillen, and Tony Zucco, are another intrinsic part of Gotham City as they often infiltrate various power and political structures and network with other types of rogues, including petty criminals and supervillains. Often overshadowed by the supervillains who have flashy or gimmicky qualities, the organized criminals are a significant threat to the city. Since they can manipulate police officers and politicians, they gain power and influence over the city's authority systems. The organized criminals' collusion with supervillains gives them an additional advantage and allows them to act on their criminal agendas with the help of powerful resources. Gotham's members of the underworld are sprinkled throughout the franchise as adversaries for Batman and Robin to face. Part of their threat includes the potential for wars between organized crime syndicates. In *Batman* #212 (Robbins and Novick 1969b), Batman and Robin work to prevent a mob war from breaking out after a hit is placed on Mr. Big. *Detective Comics* #392 (Robbins and Brown 1969) brings mobsters Scap Scarpel and Angles Moore to plot to take over Gotham after they think Angles killed Batman. The inclusion of such criminals has been historically relevant. Wars between organized criminal syndicates occurred in America in the 1960s. The Gallo/Profaci War in New York City in the early 1960s, the Coonan/Spillane War in New York City in 1966, and the Killeen/Mullen gang war in Boston in 1969 are a few examples of the historical battles between gangsters in America. In 1970, the Racketeer Influenced and Corrupt Organizations (RICO) Act was passed as part of the Organized Crime Control Act to strike against racketeering within organized crime groups. But the gangsters continue to plague Gotham both in the comics and on screen, creating continuous opportunities to intensify the underbelly of Gotham City.

Even Gotham's petty criminals may be just as impactful as its mafia dons and supervillains. When Joe Chill murders Thomas and Martha Wayne, he inadvertently creates Batman. The petty criminals also contribute to the persistent decay of the city. Gothic imaginings of the city, in particular, use "the desolate-to-threatening Gotham scene" (Uricchio 2010, 123) to breed its various criminal types. In Nolan's (2005) *Batman Begins*, Rachel exposes Bruce to the state of the crime in Gotham where organized criminals create petty criminals who then further contribute to the decay of the city. The base of Gotham rots from within, illustrating a link between criminal types and also class and crime. To fix such conditions, widespread social change is needed.

Gotham City itself is a living organism that can breed criminal offspring to maintain its perpetual, but never realized, state of decline. Susan M. Bernardo (1994, 17) uses similar rhetoric in describing the people of Gotham in Burton's (1992) *Batman Returns*: "Like their society, they know no way to deal with that which has become noxious except to throw it out. They wish to forget that this noxious thing came from them, is their offspring, their 'product.' " Those who have been rejected in the film, like Selina Kyle and Oswald Cobblepot, become supervillains Catwoman and the Penguin, respectively. Selina's boss pushes her out of a window, intending for her to plummet to her death, and when Oswald was a baby, his parents put him in a basket and set it flowing through the sewer systems. Instead of dying, these two individuals are reborn as supervillains, their new identities sprung from their social and familial rejection.

Gotham City serves as a space that fosters the generation and regeneration of supervillains, as it (in some unconfirmed way) created the Joker, who creates additional supervillains, like Two-Face, according to the Nolan franchise, and Harley Quinn.[3] Many of the supervillains of Gotham City have physical deformities (Killer Croc, Man-Bat, Mr. Freeze, etc.) that enhance their villainy and evil natures. In pre-New 52 Batman continuities, Sal Maroni throws acid at Harvey Dent's face, which causes his disfigurement. Dent, who had always defended his city, is now corrupted by it. Organized criminals maintain their own order in Gotham and then physically create the disfigured supervillain Two-Face, whose internal moral ambiguity is made visible as a result. Dent inherits criminality, then, from Gotham City's criminals, who inherit it from the city's perpetually depraved condition.

The Joker finds pleasure in trying to corrupt individuals in Gotham City. In Nolan's (2008) *The Dark Knight*, when the Joker says, "This town deserves a better class of criminal. And I'm going to give it to them," he asserts the city's prerogative for a particular criminal type. He feels confident that he knows the needs of the city and wants to fulfill that role. The Joker does not desire to destroy Gotham like some of the other supervillains, which facilitates his frequent resurgence in the Batman franchise. For the Joker, crime is a game that Gotham City encourages him to play since he can move through the city seamlessly, and he knows that Batman will always chase him. The Joker in both *The Dark Knight* and Moore and Bolland's ([1988] 2008) *The Killing Joke* is actually more concerned with corrupting individuals than destroying Gotham City. In *The Dark Knight*, he successfully contributes to Harvey Dent's conversion to murderer. *The Killing Joke* includes a Joker who tries to drive Gordon mad with naked pictures of his gravely wounded daughter. The Joker enjoys the challenge because he assumes that he understands human behavior. His criminal aspirations are not cataclysmically motivated; rather, he desires to drive individuals to moral breaking points.

In the comics, the Joker uses Joker venom as a frequent weapon of choice to cause uncontrollable laughter and death to his targets whose corpses bear a Joker grin.[4] In Chuck Dixon and Scott Beatty's ([2001–2] 2008) miniseries *Joker: Last Laugh*, the Joker uses his venom to Jokerize other supervillains. By creating living replicas, the Joker can infiltrate deeper into the city and orchestrate grander schemes. The Jokerized body becomes both an extension of the Joker's criminal power and a visible calling card at a murder scene. It also suggests that anyone can be a Joker. Thus, any citizen of Gotham can be corrupted.

With fluctuating identities, supervillains thrive best in a chaotic environment that they also help maintain through creating disorder and violence. In "Two-Face: Year One" (Sable and Saiz 2009, the police commissioner says, "Say what you want about the mob, but they have a *code*. They maintain *order*. But this new breed of criminal that's plaguing us since this *Batman* showed up? They bring out nothing but *chaos* and *madness*." Gotham City's mafia is more appealing to the commissioner because despite the crime, the mob is more controlled and organized than the supervillains, who he implies came into existence due to Batman. The supervillains who lack such a code as the mafia are larger threats because their activities are chaotic and unpredictable. Ironically, the commissioner does not acknowledge that Batman may be best equipped to battle the perpetrators. Batman is accused of instigating the arrival of these rogues, but he is the only one who can defeat them—a cyclical pattern that perpetuates the franchise.

In Nolan's (2008) *The Dark Knight*, the Joker explains his view of the world to Harvey Dent, revealing a methodology that he tries to mask by seeming to be a pure agent of chaos:

> Do I really look like a guy with a plan? You know what I am, I'm a dog chasing cars. I wouldn't know what to do with one if I caught it. You know, I just do things. The mob has plans. The cops have plans. Gordon's got plans. You know, they're schemers. Schemers trying to control their little worlds. I'm not a schemer. I try to show the schemers how pathetic their attempts to control things really are ... Nobody panics when things go according to "plan." Even if the plan's horrifying. If tomorrow I tell the press that like a

gangbanger will get shot, or a truckload of soldiers will be blown up, nobody panics because it's all part of the plan. But when I say that one, little old mayor will die, well then everyone loses their minds. Introduce a little anarchy, upset the established order, and everything becomes chaos. I'm an agent of chaos.

Because chaos is required by Gotham City, the Joker can function as an agent of chaos. Yet his agency allows his chaos to be crafted and planned. Despite his denial of such, the Joker has a very systematic approach to his plans. Langley (2012, 23) notes, "He uses order to sow chaos, developing well-orchestrated plans to foster anarchy." In this scene, the Joker claims he does not have plans and prides himself on evoking chaos while criticizing the established order. He also criticizes the hypocrisy of a system that can create the perception that a murder or explosion is acceptable if the victim(s) is disposable, exposing the selectiveness of perceived order and control. The Joker is very perceptive to how Gotham's social and even philosophical infrastructure is maintained. Kolenic (2009, 1031) observes that the Joker's chaos contrasts with the established order: "Clearly he aligns chaos with a brand of fairness, altruism, and purity as an alternative to this institutionality, which somehow makes it right and without alternative in his mind." The Joker rationalizes his behavior, which proves that it is not merely random violence. The Joker is also aware of the source of his power when he says to Dent, "Oh and you know the thing about chaos—it's fear" (Nolan 2008). Fear creates chaos, which creates more fear; thus, chaos cycles through and fuels Gotham City through a crazed criminal's exploits.

Vigilantism versus Superheroism

The supervillains and other criminals have agendas that aim to terrorize, destroy, or corrupt the people of Gotham City, while Batman aims to subvert all criminals in order to protect and defend the people of Gotham. However, the only way he can do so is by resorting to his own means, which are often not within the law. Golden Age Batman killed criminals readily—such as in *Detective Comics* #30 (Fox, Kane, and Moldoff 1939a) where Batman snaps a criminal's neck with his foot. But for the majority of his existence, he has refrained from killing—the one caveat that he can argue positions him as morally superior to the criminals that he chases and captures. Still, Batman may be accused of breaking and entering, assault, child endangerment, and other crimes. He even admits to his lawbreaking in *Red Hood and the Outlaws* Vol. 2 #6 (Lobdell and Soy 2017). Jason Todd accuses Batman's "way" as following law and order. To this, Batman starts laughing and simplifies his methods as follows: "I break into private property without a warrant and beat people up. Almost every night." Batman does not try here to defend his ways as being within the law but as essentially disregarding the law.

Batman's law-breaking and -bending raises the question as to how one can be defined as a crime fighter. He is referred to as both a vigilante and a superhero, but can he truly be deemed as both? Scholars of vigilantism have found that the term is difficult to conceptualize. Eduardo Moncada (2017, 408) argues that vigilantism in the real world is typically "a group activity" and defines the term as "the collective use or threat of extra-legal violence in response to an alleged criminal act." Nicole E. Haas, Jan W. de Keijser, and Gerben J. N. Bruinsma (2012, 390) define vigilantism as "a planned criminal act, carried out by a private citizen in response to (the perceived threat of) a crime committed by a private citizen, targeting the (alleged) perpetrator of that crime." Moncado and Haas et al.'s definitions posit vigilantism as reactionary. For Stephanie Juliano (2012, 46), "a vigilante is someone who breaks the law … in favour and/or pursuit of some form of personal justice." This explanation forgoes a specification of criminal behavior in response to crime and, instead, sees crime as enacted to achieve a larger social goal—justice. Juliano further describes the difference between vigilantes and criminals: "Criminals have no passion to achieve justice" (48). Certainly, Batman could fall under this definition as his motivation is for justice. Regarding the Batman of the 1990s under Denny O'Neil, Glen Weldon (2016, 196) finds, "His goal isn't attainable vengeance, but something that will forever lie just beyond his reach: justice." Looking back to early issues, Batman uses different language. In his original origin story in *Detective Comics* #33 (Finger et al. 1939), Batman makes his vow: "I swear by the spirits of my parents to avenge their deaths by spending the rest of my life warring on all criminals." In *Detective Comics* #38 (Finger and Kane

1940f), Batman has Dick Grayson take this oath: "And swear that we two will fight together against crime and corruption and never swerve from the path of righteousness!" In both cases, Batman separates himself from criminals based on the purpose of his plight. Ironically, though, "the path of righteousness" has become a path of resistance against the legal boundaries that would deter success in catching criminals.

Batman's interpretation of justice does not align with the law. He opposes such restraints because his definition of justice outweighs the criminal justice system. Over the years, the Bat Family has grown to include several superhero-vigilantes following Batman's philosophy and modeling his methodology. Within Edwin H. Sutherland's (1940, 6) breakdown of his theory of differential association, he argues, "In some societies an individual is surrounded by persons who invariably define the legal codes as rules to be observed, while in others he is surrounded by persons whose definitions are favorable to the violation of legal codes." Batman has become the definer of the vigilante code in Gotham City and gains followers—or family members—who act accordingly. Batman directly influences and models their learned criminal behavior, especially the several young, malleable Robins. Though Batman steers Jason Todd and Damian Wayne away from street crime and murder, respectively, the boys' relationship with Batman brings them to associate and adapt their behavior to his kind of crimes.

Scholars have discussed the problematics of conceptualizing the term "vigilante," as a variety of definitions have been offered over time without consensus. If scholars of crime disagree on aspects of the definition, then we should turn to definitions within the scope of comics studies. Peter Coogan (2006, 158) calls Batman a "dual-identity crime-fighting avenger-vigilante." He specifies, "Most avenger-vigilantes operate outside legitimate authority and base their actions on their own sense of morality and justice" (147). Batman's moral code and drive for justice both justify his entire existence and behavior. Ironically, Batman "holds himself above the law, despite the fact that he expects everyone else to obey it" (White 2019, 202). In *Batman* #284 (Reed and Tanghal 1977), chief police inspector Maddox chastises Batman for "interfer[ing] with the police and grab[bing] all the glory" after an incident where Batman stopped some criminals.

Batman responds, "I don't work against the police—nor do I work for the police ... or with the police! I work alone!" Maddox commands that Batman "follow department procedures." Batman assumes that by distancing himself from the police, he is free from their rules. But Maddox's demands that Batman follow police protocol are not because Batman broke the rules but because he took away opportunities for the police to be glorified. Maddox wants the police, rather than a vigilante, to be successful, so he tries to bind Batman to the same rules that the GCPD must follow. Batman cannot be bothered with such rules, though. Mark D. White (2019, 208) finds, "Batman embraces his nature as a vigilante to avoid many of the restrictions that official law enforcement has to deal with, and feels that he's more effective as a result." Batman will act according to what he thinks will make him the most successful as a crime fighter—even if that means that he has to become a criminal himself in order to do so.

Despite his noble intentions, Batman's methods remain controversial, especially to those who want to uphold power. For Mike S. Dubose (2007, 922), "Batman is a political liability because his morality is fiercely independent. He only fights those *he* (not the government) believes are wrong and is consequently treated as a vigilante—vigilante being the key term for those who will not fall in line to authority's domination." Dubose's language here implies that the figures of authority may not actually be morally superior. In claiming that they hold "domination," Dubose suggests a power struggle that may not actually be productive or useful but domineering. Batman abides by his own moral code, which threatens those in power because he is more successful than the criminal justice system in bringing down criminals. In *Detective Comics* #647 (Dixon and Lyle 1992), mayor candidate Armand Krol says, "It's this city's shame that a phenomenon like the Batman has arisen. It's not up to some masked vigilante to protect our citizens ... no matter how good his intentions ... no matter how noble his cause." Krol argues that an individual's moral agenda is irrelevant and that Gotham does not need a vigilante when it has other organizations that can serve the people. However, when the authorities are deficient, Batman seems to be the city's best hope.

Even though Batman has faced opposition, he also has garnered support. Katherine Marazi's (2015) definition of real-world vigilantes, specifically in regard to public perception, applies to Batman's existence in the franchise. Marazi looks at the conflicting perceptions that may arise between the authority and the people: "Vigilantes are outcasts of society as they do not act in accordance with government state laws in spite of their logic and motives occasionally being subjectively understood and viewed as acceptable by citizens who may identify with their reasons of action" (69). Throughout the franchise, there have been many occurrences when the people have supported Batman and his efforts. In *Batman* #119 (Finger and Moldoff 1958), a wealthy man builds a museum for honoring Batman and Robin on his island that he has named Batman Island. In *Batman* #126 (Finger and Moldoff 1959), Gotham erects a lighthouse in honor of the Caped Crusader, which the narration calls "a towering tribute to a great lawman." This is quite an ironic description for one who is actually guilty of many crimes, including murder. But Batman is identified and honored as a hero in such examples because he has been a successful protector of Gotham's people.

Commissioner Gordon and Batman have a history of working together, feeding one another information. Gordon accepts Batman because they are morally aligned and both want what is best for the people of the city. In *Batman* #7 (Finger and Kane 1941b), Commissioner Gordon says to a jury about Batman:

> Yes—he works "outside the law" as you call it, but the legal devices that hamper us are hurdled by this crime-fighter so he may bring these men of evil to justice. The eminent district attorney calls him a meddler with a theory—Washington, the Wright brothers, Lincoln, Edison, and others, they were "meddlers" too—who proved their theories. They made sacrifices so that we might enjoy the security and comfort we do. The Batman has done that, too!

Despite his own duty to follow the law, Gordon allows Batman's vigilantism and reiterates his existence as a fighter for justice. In comparing Batman to historical geniuses, Gordon essentially argues that Batman's vigilantism is for the betterment of society at a level beyond the capability of the average man. Gordon adds, "This man who daily risks his life to save others—who never carries a gun—who is aided by his young friend, Robin, fights crime with the courage and zeal born of love for his fellow man." Gordon justifies Batman's actions further as acts of love; in doing so, he admits the law that he has sworn to uphold is actually bendable for those who love man. To make such an argument, Gordon must believe that true criminals—those that Batman helps catch—have no regard for humankind. In this issue, Gordon also appoints Batman an honorary member of the police department even though Batman will not be bound by the department's rules.

Miller and Janson's ([1986] 2002) *The Dark Knight Returns* grapples with how Batman's role in Gotham is publicly identified and either accepted or rejected. A resident describes Batman to a reporter as "a ruthless, monstrous vigilante, striking at the foundations of our democracy—maliciously opposed to the principles that make ours the most noble nation in the world—and the kindest." From this perspective, there cannot be any flexibility with the law despite moral intentions. No one is above the law. In a news report, the Council of Mothers demands Batman's arrest, "citing him as a harmful influence on the children of Gotham" (Miller and Janson [1986] 2002). The fear that Batman will inspire other vigilantes overpowers the potential for Batman to be a positive moral influence. Because Batman has his own code, which allows for violence, he is regarded as a threat. When Ellen Yindel is appointed police commissioner of Gotham, she publicly announces her plans to issue a police warrant against Batman "on the charges of assault, breaking and entering, creating a public hazard ..." (Miller and Janson [1986] 2002). After seeing Robin with him, she later adds child endangerment to the list. Yindel does not feel the same way as Gordon, who found use for Batman in catching the criminals that his department could not. Yindel cannot give leniency to a single citizen's methods despite his successes in bringing down criminals of an arguably worse nature. Her view on the law is firm, and she does not weigh the severity of criminality.

Miller and Janson ([1986] 2002) also show public support for Batman, though, and how the media has become a platform for citizens to argue their case for or against his vigilantism. One individual says to a reporter, "Frankly, I'm surprised there aren't a hundred like him out there—a thousand people are fed up with terror—with stupid laws and social cowardice. He's only taking back what's ours." In this case, the individual does not think there would be a problem with more vigilantes. He views the problems with society and the legal system as bigger than vigilantes breaking the law. Lana Lang, the managing editor of *The Daily Planet*, says, "We live in the shadow of crime, Ted, with the unspoken understanding that we are victims—of fear, of violence, of social impotence. A man has risen to show us that the power is, and always has been, in our hands. We are under siege—he's showing us that we can resist" (Miller and Janson [1986] 2002). Lang views Batman as an inspiration for evoking change. She believes that Batman can give power to the people of Gotham to rise up and overcome Gotham's present conditions.

The public perception of Batman helps shape his identity as well. Some critics have argued that Batman cannot be strictly deemed a vigilante. Neal Curtis (2016, 108) defines superheroes in general as having "sovereign anomie" rather than being defined as antiheroes or vigilantes. For Curtis (2016, 108), "the superhero expresses a profound and deeply important problem in the execution of the law rather than simply stepping outside of it to exact their own version of justice. In effect, if we define this anomie as vigilantism then we fail to understand and continue to disavow the violence committed by a supposedly legitimate and lawful sovereign." This perspective does not place superheroes outside of the law or assume that they redefine their own version of the law. Instead, Curtis gives agency to the superhero. Wolf-Meyer (2006) also does not regard superheroes as simply lawbreakers. He argues, "Superheroes, being able to uphold 'justice' while breaking laws—what would normally be considered vigilantism—must identify themselves as existing in this liminal position of protector, allowing them to uphold the law while simultaneously defying it" (193). However, "protector" is a self-proclaimed position, and the code of protecting is also self-created. Curtis and Wolf-Meyer seem to find flexibility within the world of superheroes to allow these individuals to exist under a separate designation from any other citizens. The acceptance and encouragement of superheroes despite their lawbreaking mean that there is some kind of problem with the criminal justice system.

Throughout the history of the franchise, Batman has been portrayed as an avenger, a righteous fighter, a vigilante, and a defender of justice. Another designation that Batman may fall under is one who aims to revive the condition of Gotham City—or even

America as a whole. Referring to *The Dark Knight Returns* (Miller and Janson [1986] 2002), Richard A. Iadonisi (2013, 79) argues, "The book suggests that [Batman] is the *good* kind of criminal, the kind needed to restore order to the chaos that is America." Ironically, breaking the law is needed to restore order—at least according to the franchise. Batman infiltrates spaces that the GCPD cannot seem to access, and he succeeds in capturing criminals and supervillains, but he never does restore order. The complete restoration of order in Gotham would mean that his existence is no longer needed. The franchise is fueled not entirely by Batman but by the criminals who cannot actually be eradicated and therefore perpetuate his presence and vigilantism in Gotham.

In Nolan's (2008) *The Dark Knight*, Commissioner Gordon and Batman actually realize that Batman needs to assume a different public perception and remove himself from his role as Caped Crusader in order to try to bring peace to the people of the city. At the end of the film, Batman takes the blame for people who Harvey Dent killed (after a mental breakdown) so that the public will not lose hope in the kind of society that Dent previously promoted. Batman tells Gordon to hunt him and condemn him. When Gordon tells his son that they need to chase Batman, his son replies, "He didn't do anything wrong." Gordon explains, "He's the hero that Gotham deserves but not the one it needs right now. So we'll hunt him because he can take it, because he's not a hero; he's a silent guardian, a watchful protector, a dark knight." In this case, Batman's morality supersedes that of the villains. In refusing to kill, Batman positions himself on a superior moral echelon. Ironically, even though, as Gordon's son observes, "he didn't do anything wrong," Batman takes the blame for the murders simply "because he can take it" and sacrifices his moral reputation for the greater good of society. He understands that the people need hope in a symbol and that Harvey Dent's righteous mission and memory can provide that better than he can. Batman must be perceived as a murderer in order to best serve the people of Gotham. Gordon does not define this as heroic—that term is reserved for Dent—but as protecting and guarding the city. In order to best serve Gotham City, Batman needs to assume a false narrative. His conduct is not about justice here but about safeguarding people from truth that will hurt them. Slavoj Žižek (2012) describes Dent as "a kind of official vigilante whose fanatical battle against crime leads to the killing of innocent people and ultimately destroys him." Dent is intended to be the hero the people need because he stays within the law in contrast to Batman. But even Dent cannot uphold this image, as he becomes an actual supervillain. For Žižek (2012), "it is as if Dent were the legal order's reply to the threat posed by Batman: against Batman's vigilantism, the system generates its own illegal excess in a vigilante much more violent than Batman." But Gordon and Batman feel that the public cannot be made aware to Dent's breakdown. They need to hold on to the hope for justice that can occur within the system, not through the methods of a vigilante.

* * *

From corrupted youth to evil doctors, the Batman franchise produces a gamut of criminal types to show that anyone can become a villain. The rogues all have a strong relationship with Gotham City as they strive to gain power and territory and fight to defeat the Bat Family. Crime is normalized in Gotham City, and the recycling of supervillains ensures perpetual threats. The influence of the city, psychological disorders, or just hunger for power all drive individuals to act on their criminalistic impulses, and Gotham provides them the space to attempt to achieve their nefarious agendas. The criminals of Gotham also embody the urban anxieties of the American populace. They serve as visible caricatures of the far reaches of corruption. The criminal methods of the city's superhero and cohorts illustrate the ongoing conflict between law and morality. Thus, Batman treads in between law and order in the liminal space where he can best serve and protect Gotham's people.

Epilogue

As the Batman franchise evolves with the social trends of urban America, we will continue to see ourselves reflected in the people who populate the Dark Knight's city. In the twenty-first century, American politics tend to be greatly tied to the social dynamics and social division of American people. Perhaps Batman can unite conflicting groups in the future and continue to tackle relevant divisive issues, such as immigration, globalization, and the dissemination of news. Social media has also transformed society and allows more ways for direct influence on comic book content. Instead of readers calling a hotline to influence plot, they can tweet. Artists and writers can communicate with fans in this way as well and get immediate feedback.

The Batman multiverse is endlessly expanding and evolving. In October 2019, the CW aired *Batwoman*, a TV series in the Arrowverse based on the *Batwoman* comic book series. At the start of 2020, after Tom King ended his run of *Batman*, a new team, including writer James Tynion IV and artist Tony S. Daniel, took the reins of the series. A new film by Matt Reeves, *The Batman*, is slated to be released in 2022[1] with Robert Pattinson donning the cape and cowl. As we continue to witness new takes on old characters, we experience the social impact of the present day on popular culture as well as its influence on us. People and popular culture are indelibly linked, and both reflect one another. Gotham City and its residents remain a dark representation, a shadow, of urban America.

Notes

INTRODUCTION

1 Washington Irving is credited with first nicknaming New York City "Gotham" in the magazine *Salmagundi* in 1807. For an in-depth examination of the nickname, see Edwin G. Burrows and Mike Wallace's (1999) *Gotham: A History of New York City to 1898*. However, Bill Finger actually chose the name Gotham to separate the city's association from New York (Stamp 2014).

2 See William Uricchio's (2010) "The Batman's Gotham City™: Story, Ideology, Performance" and Jimmy Stamp's (2009) "Batman, Gotham City, and an Overzealous Architecture Historian with a Working Knowledge of Explosives."

3 See Will Brooker's (2012) *Hunting the Dark Knight: Twenty-First Century Batman*, Martin Fradley's (2012) "What Do You Believe In? Film Scholarship and the Cultural Politics of the Dark Knight Franchise," and Anthony J. Kolenic's (2009) "Madness in the Making: Creating and Denying Narratives from Virginia Tech to Gotham City."

1 YOUTH AND GOTHAM CITY: RAISING CRIMINALS, TRAINING VIGILANTES, AND INFLUENCING READERS

1 This occurred despite America so recently coming out of the Second World War where the Nazis burned books.

2 See Comstock and Scharrer (2007, 204–20).

3 See Scott Snyder and Greg Capullo's *Batman Vol. 7: Endgame* (2016).

4 Nightwing's first appearance was in *Tales of the Teen Titans* #44 (1984).

5 The only other two characters to assume the role are Carrie Kelly in Frank Miller and Klaus Janson's ([1986] 2002) *The Dark Knight Returns* and Stephanie Brown. Stephanie was only Robin for a short time (*Robin* #126–128).

2 BEYOND BATMAN: GENDER IN GOTHAM CITY

1. Wonder Woman's TV series did not debut until 1975.
2. The Equal Pay Act of 1963 "prohibits sex-based wage discrimination between men and women in the same establishment who perform jobs that require substantially equal skill, effort and responsibility under similar working conditions" (United States Equal Employment Opportunity Commission n.d.)
3. See Grayson and Robinson's (2002) *Batman: Gotham Knights* #25 and Simone and Syaf's (2012) *Batgirl* Vol. 4, #3.
4. See "Barbara Gordon" on the Batman Wiki (n.d.).

3 THE SEXUALIZED CITY: VIOLENCE, POWER, AND LIBERATION

1. See Solis (2017).
2. See Downey (2015).
3. The New 52 *Catwoman* series has been criticized for the way Catwoman is overtly sexualized, sparking several changes to art and story plans. See Tim Hanley's (2017) *Many Lives of Catwoman: The Felonious History of a Feline Fatale*.
4. Mainstream continuity has not allowed them to maintain a healthy relationship, but Selina and Bruce do get married and have a child on Earth-Two (see Bridwell and Schaffenberger's [1981] *Superman Family* #211).
5. "Don't Ask, Don't Tell" was a US military policy that permitted gay soldiers to serve as long as they were silent about their sexuality. It was in effect from 1993 to 2011.

4 PLURALISM AND IDENTITY FORMATION: RACE AND ETHNICITY IN GOTHAM CITY

1. This was also consistent with the general publishing market of the 1950s, where magazines such as *Ladies' Home Journal* and *Redbook* targeted white housewives and perpetuated gender roles. See Betty Friedan's ([1963] 2001) *The Feminine Mystique*.
2. The first interracial couple on American television was Lucille Ball and Desi Arnez in *I Love Lucy*, which first aired in 1951. The first Black and white couple on American television may have been Tom and Helen Willis in *The Jeffersons* (1975–85).

3 The film *Catwoman* from 2004 stars Halle Berry in the title role. But this Catwoman is not Selina Kyle but Patience Phillips. The film is very detached from the Batman franchise, so this version of a Black Catwoman does not offer much social commentary to regarding progressive efforts of the Batman franchise.

5 FROM THE SLUMS TO THE MANORS: GOTHAM CITY'S CLASS DISPARITY

1 Marx has been credited for the social conflict theory, though we can clearly see the arguments being made in his collaborative work with Engels.
2 See *Batman* #3 (Finger and Kane 1940e) and *Batman* Vol. 2 #44 (Snyder, Azzarello, and Jock 2015).
3 In Jeph Loeb and Tim Sale's (1996) *The Long Halloween*, Batman and Harvey Dent locate and burn Carmine Falcone's enormous stacks of cash that he has not been able to launder. They destroy money associated with criminality. Wealth gained outside of the capitalistic system is criminal wealth and therefore considered worthy of being destroyed.

6 CRIMINAL PRODUCTIVITY: GOTHAM CITY'S MOST WANTED AND MOST NEEDED

1 For further criticism of Batman through a Bakhtinian lens, see Schuy R. Weishaar's (2012) *Masters of the Grotesque: The Cinema of Tim Burton, Terry Gilliam, the Coen Brothers and David Lynch* and Cory A. Reed's (1995) "*Batman Returns*: From the Comic(s) to the Grotesque."
2 See Rucka and Raimondi (2000).
3 See Dini and Timm's (1994a) *The Batman Adventures: Mad Love*.
4 See *Batman* #1 (Finger and Kane 1940b), *Detective Comics* #475 (Englehart and Rogers 1978a), and *Detective Comics* #476 (Englehart and Rogers 1978b).

EPILOGUE

1 The movie was initially scheduled to be released in June 2021 but has been delayed due to the Covid-19 pandemic.

References

Ackerman, Spencer. 2015. "Batman Confronts Police Racism in Latest Comic Book." *Guardian*, September 15. http://www.theguardian.com/books/2015/sep/15/batman-confronts-police-brutality-in-latest-comic-book.

Andreyko, Marc, and Georges Jeanty. 2015a. *Batwoman* Vol. 2 #36, "How in the Hell Did We Get Here?, Part One." January, DC Comics.

Andreyko, Marc, and Georges Jeanty. 2015b. *Batwoman* Vol. 2 #40, "Nocturne in Red." May, DC Comics.

Andreyko, Marc, and Juan Jose Ryp. 2015. *Batwoman* Vol. 2 #38, "How in the Hell Did We Get Here?, Part Three: Tattered Memories." March, DC Comics.

Andreyko, Marc, Moritat, and Jeremy Haun. 2014. *Batwoman* Vol. 2 #34, "Night of the Hunter." October, DC Comics.

Austin, Shannon. 2015. "Batman's Female Foes: The Gender War in Gotham City." *Journal of Popular Culture* 48, no. 2: 285–95.

Azzarello, Brian, and Lee Bermejo. 2008. *Joker*. DC Comics.

Bakhtin, Mikhail. 1984. *Rabelais and His World*. Translated by Hélène Iswolsky. Bloomington: Indiana University Press.

Banisky, Sandy. 1993. "59% of Students Claim Access to Gun, Poll Says Third Say Guns Will Cut Their Lives Short." *Baltimore Sun*, July 20. http://articles.baltimoresun.com/1993-07-20/news/1993201001_1_joyce-foundation-students-handgun-to-school.

"Batgirl—Unaired Pilot." 1967. Featuring Yvonne Craig, Adam West, and Burt Ward. 20th Century Fox Television. https://archive.org/details/BatGirl-unairedPilot.

"Batman and Robin Stand Up for Sportsmanship!" 1950. Public Service Announcement. Printed in *Action Comics* #141. February, DC Comics.

"Batman: The Legacy Continues." 2005. *Batman: The Animated Series* Vol. 1 Featurette, Warner Home Video.

Batman Wiki. n.d. "Barbara Gordon." Accessed March 27, 2020. http://batman.wikia.com/wiki/Barbara_Gordon.

Beechen, Adam, and Freddie E. Williams II. 2007. *Robin* Vol. 4 #156, "The High Dive." January, DC Comics.

Berg, Christopher. 2017. "About Blue Lives Matter." *Defense Maven*, May 14. https://defensemaven.io/bluelivesmatter/pages/about-blue-lives-matter-rF54b2VNMUOrl7wfh8vRXQ.

Bernardo, Susan M. 1994. "Recycling Victims and Villains in *Batman Returns*." *Literature Film Quarterly* 22, no. 1: 16–20.
Black Lives Matter. n.d. "About." Accessed March 22, 2020. https://blacklivesmatter.com/about/.
Bonger, Willem. (1916) 1969. *Criminality and Economic Conditions*. Bloomington: Indiana University Press. https://archive.org/details/criminalityande00hortgoog/page/n12.
Bridwell, E. Nelson, and Kurt Schaffenberger. 1981. *Superman Family* #211, "Mr. & Mrs. Superman: 'The Kill Kent Contract!'" October, DC Comics.
Brody, Michael. 2007. "Holy Franchise! Batman and Trauma." In *Using Superheroes in Counseling and Play Therapy*, edited by Lawrence C. Rubin, 105–20. New York: Springer.
Brooker, Will. 2001. *Batman Unmasked: Analyzing a Cultural Icon*. New York: Continuum.
Brooker, Will. 2012. *Hunting the Dark Knight: Twenty-First Century Batman*. New York: I.B. Tauris.
Brown, Brené. 2017. *Rising Strong: How the Ability to Reset Transforms the Way We Live, Love, Parent, and Lead*. New York: Random House.
Burrows, Edwin G., and Mike Wallace. 1999. *Gotham: A History of New York City*. Oxford: Oxford University Press.
Burton, Tim, dir. 1989. *Batman*. Warner Bros.
Burton, Tim, dir. 1992. *Batman Returns*. Warner Bros.
Butler, Judith. (1990) 2007. *Gender Trouble: Feminism and the Subversion of Identity*. New York: Routledge.
Cahill, Ann. 2001. *Rethinking Rape*. Ithaca, NY: Cornell University Press.
Cameron, Don, and Jerry Robinson. 1945. *Batman* #27, "A Christmas Peril!" February, DC Comics.
Cameron, Don, and Win Mortimer. 1945. *Detective Comics* #105, "Batman: The Batman Goes Broke." November, DC Comics.
Canwell, Bruce, and Lee Weeks. 1997. *Batman Chronicles: The Gauntlet*. DC Comics.
Carlton, Bronwyn, and Staz Johnson. 2000. *Catwoman* Vol. 2 #81, "It's a Wonderful Life." June, DC Comics.
Centers for Disease Control and Prevention. n.d. *NISVS: An Overview of 2010 Findings on Victimization by Sexual Orientation*. Accessed March 28, 2020. https://www.cdc.gov/violenceprevention/pdf/cdc_nisvs_victimization_final-a.pdf.
Chun, Tze, writer. 2016. *Gotham*. Season 3, episode 8, "Mad City: Blood Rush." Aired November 7 on Fox.
Cocca, Carolyn. 2014. "Rebooting Barbara Gordon: Oracle, Batgirl, and Feminist Disability Theories." *ImageText* 7, no. 4.

Cole, Leonard A. 2012. "Bioterrorism: Still a Threat to the United States." *CTC Sentinel* 5, no. 1: 8–12. https://ctc.usma.edu/app/uploads/2012/01/Vol5-Iss16.pdf.

Collins, Max Allan, and Ross Andru. 1987. *Batman* #408, "Did Robin Die Tonight?" July, DC Comics.

Collins, Max Allan, and Chris Warner. 1987. *Batman* #409, "Just Another Kid on Crime Alley" June, DC Comics.

Comics Magazine Association of America, Inc. 1954. *The Comics Code of 1954*. Comic Book Legal Defense Fund. http://cbldf.org/the-comics-code-of-1954/.

Comics Magazine Association of America, Inc. 1971. *Comics Code Revision of 1971*. Comic Book Legal Defense Fund. http://cbldf.org/comics-code-revision-of-1971/.

Comics Magazine Association of America, Inc. 1989. *Comics Code Revision of 1989*. Comic Book Legal Defense Fund. http://cbldf.org/comics-code-revision-of-1989/.

Comstock, George A., and Erica Scharrer. 2007. *Media and the American Child*. Amsterdam: Elsevier.

Conner, Amanda, and Jimmy Palmiotti. 2014. *Harley Quinn Vol. 1: Hot in the City*. DC Comics.

Conway, Gerry, writer. 1992. *Batman: The Animated Series*. Season 1, episode 12, "Appointment in Crime Alley." Aired September 17 on Fox Kids.

Coogan, Peter. 2006. *Superhero: The Secret Origin of a Genre*. Austin: Monkeybrain.

Corsaro, William A. 2005. *The Sociology of Childhood*, 2nd ed. Thousand Oaks: Pine Forge Press.

CoSA VFX. 2014. "CoSA VFX Creates Gotham for Warner Bros. and Fox." September 23, 2014. https://www.cosavfx.com/index.php/news-blog/18-cosa-vfx-creates-gotham-for-warner-bros-and-fox.

Craig, Yvonne. 1967. "Duo to Become Terrific Trio." *Free Lance-Star* 83, no. 168 (July 19): 2. https://news.google.com/newspapers?nid=1298&dat=19670719&id=JdtNAAAAIBAJ&sjid=6IoDAAAAIBAJ&pg=5038,1721064&hl=en.

Craig, Yvonne. 1974. "1974 Equal Pay PSA with Batgirl." YouTube video, 1:02. https://www.youtube.com/watch?v=Is5vlf7nwsU.

Crawshaw, Trisha L. 2019. "Truth, Justice, Boobs: Gender in Comic Book Culture." In *Gender and the Media: Women's Places*, edited by Marcia Texler Segal and Vasilikie Demos, 89–103. Bingley: Emerald.

Crist, Judith. 1948. "Horror in the Nursery." *Collier's Magazine*. March 27.

Cronin, Brian. 2015. "When We First Met—When Did Bruce Wayne Become a BILLIONAIRE Playboy?" *CBR*. June 21. https://www.cbr.

com/when-we-first-met-when-did-bruce-wayne-become-a-billionaire-playboy/.
Cronin, Brian. 2019a. "Batman: Martha Wayne's Pearls Actually Have Their Own Secret Origin." *CBR*. January 29. https://www.cbr.com/batman-martha-wayne-pearls-secret-origin/.
Cronin, Brian. 2019b. "The 'Pearl Scene' in Batman's Iconic Origin Doesn't Make Sense." *CBR*. January 27. https://www.cbr.com/batman-pearl-scene-problem/.
Cunningham, Phillip Lamarr. 2015. "The Absence of Black Supervillains in Mainstream Comics." In *Superheroes and Identities*, edited by Mel Gibson, David Huxley, and Joan Ormrod. New York: Routledge. https://books.google.com/books?id=FsHOCwAAQBAJ&lpg=PT74&ots=YC6NKJC8O2&lr&pg=PT76#v=onepage&q&f=false.
Curtis, Neal. 2016. *Sovereignty and Superheroes*. Manchester: Manchester University Press.
Cutter, Rebecca Perry, writer. 2015. *Gotham*. Season 2, episode 6, "Rise of the Villains: By Fire." Aired October 26 on Fox.
Dan. 2012. "Class Warfare in *The Dark Knight Rises.*" *Race, Class and Gender in Film* (blog), December 8. http://dansfilmblogonraceclassandgender.blogspot.com/2012/12/class-warfare-in-dark-knight-rises.html.
Daniel, Tony S., and Ryan Winn. 2011. *Detective Comics* Vol. 2 #1. November, DC Comics.
De Beauvoir, Simone. (1949) 2011. *The Second Sex*. Translated by Constance Borde and Sheila Malovany-Chevallier. New York: Vintage.
Devore, Jennifer Susannah. 2017. "Batgirl: 50 Years Behind the Mask." In *Comic-Con International: San Diego 2017 Souvenir Book*, edited and designed by Gary Sassaman, 195–8.
Dini, Paul. 1992a. *Batman: The Animated Series*. Season 1, episode 3, "Heart of Ice." Aired September 7 on Fox Kids.
Dini, Paul, writer. 1992b. *Batman: The Animated Series*. Season 1, episode 7, "Joker's Favor." Aired September 11 on Fox Kids.
Dini, Paul, writer. 1993. *Batman: The Animated Series*. Season 1, episode 47, "Harley and Ivy." Aired January 18 on Fox Kids.
Dini, Paul, and Bruce Timm. 1994a. *The Batman Adventures: Mad Love*. February, DC Comics.
Dini, Paul, and Bruce Timm. 1994b. *Batman: The Animated Series*. Season 2, episode 9, "Trial." Aired May 16 on Fox Kids.
DiPaolo, Marc. 2011. *War, Politics and Superheroes: Ethics and Propaganda in Comics and Film*. Jefferson, NC: McFarland.
Dixon, Chuck, and Gary Frank. 1996. *Black Canary/Oracle: Birds of Prey* #1, "One Man's Hell." June, DC Comics.
Dixon, Chuck, and Mike Wieringo. 1996a. *Robin* Vol. 4 #25, "Sophomore Lethal." February, DC Comics.

Dixon, Chuck, and Mike Wieringo. 1996b. *Robin* Vol. 4 #26, "The Hard Lessons." March, DC Comics.

Dixon, Chuck, and Scott Beatty. (2001–2) 2008. Joker: Last Laugh #1–6. *Batman: The Joker's Last Laugh*. DC Comics.

Dixon, Chuck, and Staz Johnson. 1998a. *Robin* Vol. 4 #58, "The Stranger." October, DC Comics.

Dixon, Chuck, and Staz Johnson. 1998b. *Robin* Vol. 4 #59, "Brutality 101." December, DC Comics.

Dixon, Chuck, and Tom Lyle. 1992. *Detective Comics* #647, "Inquiring Minds." August, DC Comics.

Dixon, Chuck, and William Rosado. 1999. *Robin* Vol. 4 #65, "A Blessed Event." June, DC Comics.

Downey, Meg. 2015. "In Defense of Dick Grayson: Objectification, Sexuality, and Subtext." *Women Write about Comics*. December 15. http://womenwriteaboutcomics.com/2015/12/15/in-defense-of-dick-grayson-objectification-sexuality-and-subtext/.

Dubose, Mike S. 2007. "Holding Out for a Hero: Reaganism, Comic Book Vigilantes, and Captain America." *Journal of Popular Culture* 40, no. 6: 915–35.

Dullea, Georgia. 1988. "Holy Bomb Blast! The Real Robin Fights On!" *New York Times*, November 10. https://www.nytimes.com/1988/11/10/arts/holy-bomb-blast-the-real-robin-fights-on.html.

Durkheim, Émile. (1895) 2014. *The Rules of Sociological Method and Selected Texts on Sociology and Its Method*, edited by Steven Lukes. New York: Free Press.

Early, Frances H., and Kathleen Kennedy, eds. 2003. *Athena's Daughters: Television's New Women Warriors*. Syracuse: Syracuse University Press.

Education Development Center. 2008. "Bystander." Eyes on Bullying. http://eyesonbullying.org/bystander.html.

Englehart, Steve, and Marshall Rogers. 1977. *Detective Comics* #472, "I Am the Batman!" September, DC Comics.

Englehart, Steve, and Marshall Rogers. 1978a. *Detective Comics* #475, "The Laughing Fish!" February, DC Comics.

Englehart, Steve, and Marshall Rogers. 1978b. *Detective Comics* #476, "Sign of the Joker!" April, DC Comics.

Facciani, Matthew, Peter Warren, and Jennifer Vendemia. 2015. "A Content-Analysis of Race, Gender, and Class in American Comic Books." *Race, Gender & Class* 22, nos. 3–4. https://www.researchgate.net/profile/Matthew_Facciani/publication/310328448_A_content_analysis_of_race_class_and_gender_in_American_comic_books/links/5a68dccfa6fdcccd01a193c5/A-content-analysis-of-race-class-and-gender-in-American-comic-books.pdf.

Finger, Bill, and Bob Kane. 1940a. *Batman* #1, "The Cat." March, DC Comics.

Finger, Bill, and Bob Kane. 1940b. *Batman* #1, "The Joker." March, DC Comics.

Finger, Bill, and Bob Kane. 1940c. *Batman* #1, "The Legend of the Batman—Who He Is, and How He Came to Be." March, DC Comics.

Finger, Bill, and Bob Kane. 1940d. *Batman* #3, "The Batman vs. the Cat-Woman." September, DC Comics.

Finger, Bill, and Bob Kane. 1940e. *Batman* #3, "The Crime School for Boys." September, DC Comics.

Finger, Bill, and Bob Kane. 1940f. *Detective Comics* #38, "Batman and 'Robin the Boy Wonder.'" April, DC Comics.

Finger, Bill, and Bob Kane. 1940g. *Detective Comics* #39, "Batman: The Horde of the Green Dragon." May, DC Comics.

Finger, Bill, and Bob Kane. 1940h. *Detective Comics* #42, "Batman: 'The Case of the Prophetic Pictures.'" August, DC Comics.

Finger, Bill, and Bob Kane. 1941a. *Batman* #5, "The Case of the Honest Crook." March, DC Comics.

Finger, Bill, and Bob Kane. 1941b. *Batman* #7, "The People vs. the Batman." November, DC Comics.

Finger, Bill, and Bob Kane. 1941c. *Detective Comics* #47, "Batman: Money Can't Buy Happiness." January, DC Comics.

Finger, Bill, and Bob Kane. 1941d. *Detective Comics* #49, "Batman: Clayface Walks Again." March, DC Comics.

Finger, Bill, and Bob Kane. 1941e. *Detective Comics* #52, "Batman: The Secret of the Jade Box." June, DC Comics.

Finger, Bill, Bob Kane, and Lew Sayre Schwartz. 1948. *Batman* #49, "The Scoop of the Century!" October, DC Comics.

Finger, Bill, Bob Kane, and Sheldon Moldoff. 1940. *Detective Comics* #35, "Batman: The Case of the Ruby Idol." January, DC Comics.

Finger, Bill, Gardner Fox, Bob Kane, and Sheldon Moldoff. 1939. *Detective Comics* #33, "The Batman Wars Against the Dirigible of Doom." November, DC Comics.

Finger, Bill, and Sheldon Moldoff. 1958. *Batman* #119, "The Secret of Batman Island." October, DC Comics.

Finger, Bill, and Sheldon Moldoff. 1959. *Batman* #126, "The Batman Lighthouse." September, DC Comics.

Finger, Bill, and Sheldon Moldoff. 1961. *Batman* #139, "Bat-Girl!" April, DC Comics.

Finkelhor, David. 2013. "Trends in Bullying and Peer Victimization." University of New Hampshire: Crimes Against Children Research Center. January. http://www.unh.edu/ccrc/pdf/CV280_Bullying%20

&%20Peer%20Victimization%20Bulletin_1-23-13_with%20toby%20edits.pdf.

Foucault, Michel. (1975) 1995. *Discipline and Punish*. 2nd ed. Translated by Alan Sheridan. New York: Vintage Books.

Fox, Gardner, Bob Kane, and Sheldon Moldoff. 1939a. *Detective Comics* #30, "The Batman: The Return of Doctor Death." August, DC Comics.

Fox, Gardner, Bob Kane, and Sheldon Moldoff. 1939b. *Detective Comics* #31, "Batman Versus the Vampire, Part 1." September, DC Comics.

Fox, Gardner, and Carmine Infantino. 1967. *Detective Comics* #359, "Batman: 'The Million Dollar Debut of Batgirl!'" January, DC Comics.

Fradley, Martin. 2012. "What Do You Believe in? Film Scholarship and the Cultural Politics of the Dark Knight Franchise." *Film Quarterly* 66, no. 3 (Spring): 15–27.

Friedan, Betty. (1963) 2001. *The Feminine Mystique*. New York: W. W. Norton.

Gale, Bob, and Alex Maleev. 1999. *Batman: No Man's Land* Vol. 1 #1, "No Law and a New Order—Part One: Values." March, DC Comics.

Garland, Tammy S., Kathryn A. Branch, and Mackenzie Grimes. 2015. "Blurring the Lines: Reinforcing Rape Myths in Comic Books." *Feminist Criminology* 11, no. 1: 1–21.

Garneau, Eric. 2015. "Lady Haha: Performativity, Super-Sanity, and the Mutability of Identity." In *The Joker: A Serious Study of the Clown Prince of Crime*, edited by Robert Moses Peaslee and Robert G. Weiner, 33–48. Jackson: University Press of Mississippi.

Gilroy, Andréa. 2015. "The Epistemology of the Phone Booth: The Superheroic Identity and Queer Theory in *Batwoman: Elegy*." *ImageText* 8, no. 1.

Grant, Alan, and Dave Taylor. 1996. *Batman: Shadow of the Bat* #53, "Hobson's Choice. Legacy: Prelude." July, DC Comics.

Grant, Alan, and Jim Aparo. 1992. *Detective Comics* #641, "The Destroyer Part 3: A Dream Is Forever." February, DC Comics.

Grant, Alan, and Norm Breyfogle. 1990a. *Batman* Vol. 1 #455, "Identity Crisis—Part One." October, DC Comics.

Grant, Alan, and Norm Breyfogle. 1990b. *Batman* Vol. 1 #457, "Master of Fear." December, DC Comics.

Grayson, Devin, and Dale Eaglesham. 1999. *Batman: Legends of the Dark Knight* #116, "Fear of Faith, Part One: Fanning the Flames." April, DC Comics.

Grayson, Devin, and Roger Robinson. 2002. *Batman: Gotham Knights* Vol. 1 #25, "No Exit." March, DC Comics.

Haas, Nicole E., Jan W. de Keijser, and Gerben J. N. Bruinsma. 2012. "Public Support for Vigilantism: An Experimental Study." *Journal of Experimental Criminology* 8, no. 4 (December): 387–413.

Halberstam, Judith. 1998. *Female Masculinity*. Durham, NC: Duke University Press.

Hama, Larry, and Mike Deodato. 1999. *Detective Comics* #736, "Homecoming." September, DC Comics.

Hamilton, Edmond, and Sheldon Moldoff. 1956a. *Batman* #98, "The Desert Island Batman." March, DC Comics.

Hamilton, Edmond, and Sheldon Moldoff. 1956b. *Detective Comics* #233, "Batman: 'The Batwoman.' " July, DC Comics.

Hanley, Tim. 2017. *Many Lives of Catwoman: The Felonious History of a Feline Fatale*. Chicago: Chicago Review Press.

Harper, Jordan, writer. 2016. *Gotham*. Season 2, episode 14, "Wrath of the Villains: This Ball of Mud and Meanness." Aired March 14 on Fox.

Hassler-Forest, Dan. 2011. "From Flying Man to Falling Man: 9/11 Discourse in *Super Returns* and *Batman Begins*." In *Portraying 9/11: Essays on Representations in Comics, Literature, Film and Theatre*, edited by Christrophe Dony and Warren Rosenberg, 134–46. Jefferson, NC: McFarland.

Hawkins, D. Lynn, Debra J. Pepler, and Wendy M. Craig. 2001. "Naturalistic Observations of Peer Interventions in Bullying." *Social Development* 10, no. 4: 512–27.

Heller, Bruno, writer. 2015. *Gotham*. Season 1, episode 22, "All Happy Families Are Alike." Aired May 4 on Fox.

Higgins, Kyle, and Eddy Barrows. 2012. *Nightwing* Vol. 3 #8, "Bloodlines." June, DC Comics.

Holland, Charles. 2008. "Dark Knight/White Heat: The Architecture of Gotham City." *Fantastic Journal*. September 23.

Horeck, Tanya. 2004. *Public Rape: Representing Violation in Fiction and Film*. Abingdon: Routledge.

Hudson, Laura. 2013. "DC Introduces First Transgender Character in Mainstream Comics." *Wired*. October 4. https://www.wired.com/2013/04/transgender-dc-comics-batgirl/.

Hull, Robert, writer. 2016. *Gotham*. Season 2, episode 15, "Wrath of the Villains: Mad Grey Dawn." Aired March 21 on Fox.

Iadonisi, Richard A. 2013. "'A Man Has Risen': Hard Bodies, Reaganism, and *The Dark Knight Returns*." In *Graphic History: Essays on Graphic Novels and/as History*, edited by Richard Iadonisi, 72–88. Newcastle upon Tyne: Cambridge Scholars.

Ioannidou, Elisavet. 2013. "Adapting Superhero Comics for the Big Screen: Subculture for the Masses." *Adaptation: The Journal of Literature on Screen Studies* 6, no. 2: 230–8.

Ireland, Corydon. 2009. "Humanists Honor Gay Military Activist Dan Choi." *Harvard Gazette*, September 22. https://news.harvard.edu/gazette/story/2009/09/dont-ask-dont-lie/.

Johns, Geoff, Grant Morrison, Greg Rucka, Mark Waid, Keith Giffen, and Ken Lashley. 2006. *52* #7, "Going Down." August, DC Comics.

Juliano, Stephanie. 2012. "Superheroes, Bandits, and Cyber-Nerds: Exploring the History and Contemporary Development of the Vigilante." *Journal of International Commercial Law and Technology* 7, no. 1: 44–64.

K12 Academics. n.d. "History of School Shootings in the United States." Accessed March 28, 2020. https://www.k12academics.com/school-shootings/history-school-shootings-united-states#.WnUiO1MbM1g.

Kane, Bob. 1989. *Batman & Me*. Forestville: Eclipse Books.

Kanigher, Robert, and Sheldon Moldoff. 1966. *Batman* #181, "Beware of—Poison Ivy!" June, DC Comics.

Kellner, Douglas. 2013. "Media Spectacle and Domestic Terrorism: The Case of the Batman/Joker Cinema Massacre." *Review of Education, Pedagogy, and Cultural Studies* 35, no. 3: 157–77.

Kelly, Stephen. 2011. "Is Batman the Hero That Occupy Protesters Need?" *Guardian*. October 27. https://www.theguardian.com/commentisfree/2011/oct/27/batman-hero-occupy-protesters.

Kerrigan, S. J. 2011. "Christopher Nolan's Batman as Social Criticism." December 20. http://seankerrigan.com/christopher-nolans-batman-as-social-criticism/.

King, Tom, writer. 2018. *Batman* Vol. 3 #50, "The Wedding of Batman & Catwoman." September, DC Comics.

King, Tom, David Finch, Clay Mann, and Seth Mann. 2017. *Batman* Vol. 3 #24, "Every Epilogue Is a Prelude." August, DC Comics.

King, Tom, and Mikel Janín. 2017a. *Batman* Vol. 3 #12, "I Am Suicide: Part Four." February, DC Comics.

King, Tom, and Mikel Janín. 2017b. *Batman* Vol. 3 #32, "The War of Jokes & Riddles, Conclusion." December, DC Comics.

Klink, Lisa, and Guy Davis. 1999. *Batman: Shadow of the Bat* Vol. 1 #86, "Home Sweet Home." June, DC Comics.

Kohlberg, Lawrence, and Richard H. Hersh. 1977. "Moral Development: A Review of the Theory." *Theory into Practice* 16, no. 2: 53–9.

Kolenic, Anthony J. 2009. "Madness in the Making: Creating and Denying Narratives from Virginia Tech to Gotham City." *Journal of Popular Culture* 42, no. 6 (December): 1023–39.

Krafft-Ebing, Richard. 1894. *Psychopathia Sexualis*. 7th ed. Translated by Charles Gilbert Chaddock. Philadelphia: F. A. Davis.

Kupperberg, Paul, and Irv Novick. 1980. *Detective Comics* #489, "Commissioner Gordon: 'When the Inmates Run the Madhouse!'" April, DC Comics.

Lachenal, Jessica. 2014. "Why the *Batgirl* #37 Controversy Is the Conversation We Need Right Now." *Mary Sue*. December 15. https://www.themarysue.com/batgirl-37-controversy-conversation/.

Langley, Travis. 2012. *Batman and Psychology: A Dark and Stormy Knight*. Hoboken: John Wiley & Sons.

Lefebvre, Henri. (1979) 2009. "Space: Social Product and Use Value (1979)." In *State, Space, World: Selected Essays*, edited by Neil Brenner and Stuart Elden, translated by Gerald Moore, Neil Brenner, and Stuart Elden, 185–95. Minneapolis: University of Minnesota Press.

Letamendi, Andrea, and Brian Ward. 2014. *The Arkham Sessions*. Episode 33, "Robin's Reckoning: Part I." Podcast. August 28. http://thearkhamsessions.libsyn.com/the-arkham-sessions-episode-33-robins-reckoning-part-1.

Lewis, Jon, and Pete Woods. 2003. *Robin* Vol. 4 #111, "Dating for the Clueless." April, DC Comics.

Lobdell, Scott, and Dexter Soy. 2017. *Red Hood and the Outlaws* Vol. 2 #6, "Dark Trinity, Part Six: Darker Days." March, DC Comics.

Loeb, Jeph, and Tim Sale. 1996. *Batman: The Long Halloween* #1, "Chapter One: Crime." December, DC Comics.

Lucas, Mark. 2017. "Batgirl: A 50-Year Journey from the Library to the Screen." In *Comic-Con International: San Diego 2017 Souvenir Book*, edited and designed by Gary Sassaman, 173–4.

Lynch, Sarah N. 2016. "FBI Says US Police Deaths Spiked 61% in 2016." *Reuters*. October 16. *Business Insider*. https://www.businessinsider.com/r-us-police-deaths-on-duty-spiked-in-2016-fbi-2017-10.

Maggin, Elliot S., and Mike Grell. 1975. *Bat Family* Vol. 1 #1, "The Invader from Hell!" October, DC Comics.

Marazi, Katherine. 2015. "Superhero or Vigilante? A Matter of Perspective and Brand Management." *European Journal of American Culture* 34, no. 1: 67–82. doi:10.1386/ejac.34.1.67_1.

Marcia, James E. 1980. "Identity in Adolescence." In *Handbook of Adolescent Psychology*, edited by J. Adelson, 159–87. New York: Wiley & Sons.

Marx, Karl, and Frederick Engels. (1848) 1969. *Communist Manifesto*, translated by Samuel Moore in cooperation with Frederick Engels. In *Marx/Engels Selected Works* Vol. 1, 98–137. Moscow: Progress Publishers. https://www.marxists.org/archive/marx/works/1848/communist-manifesto/.

Mardorossian, Carine M. 2002. "Toward a New Feminist Theory of Rape." *Signs: Journal of Women in Culture and Society* 27, no. 3 (Spring): 743–75.

Maudsley, Henry. 1880. *The Pathology of Mind*. New York: Appleton.

REFERENCES

Meltzer, Brad, and Rags Morales. 2004. *Identity Crisis* Vol. 1 #5, "Chapter Five: Father's Day." December, DC Comics.
Meltzer, Brad, and Rags Morales. 2005. *Identity Crisis* Vol. 1 #6, "Chapter Six: Husbands & Wives." January, DC Comics.
Menza, Kaitlin. 2017. "How Bernie Madoff Took His Family Down." *Town and Country*. May 19. https://www.townandcountrymag.com/society/money-and-power/a9656715/bernie-madoff-ponzi-scheme-scandal-story-and-aftermath/.
Mert, Ceren. 2019. "Global Cities and Organized Crime: The Shifting Urban Landscape of Gotham." *Journal of Popular Culture* 52 (February 6): 153–68. doi:10.1111/jpcu.12760.
Miller, Frank, and David Mazzucchelli. (1987) 2005. *Batman: Year One*. DC Comics.
Miller, Frank, and Klaus Janson. (1986) 2002. *The Dark Knight Returns*. DC Comics.
Miniño, Arialdi, Jiaquan Xu, Kenneth D. Kochanek, and Betzaisa Tejada-Vera. 2009. *Death in the United States, 2007*. Centers for Disease Control and Prevention, National Center for Health Statistics, NCHS Data Brief No. 26 (December). https://www.cdc.gov/nchs/products/databriefs/db26.htm.
Moench, Doug. 1986. *Batman* #400, "Resurrection Night!" October, DC Comics.
Moench, Doug, and Jim Balent. 1994. *Catwoman* Vol. 2 #0, "Cat Shadows." October, DC Comics.
Moench, Doug, and Kelley Jones. 1998a. *Batman* #551, "Suit of Evil Souls." February, DC Comics.
Moench, Doug, and Kelley Jones. 1998b. *Batman* #552, "The Greatest Evil." March, DC Comics.
Moncada, Eduardo. 2017. "Varieties of Vigilantism: Conceptual Discord, Meaning and Strategies." *Global Crime* 18, no. 4: 403–23.
Montessori, Maria. (1948) 2007. *From Childhood to Adolescence: The Montessori Series* Vol. 12. Amsterdam: Montessori-Pierson.
Moore, Alan, and Brian Bolland. (1988) 2008. *Batman: The Killing Joke*. The Deluxe Edition. DC Comics.
Morrison, Grant, and Dave McKean. 1989. *Arkham Asylum: A Serious House on Serious Earth*. DC Comics.
Mulvey, Laura. 1989. *Visual and Other Pleasures*. Bloomington: Indiana University Press.
Nasr, Constantine. 2005. "Beyond Batman: Gotham City Revisited—the Production Design of *Batman Returns*." *Batman Returns*, special edition DVD. New Wave Entertainment.
Natale, Richard. 1995. " 'Batman' Paints the Town: The Caped Crusaders Are Hipper, Sleeker and Suited Up with Sex Appeal. A Colorful

Comic-Book Look Replaces Gotham's Dark Past." *Los Angeles Times*. June 13.

New York Magazine. 2009. Illustrated by Darrow and Cover Story by Steve Fishman. March 2.

New York Times. 1948. "Catholic Students Burn Up Comic Books." December 11, 18.

Newell, Mindy, J. J. Birch, and Michael Bair. 1989a. *Catwoman* Vol. 1 #1, "Metamorphosis." February, DC Comics.

Newell, Mindy, J. J. Birch, and Michael Bair. 1989b. *Catwoman* Vol. 1 #4, "Consecration." May, DC Comics.

Nolan, Christopher, dir. 2005. *Batman Begins*. Warner Bros.

Nolan, Christopher, dir. 2008. *The Dark Knight*. Warner Bros.

Nolan, Christopher, dir. 2012. *The Dark Knight Rises*. Warner Bros.

Occupy Wall Street. n.d.a. "About." Accessed March 22, 2020. http://occupywallst.org/about/.

Occupy Wall Street. n.d.b. Accessed March 22, 2020. http://occupywallst.org/.

Omi, Michael, and Howard Winant. 2015. *Racial Formation in the United States*, 3rd ed. New York: Routledge.

O'Neil, Dennis, and Chris Sprouse. 1992. *Batman: Legends of the Dark Knight* #27, "The Destroyer, Part 2: Solomon." February, DC Comics.

O'Neil, Dennis, and Dick Giordano. 1976. *Detective Comics* #457, "There Is No Hope in Crime Alley!" March, DC Comics.

O'Neil, Dennis, and Eduardo Barreto. 1994. *Batman: Legends of the Dark Knight* #61, "Knightquest: The Search—Quarry: Part Three." June, DC Comics.

O'Neil, Dennis, and Irv Novick. 1972. *Batman* #239, "Silent Night, Deadly Night!" February, DC Comics.

Ostrander, John, Kim Yale, and Luke McDonnell. 1989. *Suicide Squad* Vol. 1 #23, "Weird War Tales." January, DC Comics.

Ostrander, John, and Tom Mandrake. 2007a. *Batman* #659, "Grotesk Part 1." January, DC Comics.

Ostrander, John, and Tom Mandrake. 2007b. *Batman* #661, "Grotesk Part 3." February, DC Comics.

Ostrander, John, and Tom Mandrake. 2007c. *Batman* #662, "Grotesk Part 4." March, DC Comics.

Ostroff, Joshua. 2016. "Superhero Diversity Takes Flight as Comic Books Fight for Gender, Race and LGBT Balance." *Huffington Post*, May 26. http://www.huffingtonpost.ca/2016/05/26/superhero-diversity-marvel-comics-dc_n_9349666.html.

Patterson, Brett Chandler. 2008. "*No Man's Land:* Social Order in Gotham City and New Orleans." In *Batman and Philosophy: The Dark*

Knight of the Soul, edited by Mark D. White, Robert Arp, and William Irwin, 41–54. Hoboken: John Wiley & Sons.

Petrovic, Paul. 2011. "Queer Resistance, Gender Performance, and 'Coming Out' of the Panel Borders in Greg Rucka and J. H. Williams III's *Batwoman: Elegy*." *Journal of Graphic Novels and Comics* 2, no. 1: 67–76.

Phillips, Nickie D., and Staci Strobl. 2013. *Comic Book Crime: Truth, Justice, and the American Way*. New York: New York University Press.

Phillips, Todd, dir. 2019. *Joker*. Warner Bros.

Proctor, William. 2016. "Batgirl's Story in The Killing Joke Is Horrific, but Her Trauma Can Be Cathartic for Some Fans." *Guardian*, June 20. https://www.theguardian.com/books/2016/jun/20/the-killing-jokes-depiction-of-may-be-cathartic-for-some-readers.

Reed, Cory A. 1995. "*Batman Returns:* From the Comic(s) to the Grotesque." *Post Script* 14, no. 3: 37–50.

Reed, David Vern, and Romeo Tanghal. 1977. *Batman* #284, "If There Were No Batman … I Would Have to Invent Him!" February, DC Comics.

Robbins, Frank, and Bob Brown. 1969. *Detective Comics* #392, "Batman: I Died…A Thousand Deaths." October, DC Comics.

Robbins, Frank, and Don Heck. 1972a. *Detective Comics* #423, "Candidate For Danger!" May, DC Comics.

Robbins, Frank, and Don Heck. 1972b. *Detective Comics* #424, "Batgirl's Last Case." June, DC Comics.

Robbins, Frank, and Irv Novick. 1969a. *Batman* #210, "The Case of the Purr-Loined Pearl!" March, DC Comics.

Robbins, Frank, and Irv Novick. 1969b. *Batman* #212, "Baffling Deaths of the Crime-Czar!" June, DC Comics.

Robbins, Frank, and Irv Novick. 1969c. *Batman* #214, "Batman's Marriage Trap." August, DC Comics.

Robbins, Frank, and Irv Novick. 1969d. *Batman* #217, "One Bullet Too Many!" December, DC Comics.

Rogel, Randy, writer. 1993. *Batman: The Animated Series*. Season 1, episode 51, "Robin's Reckoning: Part 1." Aired February 7 on Fox Kids.

Rogers, Vaneta. 2012. "GAIL SIMONE on Revelations About BATGIRL's Miraculous Cure." *Newsarama*, January 11. https://www.newsarama.com/8929-gail-simone-on-revelations-about-batgirl-s-miraculous-cure.html.

Ross, Stanley Ralph, writer. 1967. "Catwoman's Dressed to Kill." *Batman*. Aired December 14 on ABC.

Rucka, Greg, and Pablo Raimondi. 2000. *Batman: Shadow of the Bat* #94, "Endgame Epilogue: Days of Auld Lang Syne." February, DC Comics.
Rucka, Greg, and J. H. Williams III. 2009a. *Detective Comics* #854, "Elegy, Part 1: Agitato." August, DC Comics.
Rucka, Greg, and J. H. Williams III. 2009b. *Detective Comics* #856, "Elegy, Part 3: Affettuoso." October, DC Comics.
Rucka, Greg, and J. H. Williams III. 2010a. *Detective Comics* #859, "GO, Part Two." January, DC Comics.
Rucka, Greg, and J. H. Williams III. 2010b. *Detective Comics* #860, "GO, Part Three." February, DC Comics.
Rude, Mey. 2014. "Drawn to Comics: We Need to Talk about the Rape in *Batwoman*." *Autostraddle*. December 2. https://www.autostraddle.com/drawn-to-comics-we-need-to-talk-about-the-rape-in-batwoman-266910/.
Rudolph, Oscar, writer. 1967. *Batman*. Season 3, episode 1, "Enter Batgirl, Exit Penguin." Aired September 14 on ABC.
Ruegger, Tom, writer. 1992. *Batman: The Animated Series*. Season 1, episode 27, "The Underdwellers." Aired October 21 on Fox Kids.
Sable, Mark, and Jesus Saiz. 2009. "Two-Face: Year One." In *Batman: Two-Face and Scarecrow Year One*. DC Comics.
Salamon, Julie. 1992. "Film: New Villains Threaten Gotham." *Wall Street Journal*, June 25, A14.
Samachson, Joseph, and Dick Sprang. 1943. *Batman* #19, "Collector of Millionaires." November, DC Comics.
Schiff, Jack, Jerry Robinson, and Fred Ray. 1942. *Batman* Vol. 1 #10, "The Princess of Plunder." April, DC Comics.
Schultz, Harrison. 2012. "Don't Occupy Gotham City: A Protester Reviews *The Dark Knight Rises*." *Daily Beast*. July 19. https://www.thedailybeast.com/dont-occupy-gotham-city-a-protester-reviews-the-dark-knight-rises.
Schumacher, Joel, dir. 1995. *Batman Forever*. Warner Bros.
Schumacher, Joel, dir. 1997. *Batman and Robin*. Warner Bros.
Scott, Suzanne, and Ellen Kirkpatrick, moderators. 2015. "Trans Representations and Superhero Comics: A Conversation with Mey Rude, J. Skyler, and Rachel Stevens." *Cinema Journal* 55, no. 1 (Fall): 160–9.
Sedgwick, Eve Kosofsky. 1990. *The Epistemology of the Closet*. Berkeley: University of California Press.
Sharrett, Christopher. 2015. "Batman and the Twilight of the Idols: An Interview with Frank Miller." In *Many More Lives of the Batman*, edited by Roberta Pearson, William Uricchio, and Will Brooker, 33–42. London: Palgrave Macmillan.

Simmons, Alex, and Dwayne Turner. 2001a. *Batman: Orpheus Rising* #1, "Mean Streets." October, DC Comics.
Simmons, Alex, and Dwayne Turner. 2001b. *Batman: Orpheus Rising* #3, "Orpheus Rising." December, DC Comics.
Simmons, Alex, and Dwayne Turner. 2002a. *Batman: Orpheus Rising* #4, "The Long Way Down!" January, DC Comics.
Simmons, Alex, and Dwayne Turner. 2002b. *Batman: Orpheus Rising* #5, "Ashes to Ashes." February, DC Comics.
Simone, Gail. n.d. *Women in Refrigerators*. Accessed March 29, 2020. http://lby3.com/wir/index.html.
Simone, Gail, and Ardian Syaf. 2012. *Batgirl* Vol. 4 #3, "A Breath of Broken Glass." January, DC Comics.
Simone, Gail, and Daniel Sampere. 2013. *Batgirl* Vol. 4 #19, "A Blade from the Shadows." June, DC Comics.
Simonson, Walter. 2007. "Legend." In *Batman Black and White* Vol. 1, 65–74. DC Comics.
Singer, Marc. 2002. "'Black Skins' and White Masks: Comic Books and the Secret of Race." *African American Review* 36, no. 1: 107–19. doi:10.2307/2903369.
Snyder, Scott, Brian Azzarello, and Jock. 2015. *Batman* Vol. 2 #44, "A Simple Case." November, DC Comics.
Snyder, Scott, and Francesco Francavilla. 2011a. *Detective Comics* #875, "Lost Boys." May, DC Comics.
Snyder, Scott, and Francesco Francavilla. 2011b. *Detective Comics* #879, "Skeleton Key." September, DC Comics.
Snyder, Scott, Francesco Francavilla, and Jock. 2011. *Detective Comics* #881, "The Face in the Glass." October, DC Comics.
Snyder, Scott, and Greg Capullo. 2011. *Batman Vol. 2* #1, "The Court of Owls Part One: Knife Trick." November, DC Comics.
Snyder, Scott, and Greg Capullo. 2012. *Batman Vol. 3: Death of the Family*. DC Comics.
Snyder, Scott, and Greg Capullo. 2014. *Batman* Vol. 2 #33, "Zero Year: Savage City." September, DC Comics.
Snyder, Scott, and Greg Capullo. 2016. *Batman Vol. 7: Endgame*. DC Comics.
Snyder, Scott, and Jock. 2011. *Detective Comics* #878, "Hungry City, Part 3." August, DC Comics.
Solis, Marie. 2017. "How the Women's March's 'Genital-Based' Feminism Isolated the Transgender Community." *Mic*, January 23. https://www.mic.com/articles/166273/how-the-women-s-march-s-genital-based-feminism-isolated-the-transgender-community.
Sosa, Iturri, writer. 2017. *Gotham*. Season 4, episode 9, "A Dark Knight: Let Them Eat Pie." Aired November 16 on Fox.

Southeast Missourian. 1949. "Pupils Burn Comic Books to Open Girardeau Drive." 46, no. 122: 1. https://news.google.com/newspapers?nid=Oc-rVwKPngoC&dat=19490225&printsec=frontpage&hl=en.

Stabile, Carol A. 2009. " 'Sweetheart, This Ain't Gender Studies': Sexism and Superheroes." *Communication and Critical/Cultural Studies* 6, no. 1: 86–92.

Stamp, Jimmy. 2009. "Batman, Gotham City, and an Overzealous Architecture Historian with a Working Knowledge of Explosives." *Life without Buildings*, June 1. http://lifewithoutbuildings.net/2009/06/on-influence-batman-gotham-city-and-an-overzealous-architecture-historian-with-a-working-knowledge-of-explosives.html.

Stamp, Jimmy. 2014. "The Cartographer Who Mapped Out Gotham City." *Smithsonian.com*, May 29. https://www.smithsonianmag.com/arts-culture/cartographer-gotham-city-180951594/.

Starlin, Jim, and Jim Aparo. 1988a. *Batman* #427, "A Death in the Family—Chapter Three and Chapter Four." December, DC Comics.

Starlin, Jim, and Jim Aparo. 1988b. *Batman* #428, "A Death in the Family—Chapter Five." December, DC Comics.

Stephens, John, writer. 2015. *Gotham*. Season 1, episode 20, "Under the Knife." Aired April 20 on Fox.

Stewart, Cameron, Brenden Fletcher, and Babs Tarr. 2015a. *Batgirl* Vol. 4 #37, "Double Exposure." February, DC Comics.

Stewart, Cameron, Brenden Fletcher, and Babs Tarr. 2015b. *Batgirl Volume 1: Batgirl of Burnside*. DC Comics.

Sutherland, Edwin H. 1940. "White-Collar Criminality." *American Sociological Review* 5, no. 1 (February): 1–12. http://www.jstor.org/stable/2083937.

Swierczynski, Duane, and Travel Foreman. 2012. *Birds of Prey* Vol. 3 #9, "Night of the Owls: Gangland Style." July, DC Comics.

Thrasher, Frederic M. 1949. "The Comics and Delinquency: Cause of Scapegoat." *Journal of Educational Sociology* 23, no. 4 (December 1): 195–205. http://innocenceprojectcdh.com/items/show/158.

To limit the exposure of children to violent video games (2005), S. 2126, 109th Cong. (December 16).

Tomasi, Peter, and Patrick Gleason. 2011. *Batman and Robin* Vol. 2 #2, "Bad Blood." December, DC Comics.

Tomasi, Peter, and Patrick Gleason. 2012a. *Batman and Robin* Vol. 2 #3, "Knightmoves." January, DC Comics.

Tomasi, Peter, and Patrick Gleason. 2012b. *Batman and Robin* Vol. 2 #8, "Black Dawn." June, DC Comics.

United States Census Bureau. n.d.a. ACS Demographic and Housing Estimates. 2010: ACS 5-Year Estimates Data Profiles. Table DP05.

Chicago city, Illinois. Accessed March 29, 2020. https://data.census.gov/cedsci/table?q=chicago%20race&g=1600000US1714000&tid=ACSDP5Y2010.DP05&layer=VT_2018_160_00_PY_D1.

United States Census Bureau. n.d.b. ACS Demographic and Housing Estimates. 2010: ACS 5-Year Estimates Data Profiles. Table DP05. New York. Accessed March 29, 2020. https://data.census.gov/cedsci/table?q=new%20york%20city%20race&g=1600000US3651000&tid=ACSDP5Y2010.DP05&layer=VT_2018_160_00_PY_D1&cid=DP05_0001E&vintage=2018.

United States Census Bureau. n.d.c. Table 14. Illinois—Race and Hispanic Origin for Selected Large Cities and Other Places: Earliest Census to 1990. Accessed March 29, 2020. https://www.census.gov/population/www/documentation/twps0076/ILtab.xls.

United States Census Bureau. n.d.d. Table 33. New York—Race and Hispanic Origin for Selected Large Cities and Other Places: Earliest Census to 1990. Accessed March 29, 2020. https://www.census.gov/population/www/documentation/twps0076/NYtab.pdf.

Uricchio, William. 2010. "The Batman's Gotham City™: Story, Ideology, Performance." In *Comics and the City*, edited by Jörn Ahrens and Arno Meteling, 119–32. New York: Continuum.

United States Congress. 2005–6. *Family Entertainment Protection Act*, S.2126, 109th Congress. https://www.congress.gov/bill/109th-congress/senate-bill/2126/text.

United States Congress, Senate, Committee on the Judiciary. 1955. *Comic Books and Juvenile Delinquency Interim Report*, March 14, 1955, S. Res. 89 and S. Res. 190, 83rd Cong. 1st Sess.–83rd Cong. 2d Sess. http://www.lostsoti.org/senatehearings.htm.

United States Department of Education. 2000. *Indicators of School Crime and Safety, 2000*. National Center for Education Statistics, October. https://nces.ed.gov/pubs2001/2001017.pdf.

United States Department of Justice. Bureau of Justice Statistics. 2013. *Female Victims of Sexual Violence 1994–2010*. March. https://www.bjs.gov/content/pub/pdf/fvsv9410.pdf.

United States Equal Employment Opportunity Commission. n.d. *The Equal Pay Act of 1963*. Accessed March 28, 2020. https://www.eeoc.gov/laws/statutes/epa.cfm.

Wandtke, Terrence R. 2007. "Frank Miller Strikes Again and Batman Becomes a Postmodern Anti-Hero: The Tragi(Comic) Reformulation of the Dark Knight." In *The Amazing Transforming Superhero!: Essays on the Revision of Characters in Comic Books, Film and Television*, edited by Terrence R. Wandtke, 87–111. Jefferson, NC: McFarland.

Warner Bros. Interactive Entertainment. 2011. *Arkham City*.

Warner Bros. Interactive Entertainment. 2013. *Batman: Arkham Origins*.

The Washington Post. 1948. "600 Pupils Hold Burial Rites for 2000 Comic Books." October 27, 1.
Wein, Len, and John Calnan. 1979. *Batman* #307, "Dark Messenger of Mercy." January, DC Comics.
Weishaar, Schuy R. 2012. *Masters of the Grotesque: The Cinema of Tim Burton, Terry Gilliam, the Coen Brothers and David Lynch*. Jefferson, NC: McFarland.
Weldon, Glen. 2016. *Batman and the Rise of Nerd Culture*. New York: Simon & Schuster Paperbacks.
Wertham, Fredric. (1954) 2004. *Seduction of the Innocent*, revised ed. Laurel: Main Road Books.
West, Candace, and Don H. Zimmerman. 1987. "Doing Gender." *Gender & Society* 1, no. 2 (June): 125–51.
Whaley, Deborah Elizabeth. 2011. "Black Cat Got Your Tongue? Catwoman, Blackness, and the Alchemy of Postracialism." *Journal of Graphic Novels and Comics* 2, no. 1: 3–23.
Wheeler, Andrew. 2012. "The Gayness of Batman: A Brief History." *Comics Alliance*. April 30. http://comicsalliance.com/the-gayness-of-batman-a-brief-history-opinion-morrison/.
White, Mark D. 2019. *Batman and Ethics*. Hoboken, NJ: Wiley-Blackwell.
Wiegman, Robyn. 1995. *American Anatomies: Theorizing Race and Gender*. Durham, NC: Duke University Press.
Willingham, Bill, and Francisco Rodriguez de la Fuente. 2004a. *Robin* Vol. 2 #124, "Good Parenting." May, DC Comics.
Willingham, Bill, and Francisco Rodriguez de la Fuente. 2004b. *Robin* Vol. 2 #125, "In the Shadow of Two Fathers." June, DC Comics.
Willingham, Bill, and Steve Scott. 2006. *Shadowpact* #5, "One Year Later." November, DC Comics.
Wolfman, Marv, George Pérez, and Jim Aparo. 1989. *Batman* #442, "A Lonely Place of Dying—Part 5." December, DC Comics.
Wolfman, Marv, and Jim Aparo. 1989. *Batman* #441, "A Lonely Place of Dying—Part 3." November, DC Comics.
Wolfman, Marv, and Jim Aparo. 1991. *Detective Comics* #627, "The Case of the Chemical Syndicate." March, DC Comics.
Wolfman, Marv, and Pat Broderick. 1989. *Batman* #436, "Batman Year 3—Different Roads." August, DC Comics.
Wolfman, Marv, and Tom Grummett. 1990. *The New Titans* #65, "Déjà vu." April, DC Comics.
Wolf-Meyer, Matthew Joseph. 2006. "Batman and Robin in the Nude, or Class and Its Exceptions." *Extrapolation* 47, no. 2: 187–206.
Woodruff, Ken, writer. 2015. *Gotham*. Season 1, episode 19, "Beasts of Prey." Aired April 13 on Fox.

Wright, Erik Olin. 2005. "Foundations of Neo-Marxist Class Analysis." In *Approaches to Class Analysis*, edited by Erik Olin Wright, 4–30. Cambridge: Cambridge University Press.

Xu, Jiaquan, Kenneth D. Kochanek, Sherry L. Murphy, and Betzaida Tejada-Vera. 2010. *National Vital Statistics Report* 58, no. 19 (May 20). https://www.cdc.gov/nchs/data/nvsr/nvsr58/nvsr58_19.pdf.

Žižek, Slavoj. 2012. "The Politics of Batman." *New Statesman*. August 23.

Index

52 #7 95

Ackerman, Spencer 106
Akins, Michael
   (Commissioner) 121
al Ghul, Ra's 159, 166
Ali (character) 150
Aparo, Jim 35, 115
Anarky 168
Arkham, Amadeus 158
Arkham Asylum 26, 158–9
Arkham Asylum: A Serious House on Serious Earth 158–9
Arkham City (video game) 159
Austin, Shannon 63, 67
Azzarello, Brian 123, 125, 155, 161

Bair, Michael 81–2, 90
Bakhtin, Mikhail 6, 162
Bane 138–41, 166
Batgirl 47–8, 54–7, 59–60, 71–5, 82
   as Betty Kane 54
   see also Gordon, Barbara
Batgirl (comic book) 9, 62–3, 70–1, 75
   Vol. 4 #3 59–60
   Vol. 4 #19 70
   Vol. 4 #37 71–5
Batgirl Volume 1: Batgirl of Burnside 71, 74–5
Batman
   attributes of 47–8, 50, 53, 56–7, 59, 75, 78, 83, 91, 94–5, 100, 120, 127, 129–30
   as detective 1, 155
   as Dick Grayson 27
   influence of 3, 9, 13–14, 18–23, 32, 34, 37–8, 109, 123, 137, 149–50, 158, 176, 179, 183
   morality and 3, 9, 13, 18–20, 22, 24, 28, 137, 177–9, 181–2
   origin of 5, 28–9, 31, 135–6, 154–5, 171, 175
   public perception of 65, 177–80
   relationships and 30, 36–7, 39, 51, 92–3, 95, 100–1, 112
   as symbol 37, 80, 93, 181
   thoughts of 21, 27, 36, 53, 56, 58, 68, 83, 92, 123–5, 135, 159
   versus adversaries 5, 7, 11, 18–19, 53, 58, 65–6, 68–9, 80, 83–4, 91, 114, 117, 128, 131, 134, 137, 139, 141, 145, 149–51, 153–4, 156–7, 162, 170–4
   as vigilante 2–3, 11, 155, 167, 174–82
   wealth and 127–8, 130–1, 137–9
   see also Wayne, Bruce
Batman (comic book)
   #1 64, 92, 135
   #3 18–20, 64, 80, 92, 129, 157
   #4 1
   #5 136
   #7 178–9
   #10 80
   #19 129, 150
   #27 149
   #49 79–80, 92
   #98 134
   #119 178
   #126 178
   #139 54

INDEX

#181 83
#210 64–5
#212 171
#214 100
#217 33
#239 136
#284 176–7
#307 136
#400 159
#408 20–1, 35, 158
#409 21–2, 158
#427 35–6
#436 35
#441 36
#442 36–7
#455 37
#457 38
#551 117–18
#552 118
Vol. 2 #33 154
Vol. 2 #44 22–3, 123–5, 158
Vol. 3 #12 30
Vol. 3 #24 100
Vol. 3 #32 100
Vol. 3 #50 29–30, 100–1
Batman (film) 3, 100, 154, 166
The Batman (film) 113, 183
Batman (TV series) 2, 4, 54, 56, 112
  "Catwoman's Dressed to Kill" 54–6
  "Enter Batgirl, Exit Penguin" 55
Batman Adventures: Mad Love 67, 158
Batman: The Animated Series 7, 68, 156, 165
  "Appointment in Crime Alley" 134–5
  "Harley and Ivy" 68
  "Heart of Ice" 99, 157
  "Robin's Reckoning Part I" 33–4
  "Trial" 154
  "The Underdwellers" 131
Batman: Arkham Origins 168

Batman Begins 4, 138, 154, 166–7, 171
Batman Black and White 6–7
Batman Chronicles: The Gauntlet 34
Batman: A Death in the Family 35–36
Batman: Death and the Maidens #4 135
Batman Family #1 82
Batman Forever 4, 100
Batman: No Man's Land 144
Batman: Orpheus Rising 115–17, 120–2, 124
Batman Returns 3, 6, 48, 65–6, 100, 146–7, 162, 171
Batman and Robin Vol. 2 #2 39
Batman and Robin (film) 4, 48, 84
"Batman and Robin Stand Up for Sportsmanship!" 109
Batman: Year One 2, 65, 81, 100, 129, 155–6, 168
Batwoman 9, 47, 51–4, 56–9, 75, 78, 86–9, 94–5, 97–8
  as Katherine (Kathy) Kane 51, 94
  see also Kane, Kate
Batwoman (comic book) 10, 86–8, 183
  #34 85, 87–8, 100
  #36 85–6, 88
  #38 88
  #40 89
Batwoman (TV series) 183
Batwoman: Elegy 58, 95–7
Beatty, Scott 173
Bermejo, Lee 155, 161
Bernado, Susan M. 171
Big Boy Daniels 19
Birch, J. J. 81–2, 90
Birds of Prey 60, 62, 69
Birds of Prey (comic) 162
Black Canary/Oracle: Birds of Prey #1 60
Black Lives Matter 123–4

INDEX

Blue Lives Matter 123–4
Bolland, Brian 59–60, 85, 163, 172
Bonger, Willem 132
Branch, Kathryn A. 89
Brody, Michael 34
Brooker, Will 93–5, 114
Brown, Brené 29–30
Brown, Stephanie 9, 43–5
Bruinsma, Gerben J. N. 175
Bullock, Harvey 160
bullying 40–1
Burton, Tim 3, 5–6, 48, 65, 100, 146–7, 154, 156, 162, 171
Butler, Judith 49, 72

Cahill, Ann J. 87, 89
capitalism 11, 108, 127–8, 130, 137–47, 149–51
Catwoman 9, 48, 56, 64–7, 69, 80–1, 83–4, 90–2, 112–13, 146–7, 156, 172
see also Kyle, Selina
Catwoman (comic book) 81–2, 90
 #1 90
 #4 84
 Vol. 2 #0 24
 Vol. 2 #81 24
Centers for Disease Control and Prevention 42
Chicago 5, 108, 114, 119, 125, 141
childhood
 in the city 23, 27, 120, 123, 132
 and crime 9, 13, 16–18, 20, 25
 development 14, 18, 28–30, 45
 juvenile delinquency and 16–17
 loss of innocence 8, 13, 18, 24, 29, 31, 34–5, 45
 and morality 13–14, 19–20, 22, 35
 trauma 13, 24, 28–30, 33–5, 37–8, 45, 165
children 8, 13
Chill, Joe 135, 138, 171
Choi, Daniel 95–6

class (socioeconomic)
 conflict 129–30, 132–3, 137, 139
 and crime 132–8, 145–51
 disparity 3, 8, 10–11, 125, 127–36, 138, 140, 142, 145
 representation of 104, 143
classlessness 11, 128–30, 137, 139–40, 144–5
Cobb, William 132
Cobblepot, Oswald 98–99, 171–2
 see also Penguin
Cocca, Carolyn 59, 61–2
Colonel Reyes 96
comic book burnings 14–15
Comics Code 9–10, 17, 51, 78–82, 94, 105–6, 110–11, 118, 122, 125–6
Comics Code Authority (CCA) 94, 106, 122
Comics Magazine Association of America (CMAA) 17
The Communist Manifesto 128–9, 133
Conner, Amanda 69, 158
"Contagion" 167
Coogan, Peter 154, 163–4, 176
Corsaro, William A. 23
"The Court of Owls" 160
Craig, Wendy M. 40
Craig, Yvonne 54–6
Crawshaw, Trisha L. 47–8, 53, 61
crime
 in the city 1–6, 9, 11, 18, 28, 111, 114, 125, 130, 134–5, 142, 144–5, 153–7, 159–63, 168–72, 182
 and class 10–11, 132–8, 142, 145–51
 fighting against 29, 52–7, 60, 62–3, 67, 79, 100, 114, 139, 141, 154–5, 170, 173, 175–6, 182
 identity and 114, 117, 151
 organized 34–5, 128, 142, 170–3

INDEX

pathways toward 9, 13, 18–27, 132, 157–8, 163, 169
and punishment 69, 80, 119, 158–9
representation of 14–18, 105–6, 114, 145, 155, 162
supervillains and 64–8, 80, 83–4, 99, 143, 154–5, 163–6, 172–4
terroristic 4, 115, 139–40, 166–8
versus vigilantism 2, 11, 32, 24, 174–82
white-collar 3, 11, 127–8, 145–9
Crime Alley 20–2, 134–5
criminality 2, 9, 11, 18, 23–4, 26–7, 80, 83, 110–11, 115, 121–3, 142, 146, 149, 155–7, 163, 165
Cronin, Brian 129, 135
Cunningham, Phillip Lamarr 105, 111–12
Curtis, Neal 180

Daggett, Roland 134
Daniel, Tony S. 183
The Dark Knight 4–5, 7, 99–100, 138, 141, 143, 154–5, 159–60, 162–4, 166, 172–4, 181–2
The Dark Knight Returns 2–3, 135, 144–5, 155–6, 170, 179–81
The Dark Knight Rises 4–5, 66, 100, 138–41
darkness 2–3, 6–7, 156
Dawes, Rachel 99–100, 138, 171
de Beauvoir Simone 50–1
de Keijser, Jan W. 175
Dent, Harvey (Two-Face) 99, 172–3, 181–2
"The Destroyer" 160
Detective Comics
  #27, 1
  #30 174
  #31 92
  #33 29, 80, 175
  #35 114–15
  #38 32, 175–6
  #39 114
  #42 133
  #47 149–50
  #49 92
  #52 114
  #105 130–1
  #233 51–3
  #392 171
  #423 57
  #424 57
  #457 134–6
  #472 168
  #489 159
  #627 115
  #647 177
  #854 58
  #859 95–7
  #860 58
  #875 25–6
  #879 27
  #881 26–8
Dini, Paul 67, 69, 158, 165
DiPaolo, Marc 3–4, 147, 165–6
Dixon, Chuck 44, 173
Downey, Meg 32–3, 79, 82
Drake, Jack 38, 42
Drake, Tim 9, 36–43
  see also Robin
Dubose, Mike S. 3, 177
Duffield, Tom 6
Durkheim, Émile 161–2

Engels, Friedrich 128–9, 131–4, 144
Esterhaus, Karl 122
ethnicity 10, 103–4, 107, 111, 113–18, 126
Eyes on Bullying 41

Facciani, Matthew 67, 104, 107–8
Family Entertainment Protection Act 17
Federal Equal Pay Law 56

femininity 8–9, 47–60, 62–3, 65–7, 69, 72, 74–5, 79–80, 94
Finger, Bill 1, 54, 150
Flannery 90–1
Fleck, Arthur 138, 165
Fletcher, Brenden 71
Fox, Lucius 138
Fradley, Martin 143
Franklin, Wayne (Grotesk) 119–20
Fries, Victor (Mr. Freeze) 99, 157

Gale, Bob 144
Garland, Tammy S. 89
Garneau, Eric 164
gay readings 51, 54, 77, 85–7, 92–100
gender
 equality 52–3, 56–7, 63, 68
 performance 9, 49, 52, 58–9, 65, 67, 72–5
 roles 9, 47, 49–50, 54, 65, 86
gentrification 10, 119, 125, 134
Gibbons, Bishop Edmund F. 15
Gilroy, Andréa 58, 97
Gordon, Barbara 26–7, 54, 57, 59–63, 70, 72, 85
 see also Batgirl; Oracle
Gordon, James (Commissioner) 25–7, 54–5, 61, 85, 100, 123, 144–5, 154, 167–9, 172, 178–9, 181–2
Gordon, James Jr. 25–8
Gotham (TV series) 4, 24–5, 31, 98–9, 141–2
 Season 2 Episode #14 31–2
 Season 4 Episode #9 148–9
Gotham City 27–8, 159
 crime and 1–6, 9, 11, 18, 28, 111, 114, 124, 130, 134–5, 142, 144–5, 153–7, 159–63, 168–72, 182
 depictions of 1–8, 11, 140–3, 155–6
 population of 10, 14, 70, 75, 108, 110, 114, 118–19, 134, 143, 167
 sections of 18–19, 20–4, 31, 121, 123–5, 127, 134–6, 138, 143–4, 157–8
Gotham City Sirens 69
Gothic 2–7, 156, 171
Grayson, Dick 18–19, 29, 32–7, 82, 176
 as Batman 27
 see also Nightwing; Robin
Grimes, Mackenzie 89
"Grotesk" 119–20
gun violence 9, 21, 42–3

Haas, Nicole E. 175
Halberstam, Judith 47, 70, 72
Hanley, Tim 64–5, 80–1
Harley Quinn (comic book) 69, 158
Harvard School of Public Health 43
Hassler-Forest, Dan 4
Hawkins, D. Lynn 40
Heller, Bruno 4–5, 24, 31, 98, 141
Holland, Charles 7
Horeck, Tanya 87
Howler, Ned 124

Iadonisi, Richard 2, 181
Indicators of School Crime and Safety 40

Janín, Mikel 30–1
Janson, Klaus 2–3, 135, 144, 170, 179
Jock 123
Joker 26–7, 35–6, 59–60, 67–9, 85, 138, 143, 147, 153–5, 158–61, 163–6, 172–4
Joker (film) 138, 165
Joker (graphic novel) 155, 161
Joker: Last Laugh 173
Jones, Kelley 117
Juliano, Stephanie 175

Kane, Bob 1, 36, 64, 150
Kane, Kate 58–9, 85–90,
    95–8, 100
    see also Batwoman
Kellner, Douglas 4
Kerrigan, S. J. 139
The Killing Joke 59–62, 85,
    163–5, 172
King, Gavin
    see Orpheus
King, Tom 29–31, 100, 183
Kitt, Eartha 112–13
Kohlberg, Lawrence 13,
    19–21, 25, 28
Kolenic, Anthony J. 164, 174
Krafft-Ebing, Richard 26
Kravitz, Zoë 113
Krol, Armand 177
Kyle, Selina 24–5, 29–30, 64–6,
    81–2, 90–1, 100–1, 113, 142,
    146, 171–2
    see also Catwoman

Lachenal, Jessica 71
Lang, Lana 180
Langley, Travis 25–6, 28, 39, 44,
    93, 174
Ledger, Heath 143, 166
Legends of the Dark Knight
    #61 129
Lefebvre, Henri 8
"Legacy" 167, 169
Letamendi, Andrea 33–4
Loeb, Gillian B. 168
Loring, Scranton 149
Luthor, Lex 168–9
Lynch, Sarah N. 124

Ma Gunn 20–2
Mace, David 15
Maddox, P. J. (inspector)
    176–7
Madison, Julie 92
Madoff, Bernie 147–8, 166
Mahoney, Tom 5

male gaze 78–9, 81–2, 84–5, 91
Maleev, Alex 144
Marazi, Katherine 177–8
March, Guillem 69
Marcia, James 14, 28–9, 31
Mardorossian, Carine M. 89–90
Marx, Karl 128–9, 131–4, 144
Marxism 10–11, 127–8, 132–3, 137
masculinity 9, 47–51, 53, 55,
    59–62, 64, 66–7, 70,
    72, 75, 94
Maudsley, Henry 11, 157–9
Mazzucchelli, David 2, 65, 81,
    99, 168
McKean, Dave 158
Mert, Ceren 141–2
Miller, Frank 2–3, 36, 65, 81, 99–
    100, 135, 144, 168, 170, 179
Mitternacht, Natalia
    see Nocturna
Moench, Doug 117
Moldoff, Sheldon 54
Moncada, Eduardo 175
Montessori, Maria 23
Montoya, Renee 97
Moore, Alan 59–60, 85, 163, 172
morality 3, 8–9, 13–15, 18–26, 28,
    35–6, 39, 45, 66, 80, 94, 115,
    136–7, 144, 148, 151, 157–8,
    160–2, 172, 175–9, 181–2
Morrison, Grant 135, 158
Mr. Freeze
    see Victor Fries
Mulvey, Laura 79
Mutants 144, 170

National Crime Victimization
    Survey 40
National Intimate Partner and
    Sexual Violence Survey 86
National School Safety Center 43
The New Titans #65 29
New York City 4–5, 69, 108, 114,
    119, 141, 158, 171
Newell, Mindy 81–2, 90

Nicholson, Jack 166
Nightwing 35, 59–60
  see also Grayson, Dick
Nightwing Vol. 3 #8 132
Nocturna (Natalia Mitternacht) 85–89
Nolan, Christopher 4–6, 66, 99–100, 138, 140–1, 143, 154, 156, 164, 171–3, 181
"No Man's Land" 121, 143–4, 156, 168–70
Nygma, Edward 98–9

Occupy Wall Street 138–40
Omi, Michael 10, 107
O'Neil, Denny 175
Oracle 47, 59–60, 62
  see also Gordon, Barbara
Orpheus (Gavin King) 116, 118, 120–2
Ostroff, Joshua 108

Page, Linda 92
Palmiotti, Jimmy 69, 158
Patterson, Brett Chandler 156
Pattinson, Robert 183
Penguin 22, 144, 156, 172
  see also Cobblepot, Oswald
Pennyworth, Alfred 31, 34–5, 39, 162
Pepler, Debra J. 40
Petrovic, Paul 95–8
Pfeiffer, Michelle 65, 67
Phillips, Nickie D. 165–7
Phillips, Todd 138, 165
Pittsburgh 5, 141
Poison Ivy 9, 67–9, 73, 83–4
police 5, 10, 32, 64, 80, 84, 90, 106, 114, 119, 121–4, 143–4, 168, 170, 176–7, 179
Professor Pyg 148–9
Proctor, William 61–2

Quinn, Harley (Harleen Quinzel) 67–9, 158

race
  in the city 10, 108, 114, 116, 118–19, 121, 124–5
  depictions of 10, 103, 105–13, 118–20, 122, 126
  and diversity 103–5, 110–11, 118, 126
  and prejudice 10, 103–6, 109–11, 113–15, 117–18, 122, 124–5
racial formation 10, 103–4, 107–8, 114, 117–18, 120, 123
Radomski, Eric 156
Ragman (Rory Regan) 118
rape 10, 77, 85–90
Red Hood and the Outlaws Vol. 2 #6 175
Reed, Cory A. 6, 146–7
Reeves, Matt 113, 183
The Return of Bruce Wayne 135
Robin 9, 14, 18–20, 22, 32–43, 45, 47, 50–1, 53–6, 69, 79, 82, 84, 92–3, 109, 129–31, 149–50, 171, 176, 178–9
  see also Drake, Tim; Grayson, Dick; Todd, Jason; Wayne, Damian
Robin Vol. 2 (comic book) 40–5
  #25 42–3
  #58 43–4
  #59 40, 44
  #60 41
  #65 44
  #111 44–5
  #124 38
  #125 38
  #156 41–2
Rucka, Greg 57, 95–6, 135
Rude, Mey 74, 85–6

Sable, Mark 161
Saiz, Jesus 161
Salamon, Julie 162
Sampere, Daniel 70
Sawyer, Maggie 85–9, 98, 100

Scarecrow 38, 156
Schultz, Harrison 139–40
Schumacher, Joel 4–5, 48, 84, 100
Sedgwick, Eve Kosofsky 96–7
Seduction of the Innocent 16, 78, 92–4, 110
  see also Wertham, Fredric
Sewer King 131
sex appeal 9–10, 64, 77–80, 83–4
sexual harassment 44–5
sexual orientation 54, 77–8, 92–100
Shadowpact 161
Shreck, Max 66, 146–7
Simmons, Alex 115, 120
Simone, Gail 59–63, 70–1
Simonson, Walter 6
Singer, Marc 104
Skyler, J. 73
Snyder, Scott 123, 125
social conflict theory 133, 136
Stabile, Carol A. 50
Stamp, Jimmy 163
Starlin, Jim 35
Stewart, Cameron 71
Strobl, Staci 165–7
suicide 9, 30–1, 41–2, 148
Suicide Squad #23 62
Superman 48
Sutherland, Edwin H. 145–6, 149, 169, 176
Syaf, Ardian 59

Talon 162
Tarr, Babs 71
teenage pregnancy 9, 43–4
Thor 48
Thorne, Rupert 168
Thrasher, Frederic M. 15–16
Timm, Bruce 67, 158
Todd, Jason 21–2, 24–5, 35–6, 175–6
  see also Robin
transgender 9, 47, 69–70, 73–5, 81

transphobia 71–74
trauma 9, 13–14, 24, 27–30, 33–4, 37–8, 45, 61–3, 73, 165
Turner, Dwayne 115, 120
Two-Face
  see Dent, Harvey
"Two-Face: Year One" 161, 173
Tynion, James IV 183
Type, Dagger 71–4

Uricchio, William 5
US Senate Committee on the Judiciary 16–17

Vale, Vicki 79–80, 92
Vendemia, Jennifer 67, 104, 107–8
vigilantism 2–3, 7, 11, 13–14, 22, 24, 28, 31, 35, 37–9, 92, 98, 100, 155, 167, 174–82
violence 11, 13–14, 17–18, 26, 39, 41–3, 77–9, 83–91, 94, 101, 111, 113, 116, 118–19, 122, 124, 128, 132–3, 136–7, 143, 158, 170, 173–5, 179–80
  against women 60–3, 90

Wandtke, Terrence R. 2–3
Warren, Peter 67, 104, 107–8
Wayne, Bruce 8, 13, 18–20, 23, 25, 28–35, 37–40, 80, 83, 92, 100–1, 123, 125, 129–31, 135, 137–40, 147, 150, 171
  see also Batman
Wayne, Damian 39, 176
  see also Robin
Wayne, Martha 24, 134–5, 171
Wayne, Solomon 160, 163
Welch, Bo 6
Weldon, Glen 2, 175
Wertham, Fredric 10, 14–17, 33, 51, 78–9, 92–4, 110
  see also *Seduction of the Innocent*
West, Candace 49, 52, 59

Whaley, Deborah Elizabeth 81, 112–13
Wheeler, Andrew 93–5
White, Mark D. 177
Wiegman, Robyn 10, 107–8, 111, 121
Williams III, J. H. 95
Winant, Howard 10, 107
Wolfman, Marv 115
Wolf-Meyer, Matthew Joseph 129–30, 137, 145, 180

Women in Refrigerators 60–1
Wright, Erik Olin 133, 136

Yeoh, Alysia 70
Yindel, Ellen 179

Zimmerman, Don H. 49, 52, 59
Žižek, Slavoj 138–40, 181–2
Zucco, Tony 33, 35, 170

www.ingramcontent.com/pod-product-compliance
Ingram Content Group UK Ltd.
Pitfield, Milton Keynes, MK11 3LW, UK
UKHW021901220326
469204UK00008B/107